Schools and Schooling in the Digital Age

This book presents a wide-ranging and critical exploration of a topic that lies at the heart of contemporary education. The use of digital technology is now a key feature of schools and schooling around the world. Yet despite its prominence, technology use continues to be an area of education that rarely receives sustained critical attention and thought, especially from those people who are most involved and affected by it. Technology tends to be something that many teachers, learners, parents, policymakers and even academics approach as a routine rather than reflective matter.

Tackling the wider picture, addressing the social, cultural, economic, political and commercial aspects of schools and schooling in the digital age, this book offers to make sense of what happens, and what does not happen, when the digital and the educational come together in the guise of schools technology.

In particular, the book examines contemporary schooling in terms of social justice, equality and participatory democracy. Seeking to re-politicise an increasingly depoliticised area of educational debate and analysis, setting out to challenge the many contradictions that characterise the field of education technology today, the author concludes by suggesting what forms schools and schooling in the digital age could, and should, take.

This is the perfect volume for anyone interested in the application and use of technology in education, as well as the education policy and politics that surround it. Many will also find its innovative proposals for technology use an inspiration for their own teaching and learning.

Neil Selwyn is Senior Lecturer in the London Knowledge Lab, Institute of Education, University of London, UK.

Foundations and Futures of Education
Series Editors:
Peter Aggleton *School of Education and Social Work, University of Sussex, UK*
Sally Power *Cardiff University, UK*
Michael Reiss *Institute of Education, University of London, UK*

Foundations and Futures of Education focuses on key emerging issues in education as well as continuing debates within the field. The series is inter-disciplinary, and includes historical, philosophical, sociological, psychological and comparative perspectives on three major themes: the purposes and nature of education; increasing interdisciplinarity within the subject; and the theory-practice divide.

Previous titles include:

Language, Learning, Context
Wolff-Michael Roth

Learning, Context and the Role of Technology
Rosemary Luckin

Education and the Family
Passing success across the generations
Leon Feinstein, Kathryn Duckworth and Ricardo Sabates

Education, Philosophy and the Ethical Environment
Graham Haydon

Educational Activity and the Psychology of Learning
Judith Ireson

Schooling, Society and Curriculum
Alex Moore

Gender, Schooling and Global Social Justice
Elaine Unterhalter

Education – An 'Impossible Profession'?
Tamara Bibby

Being a University
Ronald Barnett

Forthcoming titles include:

Irregular Schooling
Roger Slee

School Trouble
Deborah Youdell

The Struggle for the History of Education
Gary McCulloch

Schools and Schooling in the Digital Age

A critical analysis

Neil Selwyn

Routledge
Taylor & Francis Group

LONDON AND NEW YORK

First edition published 2011
by Routledge
2 Park Square, Milton Park, Abingdon, Oxon, OX14 4RN

Simultaneously published in the USA and Canada
by Routledge
270 Madison Avenue, New York, NY 10016

Routledge is an imprint of the Taylor & Francis Group, an informa business

Typeset in Garamond by Swales & Willis, Ltd, Exeter, Devon
Printed and bound in Great Britain by TJ International Ltd, Padstow,
Cornwall

British Library Cataloguing in Publication Data
A catalogue record for this book is available from
the British Library

Library of Congress Cataloging-in-Publication Data
Selwyn, Neil
  Schooling and schooling in the digital age : a critical analysis /
  Neil Selwyn. — 1st ed.
    1. Educational technology. 2. Internet in education.
    3. Education—Effect of technological innovations on. I. Title
  LB1028.3.S38886 2011
  370.285—dc22
  2010016105

ISBN13: 978–0–415–58929–1 (hbk)
ISBN13: 978–0–415–58930–7 (pbk)
ISBN13: 978–0–203–84079–5 (ebk)

Contents

Preface and acknowledgements   ix

PART I
High-tech hope and digital disappointment   1

1   Revisiting the promise of digital technology and schools   3

2   The messy realities of digital technology use in schools   22

3   Rethinking digital technology and schools   38

PART II
Making sense of schools, schooling and digital technology   53

4   Digital technology and education policy-making   55

5   Digital technology and the privatisations of schooling   68

6   Digital technology and the organisational concerns of schools   87

7   Digital technology and the lived experiences of teachers and students   102

PART III
What to do with schools in the digital age?   117

8   Reconstructing schools and schooling in the digital age   119

9   Readjusting schools and schooling in the digital age   136

References   156
Index   175

Preface and acknowledgements

This is intended to be a book for – rather than against – the educational technology community. Throughout the course of my research and writing on the topic of schools and technology I have faced occasional rebuttal of my arguments along the lines that I am somehow 'anti-technology' or pursuing some obtuse Luddite agenda. I would hope that any reader of this book would realise that this is not the case. Instead, this book simply attempts to look objectively at technology use in schools through a non-technologically focused lens. Of course, I recognise that this state of detachment is not a usual feature of educational discussions of technology, which are more commonly driven by a specialist passion for all things technological. Yet this division notwithstanding, I hope that my position as a technologically detached, mainstream observer has not led me to reach a set of disinterested or even hostile observations. My intention in writing this book was to provide a constructive rather then destructive reading of the current state of school technology use around the world. I would therefore invite readers to join me in developing critically informed – and hopefully critically enhanced – visions of the future implementation of digital technology in schools.

As will be argued throughout the book, a critical analysis is a necessary step towards developing realistic understandings of the current educational technology landscape and, perhaps most importantly, towards realising the undoubted educational potential of these technologies. The arguments made in this book are certainly not intended to be wilfully obtrusive, negative or somehow 'anti-technology'. I did not set out to write an angry diatribe against the perceived failures of technology in educational settings along the lines of the recent conservative polemics produced by Tara Brabazon, Todd Oppenheimer and the like. Rather, this book is offered as a corrective to the mainstream celebratory commentary about schools and digital technology that emanates from the mass of technologists, educationalists, social psychologists and pedagogy experts that constitute the academic educational technology community. While current debates over technologies and schools are dominated by such accounts, their usefulness is limited by a general reluctance to acknowledge the complex social structures that influence even the most innocuous application of technology in the classroom.

In taking this contrary stance, *Schools and Schooling in the Digital Age* seeks to reinvigorate a tradition of critical social analysis of education and technology that flourished briefly in the late 1980s and 1990s, but has since been eclipsed by the mass of uncritical, techno-centric writing that now dominates the educational technology literature. Indeed, anyone seeking to make sense of the contemporary educational technology landscape would do well to go back to the perceptive pre-internet analyses of 'education computing' and 'micros in schools' offered by writers such as C.A. Bowers, Larry Cuban, Steven Hodas, Stephen Kerr, Hank Bromley, Michael Apple, Hughie Mackay, John Beynon, Kevin Robins and Frank Webster. These writers all offered carefully constructed and wide-ranging critiques of the economic, political, cultural, social and historical shaping of the digital educational technologies of their time. Yet almost all these writers found their arguments ignored roundly by the mainstream academic educational technology community. Such indifference prompted most of these writers to move quickly on from the topic of educational technology – switching their attention to fields of educational inquiry that were more open to criticism than the insular and sometimes hostile world of educational technology. That the likes of Apple, Bromley, Kerr and so on are not commenting currently on the recent excesses of social media, 'semantic web' and 'cloud computing' technologies in education is a great shame – the educational technology literature is all the poorer for their absence.

While this book draws on the work, ideas and arguments of many others, ultimately I remain responsible for writing it, and so any blame, criticism or retribution should be directed solely at me. That said, there are a number of people who deserve particular acknowledgement in helping the ideas and arguments expressed in this book come to fruition – especially in challenging and refining the more extreme lines of thinking about technology and education that I have pursued over the years. As the notoriously opinionated designer Vivienne Westwood once reflected, 'I disagree with everything I used to say' (cited in Brockes 2007, p.25). While this may not be wholly accurate in my case, I hope that the shifts in thinking that this book represents when compared to some of my earlier writings reflect the need for academic writers to remain disposed to openness, provisionality, radical doubt and reworking of ideas. No doubt, if I were to write a similar book in ten years time then some of my arguments will have probably altered yet again. Yet for the time being I am content that this book contains the most salient arguments and critiques that I can make of schools and digital technology.

With this openness of thought in mind, it is only proper to acknowledge the people who have been involved in the development of my reading, thinking and writing in the area of education, technology and society. Over the past fifteen years I have benefitted immensely from writing with others on the subject – not least Stephen Gorard, John Fitz, John Furlong and Phil Brown. Throughout the duration of my writing on schools and technology many people have also offered advice and criticism. These include Keri Facer, Sonia Livingstone and Ellen Helsper. I would also like to thank academic colleagues past and present for their advice and comments on all aspects of my work. During my long time at the Cardiff School of Social Sciences many colleagues provided inspiration and support – notably Gareth Rees, Brian Davies, Sally Power, Sara Delamont, Robert Evans, Trevor Welland, Patrick White, Sara Williams, Peter Fairbrother, Jane Salisbury, Emma Renold, Ian Welsh, Harry Collins and Ralph Fevre. During my spell at the University of Bristol I was grateful for the support of Susan Robertson and Tim Rudd. My present work at the London Knowledge Lab has been helped by a number of people who should be acknowledged: Shaku Banaji, David Buckingham, Andrew Burn, Liesbeth de Block, Sue Cranmer, Natasha Gouseti, Carey Jewitt, Magdalini Kolokitha, Diana Laurillard, Harvey Mellar, Richard Noss, Martin Oliver, John Potter, Rebekah Willett and Michael Young.

Finally, I am always aware acutely of the hard work that goes into the production of any book. So in terms of the writing and production of this book I would like to thank the editors of the 'Foundations and Futures of Education' series. In particular I would like to thank Sally Power and Michael Reiss for their especially close readings of initial versions of the manuscript. I would also like to thank all of the production and editorial team at Routledge, notably Anna Clarkson and Charles Haynes, and copy-editor Sara Marchington.

Neil Selwyn
London, July 2010

Part I

High-tech hope and digital disappointment

1 Revisiting the promise of digital technology and schools

Introduction

A few years ago, in the midst of the UK government's concerted push to encourage the use of electronic smart boards in schools, I accompanied a group of Masters students (mainly international scholars from China, Taiwan, Ghana and Uganda) on a visit to a local primary school. We braved a torrential British rainstorm to observe the real-life application of the digital technologies that the group had been studying during the previous semester's module on '*E-learning in the twenty-first century*'. For our visit I had taken care to contact a school that was known locally for its enthusiasm for educational technology, and upon our arrival I was relieved to see that the school was laden with technological 'kit'. Data projectors and interactive whiteboards (the preferred term in Britain for the electronic smart board) assumed prominent positions in all of the classrooms. Desktop and laptop computers could also be found in every classroom, as well as in two large rooms that had been converted into dedicated computer suites. A number of handheld devices were also located throughout the school. In contrast to all these high-tech accessories, the school was itself housed in an austere and imposing Victorian-era building with high ceilings, huge windows and endless tiled corridors. The main classrooms had tall sloping ceilings that followed the contours of the steeply pitched roof. The overall impression was of a typical late nineteenth-century school building which was now home to some decidedly twenty-first-century schooling. In short, the school appeared to provide an excellent example of UK primary education for my Masters students to experience.

Yet it soon became clear that this combination of Dickensian and digital-age schooling was not an altogether harmonious affair – especially with regards to the school's interactive whiteboards. The school's senior management team had decided, quite sensibly, that the projector for each classroom's whiteboard needed to be suspended securely from the apex of the ceiling. The time of our visit coincided with a spate of thefts of data projectors (each with a retail value of approaching £1,000) from schools, universities and workplaces throughout the region. Unfortunately, health and safety legislation decreed that the maximum permitted length of the aluminium poles that held the projectors in place was just over three metres. Given the ceiling height of around six metres, the school was left with a number of data projectors that were suspended three metres from the ground with the attendant whiteboard fixed about one and a half metres from the ground (the minimum height it could be placed without incurring serious image distortion).

Given the height of the whiteboards from the floor it transpired that while adults were able to write on the boards and manipulate the software, everything remained out of reach for all but the tallest of the children in the school. When one member of our group enquired about the practicalities of this situation, we were proudly shown a newly painted wooden box and set of small steps that the school had procured. This makeshift platform allowed the school students to reach the whiteboard when necessary. We were told that the school's Parent Teacher Association was in the process of raising the required funds to purchase similar wooden platforms for all of the other classrooms. This, I had to explain to my group, was the UK government's digital technology policy drive in action – albeit not as seamlessly as my students had been led to believe from their readings of the academic literature.

This enforced situation of 'making do' and 'getting by' sums up the messy realities of digital technology use in twenty-first century school systems. The fact that teachers or students in this particular British school were not using the interactive whiteboards with much regularity or enthusiasm was understandable. The paucity of whiteboard use in this school appeared to be influenced by a range of issues beyond the usual explanations for low technology take-up (i.e. that teachers lack the expertise, confidence or know-how to use the technology properly, or else that they lack access to the technology). Instead, when my Masters students and I were reflecting later on our visit, we could see that (non)use of the interactive whiteboards was shaped by a range of unseen factors that were rarely acknowledged in the academic literature. After discussing the matter for a few minutes we had come up with the following factors that could be said to have some bearing on the apparent shunning of whiteboard use in the school:

- IT industry pressure to integrate whiteboards that were designed originally for office environments and adult users into school settings;
- government policy requirements to insert an interactive whiteboard in every school regardless of demand;
- the social context of the school and its environs (in the case of our visit school such issues included national health and safety regulations, and local fear of crime);
- the materiality of the Victorian buildings that many UK schools remain housed in;
- the relatively small size of primary school students in comparison to adult-sized computer hardware;
- the pragmatism of the Parent Teacher Association in finding and funding low-tech solutions to high-tech problems.

There are certainly many more issues that could be identified in addition to this initial list. The overall point of this vignette is that there are many reasons why digital technologies in schools may be 'not working' in the ways that many people believe that they should. Moreover, there are many ways that digital technologies may perhaps be allowed to 'work better' within the school setting. Getting to the heart of these debates involves paying sustained attention to a range of aspects of educational technology above and beyond the hardware and software that most obviously constitute 'the digital' – not least giving serious thought to the social relations that surround the use of digital technologies in schools. Taking a wider critical view of the 'digital' aspects of contemporary schools and schooling therefore forms the focus of this book.

This is a book about the social, cultural, economic and political aspects of digital technology and education. In particular it sets out to unpack the relationships between digital technology and *compulsory* education – i.e. schools, schooling and all other elements of the formal organised provision of education to children and young people. This is a book that attempts to make sense of what happens (and what does *not* happen) when the digital and the educational come together in the guise of 'schools technology'. The next nine chapters will identify and examine the key tensions and controversies that surround technology and schooling in the early twenty-first century, culminating in a set of suggestions, proposals and recommendations for addressing the 'problems' that appear to beset schools technology. Above all, the book sets out to develop a *critical* understanding of all these issues – offering a counterbalance to the often uncritical and unreflective academic study of educational technology over the past forty years.

Attaching the subtitle 'a critical analysis' to this book is not intended to imply a dogmatic adherence to any particular theoretical stance or viewpoint. Rather it reflects the book's ambition to take a sustained look at schools and digital technology in terms of some rather unfamiliar concepts in the academic study of educational technology. These include issues of power, politics, control and conflict, as well as matters of empowerment, equality, social justice and participatory democracy (see Gunter 2009). The book, therefore, seeks to re-politicise an increasingly de-politicised area of educational debate and analysis. It sets out to challenge the many contradictions that characterise the field of educational technology, and to develop new understandings of the forms that schools and schooling in the digital age could – and should – take.

The roots of this book lie in two simple contentions resulting from fifteen years of researching and writing about education and new technologies. First, it should be clear to all but the most zealous technophile that the much-heralded technological transformation of schools and schooling has yet to take place. As such it is perhaps time to accept that educational technology is simply not 'performing' as well as it could in formal educational settings. Second, it should be clear to even a casual reader of the literature in this area that academic discussion of educational technology is in urgent need of an overhaul. In this sense, it is perhaps time for renewed academic debate and analysis about why the use of digital technology in schools is as it is. From these contentious starting points this book sets out to offer a deliberately *critical* analysis of schools and digital technologies such as the internet, mobile telephones and other new digital media. With these thoughts in mind, the remainder of this first chapter now goes on to address some of the deceptively simple issues and assumptions that will underpin the remainder of the book's discussion – i.e. what is meant by digital technology and, most importantly, what is the significance of 'the digital' to gaining an understanding of contemporary schools and schooling?

What is 'digital technology' and why does it matter?

This book is concerned with what is diversely referred to as digital technology, information and communications technology, computerised technology and a number of other variations on the 'information technology' label. In a technical sense all of these terms refer to computer-based systems – particularly software applications and computer hardware – that can be used to produce, manipulate, store, communicate and disseminate information. From the 1980s onwards, these systems have taken many forms as digital technologies such as computers, mobile phones and the internet have converged into an ever-growing retinue of tools, artefacts and applications. Now what is referred to vaguely as 'digital technology' can actually refer to one of any number of portable, handheld and mobile devices operating a wide range of software services and applications. Recently this diversity has been furthered by the rise of so-called 'social media' and 'web 2.0' technologies – internet-based services and applications that are based around a mass socialisation of connectivity powered by the collective actions of online user communities. The rapid pace of the diversification and convergence of 'the digital' can often appear, to academic audiences at least, as an impossible phenomenon to document and analyse in a reasoned or considered manner. Most recently, for example, technological commentators have already begun to move on to herald the emergence of biotechnologies, nanotechnologies and a third generation of 'semantic web' and 'cloud computing' tools based around the 'intelligent use' of information. All told, the relatively simple label of 'digital technology' refers to an ever-changing complex of technological artefacts and tools.

However, this book is not concerned primarily with technological artefacts *per se*. The use of the term 'digital technology' also alludes to the ongoing digitisation of culture, politics, economics and society that can be associated with such technologies – what can be termed 'the digital age' for want of a better label. Rather than being seduced wholly by the technical complexity and prowess of technological artefacts that process data in binary form of 'zeroes and ones', this book's primary interest therefore lies in the things that are then done with these digital technologies. The roots of this book's concern with the 'digital age' therefore lie in the activities and prevailing ways-of-being that have come to characterise life in the contemporary digital age – at least as experienced in technologically-infused (over)developed societies in Europe, North America and much of south-east Asia. In these grand terms, then, this book's analysis of 'schools and schooling in the digital age' is intended to offer an investigation of the issues, tensions and controversies that lie at the heart of contemporary schooling. Beyond its broad interest in digital technology this book is more specifically concerned with a range of social, economic, cultural and political issues associated with the use of digital technologies that many commentators believe are set to (re)define contemporary schools and schooling. In particular, the rapid rise to prominence of the digital in contemporary education can be seen as part of a broader set of recent societal phenomena, not least the rise of a restructured free-market capitalism that lies at the heart of much – possibly all – contemporary societal change. It follows that anyone seeking to make sense of contemporary educational change pays close attention to these issues.

One of the striking characteristics of many recent accounts and analyses of the digital age is the generally transformatative (and often optimistic) ways in which the changes associated with digital technology tend to be imagined. In short, most accounts of the digital age are framed within common discourses of progress and the allure of 'the new'. Many popular and academic perceptions of digital technology appear, for example, to be animated by a belief that the digital age represents a 'pervasive sense of leaving the past behind' (Murdock 2004, p.20). In particular, many general discussions of the digital age tend to be informed by a notion that the development of digital technology represents a distinctively new *and* improved set of social arrangements in relation to preceding 'pre-digital' times. This sense of improved change can be described as the 'digital remediation' of everyday life and social processes (see Bolter and Grusin 1999), where digital technologies are seen to be reconfiguring many – possibly all – social processes and practices for the better. This is not to say that 'new' digital forms are believed to be usurping *all* practices and processes that have gone before, but rather that digitally-based activities are able to borrow from, refashion and often surpass their earlier pre-digital equivalents. For many commentators, therefore, the ready answer to alleviating or even overcoming contemporary social problems is now seen to involve some form of digitally related solution. As Steve Woolgar (2002, p.3) reflects, 'the implication is that something new, different, and (usually) better is happening'.

A prevailing faith in the ameliorative ability of digital technology is evident across most domains of human activity. At a macro level of analysis, for example, the 'flattening out' of hierarchies and the introduction of a 'networking logic' to the organisation of social relations is seen to support an open (re)configuration of society and a corresponding under-determination of organisational structures (e.g. Castells 1996; Friedman 2007). Conversely, at a micro-level the many 'affordances' of digital technology are seen to be boosting an individualisation of meaning-making and action that prompts, for example, a resurgence of more 'primitive' pre-industrial ways of life. For instance, the networking aspects of digital technologies such as the internet and mobile telephony have long been portrayed as rekindling a previously lost sense of tribalism, nomadism and communitarianism (Rheingold 1994; D'Andrea 2006). A range of claims have also been made regarding the role of digital technologies such as the internet in providing new opportunities for informal exchanges of knowledge, expertise and folk-wisdom (Sproull and Kiesler 1991), supplementing an individual's social capital (Wellman *et al.* 2001; Haythornthwaite 2005) and even 'breaking down the barriers and separate identities that have been the main cause of human suffering and war' (Mulgan 1998, cited in Robins and Webster 2002, p.247). Even overlooking the more fanciful and idealistic aspects of such accounts, the majority of popular and academic commentary concurs that digital technologies have recast social arrangements and relations along more open, democratic and ultimately empowering lines. In the (over)developed world at least, these changes are often imagined to have been wide-ranging and far-reaching. As Nicholas Gane (2005, p.475) reflects:

It would seem to me that internet-related technologies have directly altered the patterning of everyday life, including the way we work, access and exchange information, shop, meet people, and maintain and organise existing social ties. These technologies have done more than 'add on' to existing social arrangements; they have radically altered the three main spheres of social life, the spheres of production, consumption and communication.

As Gane implies, the direct alteration of everyday life is evident across all main areas of society such as business, industry, politics and polity, the family, news media, entertainment and leisure. Yet many people would argue that education has proved to be a particularly significant site for the reconfigurative properties of the digital. In particular, many people see the primary concerns of education as resonating especially closely with those of digital technology – i.e. the production and dissemination of information and knowledge through communication and interaction with others. While this affinity is seen to apply to all levels and forms of educational provision, many people would argue that compulsory schools and schooling should be seen as one of the most important and most appropriate areas of education in which the effects of the digital age are being felt.

Why look at digital technology, schools and schooling?

Having outlined this book's focus on the digital, it is also important to make clear the terms of reference for the educational aspects of discussion – in particular the notions of school and schooling. This book is concerned with what is referred to in North America and Australia as 'K12' or 'P12' education and often labelled elsewhere as compulsory schooling – i.e. the elementary and secondary schooling that is provided free of change by the state and is generally mandatory for all children and young people. Nearly all readers of this book will have attended a school for much of their childhood and adolescence. Such is the familiarity that stems from this personal experience that many people give little thought to what schools actually are and how they really work. With this thought in mind, it is worth taking a little time to clarify the terms and scope of reference that will underpin the remainder of this book's discussions.

In the most basic sense *schools* can be understood as the institutions where children and young people receive education, usually learning under the guidance of teachers. *Schooling*, on the other hand, refers to the processes of teaching and/or being taught in a school. While making this distinction may appear, at first glance, to be a little pedantic, it illustrates the need to approach schools and digital technology both in terms of structure *and* in terms of process. With regards to structure, for example, schools should be seen as physical entities whose architectural design and organisation of space and place influences teaching and learning. Moreover, schools are also characterised by a number of social and cultural structures, such as the hierarchies of roles that people adopt within the school organisation, the hierarchies of knowledge that constitute the school curriculum, and the organisation of time that constitute the school timetable. Conversely, the *processes* of schooling range from explicit processes of teaching, learning, communication and decision-making to more implicit processes of socialisation, regulation and control. In all of these aspects, schools should certainly not be seen simply as neutral contexts within which digital technologies are implemented and then used.

Indeed, as will be discussed throughout the book, schools are first and foremost regulatory environments – not least in terms of their dependence upon compulsion of attendance and subsequent coercion of behaviour. As such the intersections between digital technology and compulsory schooling entail a range of issues relating to power, control, regulation and (in)equality. These are all areas of particular relevance to a sociological view of education – making digital technology a particularly appropriate lens through which to view the social, political, economic and cultural machinations of schools and society in the early twenty-first century. In this sense, digital technology should be seen as an ideal focus for the continuation of the sociological study of schools and schooling as a 'core societal institution' (Arum and Beattie 2000). As Steven Brint (1998, p.2) described, throughout the latter half of the twentieth century sociologists developed a deep concern with questions of 'what schools are actually like, with why schools are the way they are, and with the consequences of what happens in schools'. Yet as the twenty-first century has progressed it could be argued that looking critically at the internal structures and processes of contemporary schools and schooling has ceased to be quite as compelling a topic as it once was for the researcher or writer seeking to account for the social complexities of contemporary education. The vitality and richness of the 'sociology of schools' literature that thrived throughout the 1970s and 1980s (e.g. Hargreaves 1967; Davies 1976; King 1983), and the rash of socially 'thick' ethnographic descriptions of schools produced during the 1970s and 1980s from the likes of Dan Lortie, Paul Willis, Stephen Ball, Robert Burgess and others has passed somewhat. As the neo-liberal policies of the Thatcher and Regan administrations began to take hold during the 1980s, many sociologists of education refocused their attentions away from the internal machinations of schools and schooling and turned instead towards a 'policy sociology' analysis of the dynamics of choice, diversity and the implications of educational 'marketplaces' for equity. The majority of sociological attention during the past twenty years has therefore shifted away from what goes on inside schools, and on to the processes of how people get access to schools in the first place. Educational understandings of 'the school' itself have begun to dominated by the rather less critical 'school effectiveness' movement that came to typify academic discussion of schools throughout the 1990s and 2000s. With some notable exceptions, most recent academic writing on the school has remained concerned with how best to engineer 'school improvement' and achieve 'effective' outcomes, rather than developing a necessarily critical sociological analysis.

Of course, this turn away from the individual school as a site of critical analysis could be said to have stemmed largely from the unequivocal consensus arising from the studies of the 1970s and 1980s that schools were profoundly unfair and unjust places that had relatively little bearing on the educational outcomes of pupils in comparison to the mass of influences that lie beyond the school (Coleman *et al.* 1966; Jencks *et al.* 1972). Such was the entrenched stratification of educational opportunities and outcomes associated with schooling throughout the 1970s and 1980s that schools became a rather passé topic of study among those social scientists wishing to develop critical accounts of education during the 1990s and 2000s. Similarly, in comparison to other areas of society, schools are also seen to offer a rather underwhelming case study of the technological. Sociologists wishing to gain rich insights into the dynamic nature of young people's educational technology use therefore chose to look any-where but the school setting – not least the home or purely virtual settings.

Yet, as the remainder of this book will hopefully make clear, schools continue to matter immensely in gaining an understanding of education in the digital age, if only for the amount of time that children and young people spend within the confines of the school. For better or worse, students and teachers continue to spend upwards of six hours per day at school for an average of two hundred days of the year (a figure that actually ranges from an average of 170 days a year in Sweden to over 240 days a year in Japan). With many countries increasing the age at which an individual may leave compulsory schooling, most young people will now spend far more than the '15,000 hours' that schooling was long reckoned to take out of one's lifetime (Rutter *et al.* 1979). Moreover, schools continue to be very different places in comparison to the other settings that children and young people spend their time in. For these reasons alone, the remainder of this book takes the rather unfashionable but necessary step of focusing on the people, practices, processes and places involved in contemporary schooling, and the roles that digital technologies have come to play in configurations of the contemporary school. The next eight-and-a-half chapters will therefore set about questioning what Laurence Angus terms the 'taken-for granted' of schools, schooling and digital technologies. In other words, the book will use digital technol-ogy as a lens through which to re-evaluate the everyday practice of contemporary schooling, thereby yielding insights into the 'black box' of the school, and exploring 'how the process of schooling is perceived, constituted and experienced from differ-ent social positions' (Angus 1993, p.335).

Looking beyond the hype of schools and digital technologies

The long-standing and widespread faith in the ability of digital technologies to reme-diate and even transform schools must be seen in terms of wider societal concerns over mass schooling. For at least the past forty years – if not the past one hundred and forty years – many people have tended to view the school as cause for concern rather than celebration. Well-established accounts persist in many developed coun-tries of school systems somehow 'failing' to perform as well they should. For many political and popular commentators, schools in countries such as the US and UK have long been felt to be underperforming, leading to what Stephen Gorard has termed a prevailing 'crisis account' of schooling where educational opportunities have come to be understood as increasingly polarised, and schools characterised by their apparently poor overall educational standards. As Gorard (2001, p.279) describes:

> This crisis account is a shared perspective of a loose alliance of researchers and other commentators who apparently recall some golden age of schooling, when educational standards were generally higher, and social justice was greater. Since that time, divisions . . . are supposed to have increased.

Against this background, growing numbers of people have proved all too keen over the past forty years to seize upon digital technologies as offering a ready 'technical fix' for the problem of the underperforming and failing school. The topic of schools and technology has attracted a broad range of interest groups and concerns seeking to speak on its behalf. On the one hand are a large number of enthusiastic teachers and other practitioners who make extensive use of digital technology in their work. Outside of schools exist a growing group of professional 'educational technologists' who develop technology applications and tools, accompanied by a growing cadre of 'learning technologists' responsible for their pedagogical design and implementation. These voices are complemented by ranks of academic researchers and writers who evaluate the use of digital technology in schools – often working within university departments of education and initial teacher training. These interest groups are accompanied by a sizable community of policy-makers with power to influence or determine schools technology policies and practices at a national and international level – not least civil servants, policy advisers and politicians. Correspondingly, a multitude of commercial providers and IT industry actors are responsible for the 'selling' of educational technologies to schools. Finally are a wide range of advocacy groups concerned with schools technology on behalf of parents, employers, community groups and so on. As a whole, all these interests cumulate to produce a continuous and vociferous 'buzz' relating to what schools technology is and what schools technology is capable of.

The expectations and promises emanating from these advocates have often taken a distinctly exaggerated and evangelical air. Indeed, discussion of schools technology has often bordered on the hyperbolic as sections of the education community have felt drawn towards what Robert Boody (2001) describes as 'the siren songs of technology'. Of course, this privileging of the technological is by no means a recent occurrence in educational discourse – as illustrated by Larry Cuban's (1986) synopsis of educational enthusiasm for all manner of early twentieth-century technologies from the film strip to the wireless radio. Yet as this book's remaining discussion will regularly attest, digital technologies have generated particularly high levels of hyperbole from a diverse range of interests and actors. For example, ever since their emergence computerised technologies have been portrayed as allowing learners to break free of the physical confines of classroom-based teaching and to facilitate boundless access to 'better' forms of learning on an any-time, any-place, any-pace basis (Suppes 1965; Bennet and Bennet 2008). Some educational technologists have gone as far as to anticipate the digitally-driven 'blowing-up' of the conventional school (see Papert 1984). In this respect, much faith continues to be vested in digital technologies as a catalyst for a substantial, possibly total, re-engineering of school-based modes of teaching and learning.

What is perhaps most notable about this 'hyping' of digital technology is its persistence and durability across decades, regardless of the specific tools or applications concerned. The past three decades have seen the regular advancement of arguments, for example, that individuals can learn through the 'hard fun' of creating and playing computer games rather than being subjected to the 'teaching disabled' pedagogies of the conventional classroom (Negroponte 1995; Shaffer 2008). The excitement over the transformative potentials of electronic white-boards and smart-boards that dominated discussions of educational technology in the early 2000s was later eclipsed by excitement over the use of personalised 'learning spaces' and 'learning platforms' in schools – leading educational technologists and academic commentators alike to proclaim yet again that 'we are on the verge of profound change' (Connell 2007, p.7). More recently, so-called 'social media' tools and applications prompted claims during the latter half of the 2000s that these technologies constituted 'the future of education' (Hargadon 2008), with educational technology once again promising 'the creation of a more just, human, inclusive society, where the development and transformation of teaching and learning services social and emotional as well as economic ends' (Sutherland *et al.* 2008, p.5).

The cyclical nature of these celebratory accounts should be seen against the long-standing tendency in Western societies to view digital technology as a general technical fix for social problems. The application of technological solutions continues to be a central tenet of governments' thinking when it comes to managing what Bogin (2009, p.51) terms 'the inner contradictions of the riskless, socially engineered society'. Technology therefore forms a key element of policy responses to issues as diverse as the worldwide financial crisis of the late 2000s to the ongoing concerns over disease management and environmental decline. Yet the scope of these examples notwithstanding, there is a sense that education is particularly susceptible to the promise of the 'technical fix'. As Kevin Robins and Frank Webster (1989) observed towards the end of the 1980s, there has been a notable tendency throughout the history of education to approach new technologies in an uncritical manner as a ready corrective to social issues, only later to ignore the often ineffective or unsustainable outcomes that arise as a result of their use. Over twenty years on, Robins and Webster's thesis would appear to be as prescient as ever, with many practitioners, policy-makers and academics appearing to be seduced by the overriding belief that the most serious problems that confront schools and schooling require technical solutions.

Of course, this is not to argue that such hyperbolic accounts of digital technology and education have been wholly welcomed by all sectors of the education community. While many people in education may concur with such eulogising, others have remained rightly sceptical of the notion of a technological transformation of schooling. Following this lead it would be wise to approach these strains of intense enthusiasm for educational technology with caution. Indeed, many of the claims just outlined are perhaps best seen as little more than what Henri Lefebvre terms as 'techno-hype' – i.e. 'an intensification of technological modernism and an expectation of novelty, in a kind of frantic fervour for a different society, the product of computer science, telematics and so on' (Lefebvre 1981, p.91). In this sense, it could be prudent to be a little more circumspect about the educational promise of digital technology than has often been the case in the arguments presented so far in this chapter.

Considering the specific hopes for schools, schooling and digital technologies

In many respects, the incessant 'hyping' of the educational potential of technology should be seen as part of the wider tendency in contemporary society towards a 'techno-romantic' or 'techno-utopian' reading of the technological. As Chris Bigum and Jane Kenway (1998, p.378) highlighted, there continues to be a noticeable tendency within education discourse towards what can be termed a technological 'boosterism', i.e. visions of educational technology that are:

characterised by an unswerving faith in the technology's capacity to improve education and most other things in society, often coupled with a sense of inevitability concerning the growth and use of computer technology. They have few doubts about the educational merits of their vision for change.

Such extreme evangelism is accompanied, inevitably, by negative reactions from some other commentators – what Bigum and Kenway identified as an attendant set of 'doomster' discourses that 'see much damage to society and education arising form the uncritical acceptance of new media forms [. . .] nostalgic for the period when these technologies did not exist or for the practices and institutions that are being replaced by new technologies' (Bigum and Kenway 1998, p.386). Although less prominent than the booster point of view, a residual 'doomster' rhetoric has persisted over the last forty years with regards to schools and digital technology. Perennial concerns have been raised, for example, over the intellectual 'dumbing-down' associated with students' and teachers' use of digital technologies to access information and knowledge (Keen 2007; Brabazon 2007). Similarly, biologists and psychologists continue to point towards technology-related declines in children's cognitive skills and mental performance, as well as the unbalancing of hormonal levels (Sigman 2009; Greenfield 2009). Aside from these supposed detrimental effects on intellect, cognition and 'traditional' skills and literacies, fears continue to be raised that digital technologies may be contributing to an increased disaffection among students for schools and classroom-based learning. For example, school students have been described as being more interested in using digital technologies such as the internet or mobile telephony for self-expression and self-promotion than for actually listening to and learning from others. These concerns have prompted some commentators to point to the digital acceleration of 'a culture of disrespect' between students and their schools and teachers (Bugeja 2006).

While persistent and often compelling, it is worth maintaining a sense of perspective on the significance of these booster and doomster traditions. These rather exaggerated and polemic debates over the utopian and dystopian extremes of schools technology take place largely at the margins of educational technology thinking. Instead, most debate over the potentials and possibilities of educational technology takes the form of a rather more grounded set of articulations relating to specific educational advantages of technology use. These can be seen as a widely accepted set of specific hopes (rather than abstract hyperbole) for schools, schooling and digital technology. In brief, the specific educational advantages of digital technologies are seen to take a number of forms – all concerned broadly with changes that digital technologies can bring to learning, learners and the settings within which they learn. All these perceived benefits are worth considering in further detail.

i) Hopes for better learning

Perhaps the most pervasive hopes for digital technology and education centre around perceptions of the 'better' forms of education that technology use can yield for individual students. As such, the specific educational merits of digital technology have tended to be expressed through a set of distinct articulations concerning the empowerment of individual learners – not least the improvement of learning processes. Indeed, one of the most prominent strands of thinking in this respect is the perception that digital technologies offer a ready basis for learning to take place as a socially situated, communal activity. In particular, internet-based technologies are often seen to readily support socio-cultural and constructivist forms of learning that are 'situated' within networks of objects, artefacts, technologies and people. Technology-based education has long been felt, for example, to chime with Vygotskian notions of 'authentic' learning where knowledge is constructed actively by learners with the support of communal social settings. A great deal of attention has been paid recently to the personalised and socially situated forms of learning (intended or otherwise) that can be found within learners' participatory experiences in the co-construction of online knowledge (e.g. Lameras *et al.* 2009; Luckin 2010).

These arguments highlight the totemic role that digital technologies now play for many academic commentators who believe learning to best take place within networks of learners and objects that are involved with the creation as well as consumption of knowledge. As such, the valorisation of the social dynamic of learning within recent educational thinking (itself prompted by the rise of socially-focused theories within cognitive psychology) now encompasses the personalised and socially situated forms of learning seen to be implicit within much contemporary technology use. In this sense, as Charles Crook reasons, digital technologies such as social web applications are seen to offer learners

> a more participatory experience . . . This is largely about making more opportunities for the user to publish and communicate. It is about uploading rather than downloading. About co-ordination, rather than delivery. So, for learners: it's about more audience, more collaboration, more resource (Crook 2008, p.30).

The centrality of digital technologies to socio-cultural views of learning is perhaps reflected most explicitly in the emerging learning theory of 'connectivism'. Here learning is framed as the ability to access and use distributed information on a 'just-in-time' basis (see Siemens 2004). From this perspective, learning can be primarily conceived as an individual's ability to connect to specialised information sources or 'nodes' as and when required. In this sense, an individual's existing knowledge is seen to be of lesser importance than their ability to nurture and maintain these potential connections to future knowledge. As George Siemens (2004, n.p.) puts it, learning is therefore conceived in terms of the 'capacity to know more' via digital technologies such as the internet, rather than a reliance on the accumulation of prior knowledge in terms of 'what is currently known'. Similar claims have been made with regards to the 'fluid' nature of digitally-supported intelligence, described as 'the ability to find meaning in confusion and to solve new problems, independent of acquired knowledge' (Cascio 2009, n.p.). All told, digital technologies are seen to have changed the nature and form of learning, as well as what it is to be a learner.

Some authors have also argued for distinct biological and neurological changes to the ways in which generations of technology-using learners are now able to learn and process information. The technologist Marc Prensky, for one, has spent much time detailing what he sees as the technology-induced capacity of young people to 'think and process information fundamentally differently from their predecessors' (2001, p.1). These claims are grounded in an emerging body of scientific evidence that suggests that young people's working memory and perceptual learning can be enhanced through engagement with digital technologies (see Small and Vorgon 2008). It is argued, for example, that cognitive and neurological benefits are evident in the ease with which children and young people are able to learn at high speed, make serendipitous connections, process visual and dynamic information and learn through digitally-based play and interactions (Prensky 2001). As Prensky (2008, n.p.) speculates, 'within the working lives of our students, technology will become a billion times more powerful, likely more powerful than the human brain'.

ii) Hopes for fairer learning

As these latter sentiments suggest, many commentators perceive the specific educational potentials of digital technologies in decidedly transformatory terms. Aside from the cognitive and intellectual benefits of digital technology use, this transformatory tone is continued in the view that digital technologies are capable of fostering an increased democratisation of educational opportunities and outcomes. The perceived capacity, for example, of the internet to enhance the 'goodness of fit' between education provision and individual circumstance is seen to lead to forms of schooling that are more egalitarian and less compromised than would otherwise be the case. Here it is argued that learners can enjoy access via the internet to a more diverse range of learning opportunities both inside and outside of the classroom. Crucially these enhanced opportunities are seen to be accessible regardless of geographical proximity or socio-economic circumstance. For example, digital technologies have been portrayed as a ready means of providing a high quality universal education for all children throughout the developing world via the creation of so-called 'Mega-Schools', i.e. schooling provided through a combination of distance learning and community-based support (Daniel 2010). Much has also been written about the internet's capacity to stimulate episodes of informal learning through access to vast quantities of information – what has been described in some quarters as a realisation of 'the dream of the universal library' (Kruk 1999, p.138).

These discourses of democracy are also evident in the widely-held belief that digital technologies offer an opportunity for schools and teachers to (re)connect with otherwise disaffected and disengaged learners. As Mason and Rennie (2007, p.199) reason, 'shared community spaces and inter-group communications are a massive part of what excites young people and therefore should contribute to [their] persistence and motivation to learn'. Similarly, much popular and academic commentary has celebrated (at least implicitly) the capacity of digital technologies such as the internet to recast social arrangements and relations along open and democratic lines. As Solomon and Schrum (2007, p.8) concluded with regards to the second wave of 'social' internet applications that emerged throughout the 2000s, 'everyone can participate thanks to social networking and collaborative tools and the abundance of web 2.0 sites . . . The web is no longer a one-way street where someone controls the content. Anyone can control content in a web 2.0 world'.

In this sense digital technology has been welcomed by some radically minded practitioners and academics as one of the latest vehicles in progressive educational aspirations. As Douglas Kellner (2004) put it, digital technology has been welcomed as a ready means of achieving 'a more democratic and egalitarian society'. Social media and other internet applications, for example, have been promoted by some academic commentators as supporting an 'educational superabundance' where students can engage in levels of learning that far exceed the demands of utilitarian schooling. As Juha Suoranta and Tere Vadén conclude, in this sense digital technology can act as 'a means for revolutionary ends' – that allow individuals to transcend the limitations of conventional schooling and educational expectations (Suoranta and Vadén 2010, p.177).

iii) Hopes for individualised and informalised learning

As these preceding examples illustrate, much of the enthusiasm for technology use in schools centres on the increased empowerment of the individual learner. In particular, digital technologies are seen to enhance students' control over the nature and form of what they do, as well as where, when and how they do it. For example, the internet is described as supporting the capacity of individual students to build and maintain connections with various components of their schooling – what is often presented as the 'personalisation' of learning. This notion of technology-supported personalisation sees the reversal of the logic of education provision 'so that it is the system that conforms to the learners, rather than the learner to the system', with learners therefore (re)positioned at the centre of networks of learning opportunities (Green *et al.* 2006, p.3). These accounts of the technology-supported repositioning of the individual learner at the centre of their schooling are plentiful. As Nunes (2006, p.130) concludes, contemporary forms of technology-supported education are now believed widely to

> conflate access and control; transmission in other words is figured as a performative event in the hands of the student, thereby repositioning the student in relation to institutional networks. To this extent, the [student] is anything but marginal; as both the operator that enacts the class and the target that receives course content, the student occupies a metaphorical and experiential centre for the performance of the course.

These sentiments also chime with a general enthusiasm among many academics and learning technologists over the informalisation of learning that digital technologies afford – i.e. learning that is often spontaneous, somehow more natural and often less forced than is usually the case in formal education settings (Sefton-Green 2004). Mimi Ito and colleagues (2008), for example, have described how digital technologies provide young people with the opportunity to 'mess about' in a variety of ways, occasionally compelling them to immerse themselves in intense periods of self-directed learning activity – what these authors refer to as 'geeking out'. In this sense the technology-supported learner is celebrated as being no longer the passive recipient of learning instruction but cast instead into an active role of (re)constructing the nature, place, pace and timing of the learning event.

Learners of all ages are therefore seen to benefit from a distinct individualisation of their learning that derives specifically from digital technology use. As such, upcoming generations of school students are portrayed as autonomous *and* highly sociable learners. This combination of individualisation and sociability is often presented as giving children and young people a propensity to question, challenge and critique their engagement with formal education. These are individuals who 'typically can't imagine a life where citizens didn't have the tools to constantly think critically, exchange views, challenge, authenticate, verify, or debunk' (Tapscott and Williams 2008, p.47). The inherently sceptical but highly sociable worldview is portrayed as leading some children and young people to construct alternatives to the core values of traditional institutions and structures. Instead of kowtowing to the linear restrictions and requirements of formal schooling, young people are described as now having the ability to self-organise and provide such services for themselves. As Tapscott and Williams (2008, p.52) suggest, digital technologies thereby foster a tendency for some young people, at least, to no longer be 'content to be passive consumers, [but] increasingly satisfy their desire for choice, convenience, customisation, and control by designing, producing, and distributing products themselves'.

iv) Hopes for enhanced teaching and pedagogy

Of course, digital technologies are seen to bring a number of enhancements and improvements to schools and schooling above and beyond the context of the individual learner – not least benefits in terms of the role of the teacher. Digital technologies have long been seen as supporting teachers in the more procedural elements of their job, as well as allowing them to guide students towards more successful learning outcomes. Indeed, the framing of various technologies as 'the teacher's friend' has had an enduring appeal over the recent history of educational technology (Shoup 1984; Haigh 2007). In terms of supporting the bureaucratic and administrative aspects of teaching, for instance, digital technologies are believed widely to support teachers and teaching in a number of ways – not least their role in reducing teacher workloads and their support in the tracking and monitoring of learner progress, the management of learning materials, and the provision of formative and summative assessment of learners and learning. All of these administrative and procedural 'scaffoldings' are seen to culminate in the substantive improvement and 'freeing-up' of teachers' ability to teach (see Selwood 2005).

Besides these administrative and procedural forms of support, digital technologies are also seen to offer a number of pedagogical advantages to school teachers. It is argued, for example, that digital technologies support teachers in planning and preparing their teaching in more diverse and informed ways. Digital technologies are also seen as an innovative means of allowing teachers to enhance their own learning about their subject areas, and in more general terms to advance professional knowledge about the process and practice of teaching (Somekh 2007). Crucially digital technologies such as the internet are seen to provide teachers with access to resources and collegial support beyond the limitations of their immediate circumstances. Classroom-based technologies such as the interactive whiteboard are also seen to provide teachers with opportunities to alter their styles of teaching and modes of delivery. For example, it is argued that through the use of digital technology teachers can switch between individualised to communal and communicative forms of pedagogy, thereby moving the role of the teacher from one of an organiser of learning activities to one of a shaper of quality learning experiences. Amidst all of these changes, most educational technologists are careful to emphasise the continuation of the role of the teacher at the centre of the pedagogical process. As David Guile argues, most technology-enhanced gains in learning and achievement 'occur primarily because teachers have designed new contexts as well as new learning processes to support learning' (cited in Reynolds *et al.* 2003, p.152).

v) Hopes for enhanced management and organisation of schooling

In considering the specific educational hopes regarding digital technology use, a number of institutionally-related issues also present themselves. In particular digital technologies have been welcomed as a ready means through which to transform school organisation and leadership, and hasten the management of change within schools. Many practitioners, academics and policy-makers, for example, see digital technologies as hastening the 'flattening-out' of hierarchies and decision-making processes within schools – thereby making them more democratic and efficient organisations (see Shuttleworth 2003). Digital technologies are seen to allow school leaders to motivate and support individual teachers, and thereby influence and empower them to achieve personal and institutional change – not least through technology-based professional development and training. This technology-supported inclusion of individuals within the organisational processes of the school is felt to encompass all members of the school, allowing schools to become 'learning communities' where all members of the school are given a more participative role in the schools' affairs. Much enthusiasm has been directed towards the role of digital technology in supporting 'whole school democracy', where technologies are used for consultative activities and practices. Growing support is being expressed, for example, for technology-based democratic structures and mechanisms such as inter-school virtual communities, school councils and other classroom-based 'e-democracy' activities. All of these applications highlight the potential of digital technologies to give school students, teachers and managers the opportunity to set their own agendas and participate in the organisation of their school life.

The managerial and administrative advantages of digital technologies for the school are also seen to be many. As with many other areas of business, technology is seen as an integral element of schools becoming more 'efficient' organisations – both in terms of their specific day-to-day administrative functions and more general managerial goals of promoting high quality teaching, learning and assessment and increasing student 'performance'. These administrative benefits range from the use of information systems to record and monitor the progress of learners, as well as the provision of information to and from external agencies such as school districts, central government, examination authorities and, of course, parents (Newton 2005). Digitally-based 'institutional technologies' are therefore implicated in many of the processes and practices of educational management and leadership. These include the integral role of technology in planning and budgeting, organising and staffing, developing policies and setting visions, setting instructional standards, running payrolls and communicating with parents and other 'stakeholders' and 'end-users'.

In all these respects, digital technologies are seen to allow schools to make more efficient use of resources than would otherwise be possible – offering an ideal means to help school organisations to become more flexible, adaptable and entrepreneurial in their business dealings. As Bromley (2001, p.41) argued with respect to the financial and resource management of schools, digital technology offers a compelling promise to enhance schools' 'ability to 'produce' more efficiently, to yield a higher level of measurable student performance with little or no increase in funding . . . enabl[ing] more learning to happen without hiring more teachers'. Indeed, such promises are reflected in the recent enthusiasm for the role of digital technologies such as the internet to allow schools to extend their engagement with the communities in which they are located in what is often referred to as an 'extended school' approach (Austin and Anderson 2008; Grant 2009).

Conclusions

Of course, many thousands of books have been dedicated to exploring the promises and potentials, hopes and hypes of digital technologies in education. As even the brief examples discussed in this chapter should make clear, schools have long been party to a seductive cocktail of claims, promises and contentions made on behalf of new and emerging digital technologies. While the polemic hype surrounding digital technologies may have abated somewhat since the 1980s and 1990s, educational hopes for the transformatative power of new technologies have solidified into a set of specific articulations pertaining to wider theories of what schools are and how they operate. Although most people are now quite rightly cautious of grand claims concerning the *complete* transformation of schools, many academic and political commentators, technologists, industrialists and practitioners continue to adhere to a set of more specific beliefs about the presumed 'benefit' and inherent advantages of technology use in schools. As the latter half of this chapter has illustrated, a number of specific legitimating rhetorics now surround schools' use of digital technology – not least a belief in technology supporting more 'efficient' forms of schooling. As such, digital technology lies at the heart of the ongoing reconstruction of contemporary schooling in the minds of many education 'stakeholders'. As Stephen Ball argues:

> schools are becoming new kinds of spaces and places as they are rebuilt and re-designed, figuratively and literally. They stand for, are icons of, new policy, new modalities of learning – the products of a re-imagineering. They have new kinds of social and architectural ecologies, which promise new kinds of

learning experience, in technologically rich, flexible learning environments (Ball 2007a, p.189).

In this sense, many of the debates and discussions surrounding schools and digital technology are not concerned with the actual technical capabilities of digital technologies *per se* – rather they relate to wider imaginings of how schools may be altered and adjusted in line with the needs of contemporary society. As many of the examples in this chapter have shown, it is perhaps not surprising that the claims and promises associated with digital technology and schools run parallel with many of the wider concerns currently dominating educational thinking – such as social constructivist and socio-cultural theories of learning, the modernisation and rationalisation of public sector organisations, the raising of standards and effectiveness, individualisation and personalisation of services and so on. The enrolment of digital technologies into all of these debates therefore lends a distinctly technocratic air to how contemporary schools and schooling are being imagined – with many discussions imbued with what Henri Lefebvre called the 'dual fetishism of competence and performance' (Lefebvre 1981, p.24).

While understandable, the rhetorical attractions of the general *idea* of digital technology (rather than the specific capabilities of any specific technology *per se*) have led to a situation where the actual uses of digital technologies in schools are rarely given sustained critical attention. The past forty years have seen a maturing and a normalisation of the benefits of digital technologies in mainstream educational thinking. As such, the status of digital technology as a generally 'good thing' has become something of an orthodoxy within educational thinking about schools and schooling – i.e. part of a commonsense consensus where digital technologies have become 'gradually accepted and virtually un-noticed', often without 'those who are affected registering the fact' (Lefebvre 1981, p.78). Whereas a distinct resistance to information technologies in some segments of the educational community may have existed during the 1980s and 1990s, most academics and practitioners have now moved beyond a disinterested acceptance of digital technology to a deep-rooted and widely held belief in the inherent benefits of technology for education. As such, digital technology use has now achieved the status of an integral and institutionalised part of the fabric of contemporary education – something that barely requires thinking about, or even, acknowledging.

In this sense, the technocratic orthodoxy that has grown up around schools and digital technology can be seen to have assumed what David Nye (2007, p.29) terms the status of being 'ideologically invisible', with its presumed ideals of efficiency and rationality all now accepted largely without discussion. This normalisation of educational technology over the last twenty years or so into an unquestioning orthodoxy is something that certainly requires scrutiny and reconsideration. While the promises, hopes and beliefs for digital technology described in this chapter may have a strong intuitive appeal, the ease with which these commonsensical 'stories' of the benefits of digital technology for schools are repeated and 're-told' throughout educational discussions and debates should be cause for some alarm. As Ng (1997, p.44) contends, despite often being uncritical, episodic and disjointed, common sense thinking in education is primarily powerful 'because it is taken for granted'.

One of the central themes for the remainder of this book, therefore, will be not to take anything that is said about digital technology and schools for granted. Indeed, as Chapter 2 will now go on to argue, the perceived benefits and advantages of schools technology are not something that the educational community can afford to take as given or see as benignly neutral. Despite the many efforts that have been made over the past thirty years or so to implement and integrate digital technologies into schools and schooling, many of the claims and presumptions made on the part of digital technology have simply not come to fruition. As such, anyone wishing to make sense of schools and schooling in the digital age faces a pressing need to contrast the many promises surrounding digital technology in education with the rather more compromised realities of digital technology use 'on the ground'. With this thought in mind, Chapter 2 now goes on to explore what was termed at the beginning of this chapter as the 'messy' realities of schools and digital technology.

2 The messy realities of digital technology use in schools

Introduction

As Chapter 1 has just illustrated, the use of digital technology in schools is a matter of intense conviction and passion for many people. Above and beyond the general belief that digital technology is inherently a 'good thing' for education in the twenty-first century, a set of more specific transformative claims are advanced to justify the reorientation of schools and schooling along digital lines. While the imperative to make best use of digital technologies in schools may appear irrefutable, it is important to remain mindful of the symbolic role that technology often plays in discussions and debates over societal change and improvement. In this sense, many of the promises, claims and justifications outlined in Chapter 1 are best seen as inspirational and exhortative rather than actual accounts of schools and digital technologies. Schools technology – like educational technology in general – is as much a focus for wish fulfilment as it is for accurate forecasting and reasoned analysis.

Having reviewed the many promises and hopes that surround schools technology this next chapter goes on to consider the rather more compromised realities of digital technology use in school systems around the world. Despite the rather grand claims that tend to be made for digital technology, all but the most zealous of educational technology 'hucksters' (to borrow a phrase from Theodore Roszak) would concede that the actual implementation and use of digital technology in school settings is somewhat less extensive and sophisticated than it could be. Indeed, growing numbers of academic commentators and educational technologists are now beginning to view schools as a distinct impediment to realising the educational potential of digital technology. While schools could not be said to be failing completely to make good use of digital technology, many commentators would nevertheless argue that schools often fail to make sustained 'best use' of digital technology. Thus, despite the increasing prominence of digital technology in school settings, growing numbers of academic accounts now discuss the school as a site of technology use in ambivalent and sometimes antagonistic terms. This chapter will now go on to explore what many people now see as the satisfactory, and the less satisfactory, elements of technology use in schools.

The rise of digital technology use in schools

In terms of resourcing and funding, digital technology is now a significant element of education systems around the world. After years of being a peripheral aspect of education provision, the last fifteen years have seen digital technologies such as the computer and the internet become prominent features of education systems in most developed and developing countries. Practically every developed country now has a detailed 'educational ICT strategy' based around the broad aim of encouraging and supporting schools' use of computers, the internet and other digital technologies. These strategies and initiatives most commonly involve dedicating significant amounts of funding towards computer hardware and internet connectivity, thereby ensuring that internet access is available in all parts of the school and that sufficient computer access is available for pupils and teachers to use. Much effort is also put into the technological training of novice and experienced teachers alike, as well as adjusting school curricula to include technology use where possible. From Ethiopia's ICT in Education Implementation Strategy to Estonia's Learning Tiger Programme, digital technology forms a central part of the improvement and modernisation of education systems around the world.

Unlike similar technology drives throughout the 1980s and 1990s, one of the key features of these national ICT strategies and programmes is that they are now directed at all levels and all aspects of the school system. As the 2010s progress, the widespread use of digital technology is as important an issue for primary and pre-school education as it is for secondary schools. For example, early years and elementary school technology use is a key component of the Singapore ten-year master plan – Intelligent Nation 2015. The current New Zealand Digital Strategy has an explicit focus through the Applying Foundations for Discovery: Supporting Learning in Early Childhood through ICT framework – seeking to use digital technologies 'meaningfully in early childhood education services to help children grow up as competent and confident learners and communicators' (New Zealand Government 2008, p.23). Similarly, the Australian Government's Digital Education Revolution strategy supports the development of fibre broadband connections to all Australian schools, and the provision to all students and teachers of online curriculum tools and resources. Most European countries have similar plans for the development of digital technology use throughout their school systems – from the French Digital Strategy to the extensive Austrian Future Learning strategy based around the use of wikis, blogging and ePortfolios.

The outcomes of these national efforts to boost the use of digital technologies in schools have been impressive in many respects. In terms of resourcing, for example, digital technologies now constitute a substantial presence in many classrooms of many schools in the developed world. Any adult visitor to a school would certainly notice an array of technologies that would not have featured in their own childhood experiences of schooling. If the outcomes of national ICT drives are judged in terms of the broad stated targets that usually accompany such policy-making, then most of the goals relating to getting digital technologies into schools tend to be met and often exceeded. Certainly in terms of most governments' central concerns of introducing digital technologies across school systems on a widespread basis, the national technology drives outlined above have all been highly successful. The substantial increases in funding, resourcing and support initiated by these policies are seen to have led to the dissipation of barriers to digital technology use in most areas of schooling. In a country such as the UK, for instance, the ratio of pupils to computers in primary education fell from 107 pupils per computer in 1985 to around six pupils per computer by the end of the 2000s (BESA 2009). Similarly, the ratio of pupils to computers in UK secondary education fell from 61 pupils per computer in 1985 to around three and a half pupils per computer by the end of the 2000s. These changes are even more pronounced in countries such as Singapore, Korea, Finland and Denmark, where pupil to computer ratios are closer to one computer for every two pupils.

Aside from issues of technological procurement and provision, there is plenty of evidence of these technologies being used in schools by students and teachers alike. Curricular guidelines in many countries and regions now include compulsory technology components. Many aspects of schoolwork now involve the presentation of coursework and project work by students via word-processed documents and slide-show presentations. Recent surveys suggest that teachers now have higher levels of technological confidence and are more likely to make regular use of digital technologies in their teaching than ever before (Barker and Gardiner 2007; BESA 2009). The past ten years have also seen schools in many countries taking responsibility for their own technology procurement beyond state funding. In the UK, for example, rising government funding for digital technology throughout the 2000s created a large capital infrastructure that led to most schools supporting technology use with their own funds by the end of the decade (Mee 2007a). By 2009, primary schools in the UK were spending annually £320 million on digital technology hardware and infrastructure alongside £76 million on curriculum software and content. Similarly, the secondary sector was spending annually £281 million on hardware and infrastructure alongside £51 million on curriculum software and content – all significant increases from just five years before.

A substantial – if not wholly convincing – evidence base exists to provide support for the beneficial outcomes of the increased financing, resourcing and use of digital technologies in schools that took place over the 1990s and 2000s. In terms of gains and improvements in learning, for example, a range of studies has sought to highlight the learning outcomes of digital technology use in schools. Trucano's (2005) review of evidence for the World Bank outlined a number of areas where digital technology use could be said to be influencing school-based learning in a positive manner – pointing towards apparent gains in areas such as student achievement and student performance in standardised tests in areas such as reading and mathematical skills. This review also highlighted the perceived benefits of digital technology use – with many students and teachers reporting that using digital technologies made for more effective, autonomous and motivated forms of learning. A similar review by Condie and Munro (2007) also pointed towards a general consensus among teachers that technology use led to enhanced motivation and engagement, independent learning and autonomy among students, as well as the development of collaborative learning and communication skills. Perhaps most importantly, these were all seen as outcomes 'which can contribute to improved knowledge, understanding and skills. This can, in turn, have an impact upon attainment' (Condie and Munro 2007, p.22).

The problems of digital technology use in schools

The above evidence notwithstanding, a large body of research findings and data exist to contradict the notion that all is well with schools and schooling in the digital age. As reasoned at the end of Chapter 1, even the most enthusiastic of proponents of schools technology would concede that the realities of digital technology use in schools often fail to match the rhetoric. While recent years may have seen substantial increases in the physical presence of digital technology in school settings, the much promised technology-led 'transformation' of education systems has nevertheless failed to mate-rialise. Although digital technologies and other personalised technologies may well have undoubted potential to support students, teachers and schools, it seems that this potential is being realised only on occasion. As Diana Laurillard (2008, p.1) has observed wryly, 'education is on the brink of being transformed through learning technologies; however, it has been on that brink for some decades now'.

Indeed, the school is portrayed regularly within the academic research litera-ture as a relatively compromised site of digital technology use. A substantial body of empirical research has documented a faltering and often awkward integration of digital technology into the formal organisational structures of schools over the past three decades (see Law *et al.* 2008 for an international overview). Numerous surveys, reports and statistical analyses confirm that while the physical presence of digital tech-nology in school systems may continue to rise, its bearing on institutional practices and processes remains limited and often focused on matters of school management and administration rather than teaching and learning. More often than not, uses of digital technologies such as the computer and internet vary significantly between dif-ferent schools, subject disciplines and levels of study. The use of digital technology by individual students also continues to be delineated along lines of gender, income, race, disability and geography.

These inconsistencies in the levels of technology use in schools carry over into the *nature* of this use. Many teachers' use of digital technology at school, for instance, continues to be focused on the passive delivery of information through interactive whiteboards and the bounded use of virtual learning environments and 'managed learning systems'. Similarly, students' in-school uses of digital technologies remain dominated by the 'cut-and-pasting' of online material retrieved from search engines such as Google into Microsoft Word documents and PowerPoint presentations (see Luckin *et al.* 2009b; Selwyn *et al.* 2010). While these can all be considered valid educa-tional uses, the picture emerging from the research literature is of a largely bounded and restricted engagement with technology within school settings. For example, stu-dents' *and* teachers' in-school uses of the internet are often reported to be hampered by a host of blocking procedures and other exclusionary practices of surveillance and filtering (Hope 2008). Significantly, many of the key processes in the day-to-day busi-ness of schools such as formative and summative assessment and communication between staff, students and parents appear to remain relatively unchanged by digital practices. In this sense, digital technology use within school settings continues to be largely formalised and bounded in nature, leading some commentators to conclude that schools offer little more than an artificial facsimile of 'real world' technology use.

As Bigum and Rowan (2008, p.249) contend, schools technology is often little more than a 'pretend', 'fabricated' and 'inauthentic' version of the digital practices and processes that take place elsewhere in society.

Thus while the amounts of financing, resourcing and training now being devoted to the use of digital technology in schools remain considerable, evidence of any increased effectiveness and change 'on the ground' is less certain. Despite repeated attempts by policy-makers, IT firms, researchers and educators to identify 'impacts' and 'effects' of the recent growth of digital technology use in schools, tangible evidence for sustained beneficial change has proved elusive. Even when digital technologies *are* being used in what could be considered appropriate and equitable ways, there is little to suggest that this is resulting in sustained educational benefit (see Brush 1999; Becker 2000; Madden *et al.* 2005; Dynarski *et al.* 2007). Thus digital technology use in schools has often been associated with what Goodson *et al.* (2002, p.138) term as the paradox of 'more producing less' – i.e. the notion that

> an abundance of new technologies may result in lower quality learning than we might reasonably expect to have otherwise occurred. Alternatively, it may result in mis-learning, frustrated learning, confused learning and so on.

This apparent lack of transformation was illustrated throughout the 2000s when a number of separate quasi-experiments in Israeli, German, Dutch and Columbian high schools all reported non-existent or even negative correlations between levels of computer use and students' examination performance, test-scores and other measures of 'learning' (Angrist and Lavy 2002; Lauven *et al.* 2003; Fuchs and Woessmann 2004; Barrera-Osorio and Linden 2009). At the very least, these large-scale studies and others like them begin to raise doubts over many of the more strident claims for improved learning and teaching highlighted in Chapter 1.

Explanations for the apparent failure of digital technology in schools

In fact it could be argued that the apparently uneven showing of digital technology use in schools should raise more than just doubts in the minds of anyone concerned with educational technology. Indeed, the generally inconclusive nature of such studies is leading growing numbers of academic commentators to conclude that the schools technology of the early twenty-first century has now reached something of an impasse – belying its outward appearance of being a high-profile, well-funded and well-resourced element of contemporary education. It could be argued that in spite of the billions of dollars directed towards it, digital technology has somehow contrived to remain a marginalised and superficial aspect of the daily to-and-fro of school life – at least in terms of the use of digital technology for learning. Authors such as Larry Cuban have pointed towards a 'high access, low use' paradox where digital technology has become a highly symbolic but, in practice, highly peripheral element of the drive towards more efficient, standardised and modern forms of education (Cuban *et al.* 2001). The apparently established trend of 'no significant difference' in terms of digital technology and learning outcomes has even prompted some critics to question openly the value of educational technology. As Michael Apple (2004, p.513) concluded, perhaps it should be acknowledged that governments have been simply 'wasting money on computers in schools' and serious questions be asked of why school systems in so many countries have apparently reached this predicament.

Increasing numbers of educational commentators have therefore started to search for reasons that may underpin the obvious discrepancy between the rhetoric and realities of technology investment in schools. As is often the case with debates over the 'failures' of public education, most aspects of the school system have been implicated at one time or another with the continued modest showing of digital technology in schools. Yet as is also often the case with educational controversies, 'blame' has tended to be attributed most readily to the perceived shortcomings of educational practitioners and institutions. In fact, a large number of practice-based reasons have been advanced over the past thirty years or so for the poor showing of digital technology in schools. For instance, school buildings have been criticised as being architecturally unsuitable for widespread networked and wireless technology use. Teachers have been deemed to be too old, incompetent or disinterested to integrate digital technology into their teaching. Students have been judged to lack the skills or application to make the most of educational (rather than leisure) applications of the internet and other digital devices. School leaders and administrators have been accused of lacking the required direction or foresight to make the most of the increased levels of technology-related funding that they have received. School curricula have been observed widely as being too rigid and entrenched in 'pre-information age' ways of thinking. School assessment procedures are seen to be overly concerned with the development and assessment of scholastic aptitude rather than 'softer' or creative skills. All told, the emerging received wisdom among some academic commentators and educational technologists is that schools and those within them lack what it takes 'to go with the technological flow' (Dale *et al.* 2004, p.456). Given the severity of some of these positions, it is worth examining these various 'discourses of deficit' in more detail.

Schools as conservative institutions

Much of the prevailing criticism of schools' unsatisfactory use of digital technology is built upon the notion that schools are over-conservative, monolithic and unwieldy institutions that are actively resistant to change and innovation. A cursory reading of the academic literature on educational technology over the past thirty or forty years soon reveals a growing sense of acute frustration as schools are portrayed as restricting and even emasculating the potential of digital technology. Indeed the notion that digital technologies have 'languished in formal schooling' (Wilhelm 2004, p.96) can be found throughout the academic literature on educational technology – usually rooted in a set of assumptions about the fundamental and intractable 'fixed' nature of schools as organisations. These accounts relate to what Carolan *et al.* (2003, p.2) identify as 'the post-industrial conundrum' – i.e. 'the match (or mismatch) between the dominant model of schooling, a model developed in the nineteenth and early twentieth centuries, and the experiences of children and adults in other sectors of twenty-first century society'.

In this sense, many academics, technologists, industrialists and even some practitioners are now beginning to highlight what they see as the fundamental incompatibility
between digital technology and what is referred to as the 'Henry Ford model of education'
or 'industrial-era' schooling (e.g. Whitney *et al.* 2007). Such critiques hark back to Alvin
Toffler's depictions throughout the 1960s and 1970s of the epistemologically and technologically outmoded 'industrial-era school'. Here Toffler (1970, p.243) decried schooling as an anachronistic by-product of 'that relic of mass production, the centralised work
place' – pointing to factory-like examples such as schools' reliance on rigid timetables
and scheduling, as well as their emphasis on physical presence and ordering of people
and knowledge. Forty years on from Toffler's initial observations, many educational
technologists continue to decry the 'cookie cutter' industrial-era school as a profoundly
unsuitable setting for the more advanced forms of learning demanded by the knowledge
age and post-industrial society (e.g. Miller 2006; Warner 2006; Kelly *et al.* 2008). As the
educational technologist Robert Pearlman was led to proclaim in frustration:

> Hasn't it been long enough? Over 100 years of public mass education, nearly 10
> years into the new century, you still see the 30-student same-look classrooms
> with students sitting in rows and columns listening to teachers and doing monot-
> onous worksheets (Pearlman 2009, p.14).

Such criticisms are as diverse as they are damning. At one extreme, as Tom Bentley
(2000, p.357) put it, very little that takes place within a school can be seen to be of particular relevance or use to modern society: 'as organisations are restructured around hori-
zontal divisions of labour, ICT capacity and networks rather than hierarchies, the habits
and routines developed in school are less useful in the real world'. In particular, schools'
continued reliance on broadcast pedagogies of various kinds, structured hierarchical
relationships and formal systems of regulation is seen to leave them as often incapable
of responding adequately to the challenges posed by new digital technologies. Carmen
Luke (2003, p.398) has argued that twenty-first century educators are failing increasingly
to 'come to terms with the contradictions' between the technological complexities and
fluidities of contemporary learning and the persistence of a model of schooling 'based
on static print/book culture and competitive individualism where learning is geographi-
cally tied to a desk . . . and old-style transmission and surveillance pedagogy'.

The conclusion therefore reached by many commentators is that schools, at best,
assimilate and incorporate digital technology use into their existing, well-established
practices and ways-of-doing. As Wilhelm (2004, p.3) puts it, schools technology
adoption is seen to be 'largely hewn to established practice'. Indeed, some educational commentators have been led to express something of a begrudging admiration
for schools' apparent ability to resist the potential disruption of digital technology
and preserve the contemporary technology-based classroom as a 'normalised and
controlled [an] environment' as it was in pre-digital times (Muffoletto 2001, p.4). As
Bigum and Rowan observe:

> To date, schools have managed to domesticate much of what has emerged in the
> technical landscape. There is a well-established pattern of applying or integrating

new technologies into existing practices or, if the new poses risks or threats, to ban or limit its use. 'Integrate' continues to be the verb used to talk about [digital technologies] and classrooms. The logic is to fit the new into the pre-existing, to integrate. [. . .] Oddly, formal education is the only field in which this way of thinking about ICTs is commonplace. Banks, airlines, government bureaucracies or the military don't talk in terms of integration. They do, however, make use of ICTs to rethink and rework the way they do things. An integration mindset privileges existing ways of doing things. It reflects a view of linear, manageable change and, to date, has allowed teacher education and schools to keep up technical appearances (Bigum and Rowan 2008, p.247).

Many of these criticisms reflect more general explanations of schools' apparent resistance to planned change and innovation. A large body of research and writing on the topic of school improvement has highlighted how over-developed bureaucratic structures and systems of governance leave the school as an 'ineffective organisation that depresses student performance' (Meier *et al.* 2000). Some school improvement and school effectiveness researchers point to the 'sacred norms' centred around shared expectations for professional behaviour and professional purpose that are embedded in a school's culture (Corbett *et al.* 1987). While impacting on all areas of school change and development, it is felt that these normative restrictions are exacerbated especially in the case of digital technology. In short it is now believed increasingly that the industrial-era school is unable to deal with the challenges posed by digital technologies for a number of structural reasons – including the continued reliance on 'broadcast' pedagogies and linear hierarchical relationships to facilitate learning and access to knowledge. As the sociologist Manuel Castells was led to conclude, 'education is the most conservative system as to changing anything since the Middle Ages [. . .] the rules, the format, the organisation of the schools are completely different in terms of interactivity and hypertextuality' (Castells 2008).

The digital disconnect between students and their schools

As far as some academic commentators are concerned, this perceived gulf between school culture and the contemporary 'technoculture' exists most obviously in terms of the generational and technological 'disconnects' that can be observed between the ways that people use technology in their 'everyday lives' and the ways in which technologies are used in schools. This is felt especially to be the case with current generations of young people. Indeed, research studies in North America, Australasia and northern Europe throughout the 2000s and into the 2010s portray a relatively extensive and expansive use of digital technologies by children and young people *outside* of the classroom and schoolhouse. In countries such as the UK, for example, domestic usage levels of the internet, mobile telephony and computer gaming now exceed 90 per cent of older children and adolescents. In terms of internet use, recent statistics confirm that the majority of young people in northern Europe and North America maintain profiles on social networking sites, download music and videos, and communicate with friends using a range of computer-mediated channels such as instant messaging and chat rooms (see Luckin *et al.* 2009a; Ofcom 2009). While these 'head-line' figures give little indication of the rather mundane and unspectacular nature of much of this use, it would be fair to conclude that young people's engagements with digital technologies in domestic settings are generally more advanced than their use of technology in school (Livingstone 2009). As Mimi Ito and colleagues reason, young people's technology use at home is now perhaps best seen as a multimedia 'ecology' where 'more traditional media, such as books, television, and radio, are 'converging' with digital media, specifically interactive media and media for social communication' (Ito *et al.* 2008, p.8).

Above all, there is a growing sense that young people's uses of technologies in everyday life are supporting and facilitating a set of rather different practices and dispositions than may have been the case in the twentieth century. A popular charac-terisation of upcoming generations of school students is that they are 'digital natives' – i.e. individuals who have grown up in a world of computers, the internet and mobile telephony, and as a result lead lifestyles that are reliant upon the affordances of digital media. The lives of current generations of technologically attuned students are seen to be entwined with new cultures of digitally-based creativity, collaboration and commu-nity. For many of these individuals, digitally-mediated everyday life is characterised by constant change, with commentators talking of a technologically-assisted fluidity and flexibility which lies at the heart of leading a mobile, 'liquid' and 'hyper-complex' way of being (Bauman 2005; Qvortrup 2006; Urry 2007). Crucially, these digital natives are seen to expect such characteristics to be woven into all aspects of their lives – not least the ways in which they learn and are educated. As Marc Prensky (2001, p.1) was warning a decade ago, 'our students have changed radically. Today's students are no longer the people our educational system was designed to teach.'

As Prensky intimates, unpinning this reading of the changing nature of children and young people is a sense of a fast-growing 'digital disconnect' between students and their education institutions. A host of research studies have shown that students' uses of technology at home and in the community are almost always 'richer' than those uses inside schools. These differences are apparent in the quality as well as the quantity of technology use – with home use of digital technologies seen to involve a rich and fluid process of multi-tasking, as opposed to the 'one task at a time' approach favoured in schools. In this sense school students are described increasingly as facing a regulated and constrained set of digital experiences when inside their schools which are limited in terms of resources, relevance, time and support. As Levin and Arafeh (2002, p.ii) concluded at the beginning of the 2000s:

> students report that there is a substantial disconnect between how they use the internet [at home] and how they use the internet during the school day and under teacher direction. For the most part, students' educational use of the internet occurs outside of the school day, outside of the school building, outside the direction of their teachers.

The continuation of these trends as the twenty-first century progresses has prompted some commentators to highlight the increased disaffection and disconnection among the student body with their schools' use of technology and, it follows, their overall experience of schooling. Bill Green's description of technology-influenced 'aliens in the classroom' (Green and Bigum 1993) has gained in significance over the last twenty years, with many recent academic studies now pointing towards a distinct technology-influenced alienation and disenchantment among current cohorts of school students. As Nicola Johnson was led to conclude from her study of Australian teenagers' views of schooling, 'some of the participants view school as irrelevant because the scholastic view found in school is also irrelevant and does not relate to students' reality. The current day out-of-school learning and the participants' technological interests further exacerbate the divide between the relevance and reality of school to their daily lives and future existence' (Johnson 2009, p.68).

The technical inefficiencies of teachers

All these depictions of the 'digital native' convey a range of attendant implications for generations of adults as well as the institutions and organisations that seek to work with children and young people. In particular, the portrayals of current generations of young people outlined above all imply a profound disempowerment of older generations of teachers. Marc Prensky (2001) and others describe adults born before 1980 as 'digital immigrants' who have been forced to adapt to a world of digital media after (many) years of leading 'pre-digital' lifestyles. Such claims imply that adults lack the technological fluency of younger generations and find the skills possessed by them unfamiliar and often foreign (Long 2005). As Prensky (2005, p.8) concludes:

> I refer to those of us who were not born into the digital world as 'digital immigrants'. We have adopted many aspects of the technology, but just like those who learn another language later in life, we retain an 'accent' because we still have one foot in the past. We will read a manual, for example, to understand a program before we think to let the program teach itself. Our accent from the pre-digital world often makes it difficult for us to effectively communicate with our students.

As such, the disconnect and deficiency explanations outlined above carry over into a set of dis-satisfactions about the abilities and aptitudes of teachers. A distinct tension is evident throughout the digital native literature between 'the generations who grow up with these ways of thinking' (Leadbeater 2008a, p.20) and the 'often web-illiterate' adults in their lives (Keen 2007, p.207). Many commentators are therefore led to construct a dichotomous 'them' and 'us' argument where teachers and schools are positioned as incompatible with the requirements and expectations of the children and young people that they seek to work with. It has been argued, for instance, that schools face a growing 'legitimacy crisis' with the young (Kenway and Bullen 2005). In particular, the digital native way-of-being is seen to be incompatible with the many formal and informal systems of regulation and control which frame students' relationships and connections with teachers, not least a continued reliance on linear hierarchical relationships to facilitate communication, learning and access to knowledge. In this sense, out of all the adults involved in the lives of children and young people, teachers are portrayed as being some of the most 'poorly placed to deal well with the social, cultural and economic changes that derive from the continuing use of these [digital] technologies' (Bigum and Rowan 2008, p.250).

Of course, such criticisms are not unique to the technological aspects of teaching – teachers have long being described as conservative and generally resistant to change in many of their practices (Lortie 1975). Yet there is a sense that digital technologies certainly exacerbate these general tendencies within the teaching profession. At best, then, the majority of teachers are still felt to be 'cautious onlookers' when it comes to digital technology as opposed to a minority of 'enthusiastic innovators' (Crook 2008, p.34). Elsewhere teachers have been observed to vary considerably in their ability to incorporate digital technology in their practice. While a minority of teachers are seen to be able to 'assimilate' and actively incorporate a range of digital technologies into their teaching, others are seen at best to reach a pragmatic 'accommodation' of technology into their existing modes of working or, at worst, display a recalcitrant use and 'retreatism' (John and La Velle 2004, p.323). According to John and La Velle (2004) such responses to technology usually involve various subtle reactions to 'the challenge' presented by digital technologies. That said, some teachers can still be said to display explicit outright negative reactions to the perceived threats of technology in their classrooms:

> the conservative profession of teaching has mediated the introduction of new technologies to render them 'safe' . . . This may be partly a distrust of novelty and partly a lack of basic familiarity with the ways of new technology, but a major reason could be the threats the technology poses to teachers' existing practices and to the perceived maintenance of control (Williams 2008, p.220).

This analysis raises the wider point of what Andrew Feenberg (2008) calls 'humanistic opposition' to educational technology – i.e. a set of sometimes negative responses based upon personal and social (rather than technical) issues. In this sense some teachers' reactions to using digital technology in their teaching may be based around an emotional or moral response to the welfare of their students and the integrity of their learning. That said, for many authors digital technology use in the classroom often comes up against more basic issues of self-interest, such as teachers' reluctance to challenge or resist dominant structures of traditional schooling and thereby 'upset the field that they are placed in and the legitimacy of that praxis' (Johnson 2009, p.68). It is suggested, for example, that many teachers have a vested interest in maintaining arrangements and structures that ensure their employment and financial security, and not altering arrangements that may destabilise or subvert their authority, status and control in the classroom. In contrast to the claims made in Chapter 1, all of these perspectives position teachers and technologies in rather oppositional roles, with the (non)use of digital technology in the classroom centred on concerns over the technological devaluing or even outright replacement of the teacher's role in the classroom and the school context.

Inadequate political support for technology in schools

A final set of rationales for the relatively poor showing of digital technologies in schools focuses on the deficiencies of policy-makers and policy-making. As outlined at the beginning of this chapter, schools technology is now a major component of state policy-making in most developed and many developing countries. Yet although these policies may well have been successful in increasing the physical presence of computer hardware and software in schools, they have perhaps failed to achieve the transformation of teaching and learning, schools and schooling that their supporters would have hoped and expected. A growing response among some academic commentators for the lack of noticeable transformation of schools is that the policies themselves can be said to be at fault. Indeed, much of educational technology policy-making outlined at the beginning of this chapter can be – and has been – criticised as being fundamentally at odds with the structure of the school organisations it is meant to be located within.

In part this is a long-standing criticism of educational policy-making in general. As Ladwig (1994) points out, the field of educational policy is noticeably discrete from that of education, with the intended outcomes and anticipated rewards often having very little to do with educational practices and the concerns of educators. This general observation notwithstanding, many commentators feel that there is a particular disconnect between education policy-making and technology-based practice. For example, some more technologically-minded commentators have pointed towards 'current gaps' between the 'closed' nature of technology use as enshrined in national policies and the democratic aspirations that many technologists have for the 'opening up' of learning beyond the school (Marshall 2005, p.158). Conversely other academic commentators have criticised national school technology policies for a lack of consideration for the realities of the classroom – arguing that such policy-making has often lacked an 'ethos that values ICT for classroom practice' (Younie 2006, p.400). These critics have pointed towards the reduction of teaching and learning within national policy-making to matters of 'delivery', with the role of the teacher reduced simply to one of delivering the means with which to digitally learn and, conversely, the role of the student often reduced to one of passive consumer of tightly defined, controlled and bounded forms of official curricular 'knowledge'. In terms of governance most educational technology policy drives and agendas have therefore been criticised as retaining the essentially 'controlling at a distance' model of the state which is exercised by many Western countries (Hall 2003).

All these criticisms focus on the limited nature of educational technology policy-making as a fundamentally 'top-down' process. Critics have long bemoaned the government-sponsored 'dumping' of hardware into schools, conveying a sense that digital technologies have tended to be 'inserted into' rather than 'integrated with' school cultures and practices. As such it is argued that national strategies and initiatives lack an ability 'to meet local needs of specific schools and teachers who may be operating in very different conditions' (Younie 2006, p.399). The national-level policy environment in many countries has been criticised as stymieing schools' and teachers' capacity to innovate – instead fostering strategies of compliance and risk aversion that have become seen as the main barriers to more expansive uses of technology (Mee 2007a). As Oliver Boyd-Barrett (1990, p.170) observed over twenty years ago:

> The literature on educational innovation is replete with accounts of the failure of centrally-generated and imposed curriculum innovations, especially where these have had only a 'pump-priming' character, but more generally where they have not been able to carry the understanding and commitment of practising teachers. There has been a scepticism in the literature about 'top-down' or 'centre-periphery' approaches to educational change. Such approaches all too often have been under-resourced, badly understood or simply unpopular at institutional or classroom levels.

Looking beyond the apparent 'clash' between schools and technology

All of these issues feed into the long-standing disappointment felt among many academic commentators, educational technologists, industrialists and even some practitioners concerning the relatively constrained and compromised use of digital technology within schools. As the opening two chapters of this book have shown, while appearing to be a high profile, well-resourced and integral element of education provision, in reality digital technology could be said to remain a marginalised aspect of the day-to-day milieu of contemporary schools and schooling. This has led to a feeling that schools and digital technology tend to suffer from a fundamental 'clash', where (to update a phrase from Larry Cuban) 'digital technology meets classroom – classroom wins'. While these disappointments are certainly understandable, viewing technology and schools in terms of a series of inevitable and often intransient 'clashes' has tended to result in discussions over schools technology taking the form of a rather unhelpful 'blame game'. As much of the material presented in this chapter implies, teachers, schools and policy-makers are often cast as fundamentally lacking the necessary digital dispositions and understandings required to make 'effective' use of technology. These criticisms are used by some to justify the outright dismissal of schools as technology 'ghettos' (Green and Hannon 2007) or the portrayal of teachers as outmoded, obstructive or ignorant. At best, such arguments transfer a set of what Convery (2009, p.30) terms 'dangerous moral imperatives' onto teachers and schools to change their practices and processes in line with the 'affordances' of digital technology. At worst such thinking leads to an unhelpful set of rejectionist conclusions where schools and schooling are branded irrelevant to contemporary digital society.

As will be discussed in more detail throughout this book, a distinct rejectionist line of thinking underpins much discussion and writing about educational technology and school-aged learners. Indeed, authors such as Seymour Papert have long promoted arguments that schools and schooling are 'are relics from an earlier period of knowledge technology' (Papert 1998, n.p.) and that new technology will 'overthrow the accepted structure of school, the idea of curriculum, the segregation of children by age and pretty well everything that the education establishment will defend to the bitter end' (Papert 1998, n.p.). This sense of terminal incompatibility was perhaps best encapsulated in Lewis Perelman's (1992) early observation that any attempt to integrate computing into schools 'makes about as much sense as integrating the internal combustion engine into the horse'. Twenty years later polemic of this sort can be found throughout mainstream thinking about technology and education, with many commentators willing to denounce the school as an anachronistic relic of the industrial age that has been rendered obsolete by contemporary digital technology.

While staunch defenders of present forms of schools technology can be found (especially among practitioners, school leaders and policy-makers) there is a creeping sense in academic educational technology circles that industrial-era schools as they currently exist are not a part of a credible solution to improving learning in the digital age. The advantage of attributing blame in this direct manner is obvious, as it isolates a neat set of institutional and practitioner deficits that, in theory, should be susceptible to change through further policy directives and funding streams. Many countries are therefore witnessing the emergence of a 'second wave' of schools technology initiatives being launched in an attempt to remedy these perceived problems, usually taking the form of vast programmes of online content commissioning, school renewal and rebuilding as well as more targeted programmes of teacher training. Policies and interventions are also being introduced to encourage or even coerce families to gain and sustain internet access with a view to enhancing children's schooling outside of the school setting.

These political efforts are certainly logical in their response, as part of the lack of 'success' of schools technology surely *does* lie in the shortcomings of schools, practitioners and those that they serve. Some teachers undoubtedly *do* lack the confidence, skill or energy required to successfully blend digital technology into their teaching. Some students probably *are* too intransigent and disengaged to use technology for conventional 'educational' purposes. Many ageing school buildings and infrastructures undeniably obstruct the fluid, networked use of technologies. But if these were the *only* reasons behind the relative ineffectiveness of digital technology use in schools then, given the unprecedented amount of policy attention afforded to it over the 1990s and 2000s, more signs of improvement would surely have been apparent by now. In fact, it could be argued strongly that so much time, effort and funding has been put into making digital technologies 'work' in schools and classrooms over the past twenty years that these reasons of deficiency *cannot* solely account for the apparent failure of digital technology in contemporary schooling.

Conclusions

It is clear even from this brief overview of the literature, that a more nuanced reading of schools and schooling in the digital age is required. Rectifying the recurrent 'failure' of digital technology across many of the school systems of the developed and developing world alike is surely not as straightforward as isolating, highlighting and then correcting a set of 'deficiencies' in teachers, schools and policy-making. The readings of schools and digital technology presented in this chapter are undoubtedly justified in many ways, but all lead to overly simplistic conclusions based around a series of technical adjustments to the people, processes and practices that constitute schools and schooling. As such, much of the current discussion and debate about schools and digital technology follows a decidedly technocratic logic – first that technology is inevitably going to change schools for the better and, it therefore follows, that the main role for any analyst of educational technology is to identify the barriers, impediments and deficiencies that are delaying and opposing the march of technological progress. As Boody (2001, p.7) points out, many of these arguments about the benefits of digital technology in schools take the form of 'means-end thinking' – i.e. thinking that starts from a given end and then strives to find the means of accomplishment. While this unhindered 'can do' approach is often welcomed in technology and policy circles, such thinking is flawed in its failure to consider fully the nature and value of the end, the by-products or unintended consequences of its implementation or the connections between this given end and other important ends. From this perspective, such 'means-end' thinking about technology and education is as reductive as it is seductive.

It is clear from this book's brief discussion so far that the issue of schools technology extends far beyond being simply a technical affair that requires finding the most suitable means to a predetermined end. It should already be apparent that adopting such a narrow perspective on schools and technology introduces a number of unhelpful silences into the debates around schools in the digital age – not least shifting the locus of critique away from the systems and structures of schooling, and making light of the many contradictions and conflicts that surround the use of digital technologies in schools. Indeed, the use of digital technologies in schools is clearly a site of intense conflict and struggle. In this sense it would seem sensible to suggest that any analysis of schools' (non)use of digital technology must concentrate on the *politics* of schools technology and thereby question and challenge some of the transformatory discourses that surround the 'ends' of technology use in school – not least the major assumption that digital technology can transform social relations. As Henri Lefebvre observed:

> This merits very serious consideration. Computer science and telematics are certainly going to alter social existence. They have already begun to do so. Communication has been an important – possibly essential – phenomenon in social practice since the beginning of history and prehistory. Will computer science, with its repercussions and related disciplines, go so far as to transform everyday life? To transform the social relations of production, reproduction and domination? That is the issue. (Lefebvre 1981, p.136).

From this perspective, the current discussions and understandings outlined so far in this book can be said to provide, at best, only partial accounts of schools and digital technology. The need remains, therefore, to redress some of the silences and gaps in prevailing educational understandings of the digital technology, and set about developing *critical* accounts of the complex and often compromised realities of learners' *actual* uses of digital technology. In particular, more attention needs to be paid to the structures, boundaries and limitations of digital technology use in schools that lurk beneath any illusion of enhanced freedom and empowerment. With these issues in mind, the remainder of this book seeks to (re)appraise the supposed promises and problems of digital technology use in schools, and return to Steven Brint's (1998) basic questions of developing a sociological understanding of schools and schooling – i.e. what is digital technology use in schools actually like? Why is digital technology use in schools the way it is? What are the consequences of what happens with digital technologies in schools? Chapter 3 now goes on to consider a suitable theoretical approach to frame such an analysis.

3 Rethinking digital technology and schools

Introduction

A clear distinction has emerged between Chapter 1's discussion of the high-powered rhetoric concerning what schooling in the digital age *could* look like and Chapter 2's discussion of the rather more varied realities of what schooling in the digital age *does* look like. The contrast between these two discussions highlights a longstanding and deep-rooted weakness in academic thinking about digital technology and education. As a forward-looking and fast-changing field of study, many educational technology commentators, writers and researchers tend understandably to focus on 'state-of-the-art' issues. As the last two chapters suggest, much effort is directed towards exploring the learning potential of emerging technologies and much time is also devoted to debating and developing forms of teaching and learning 'fit' for the digital age. Other concerns and preoccupations include issues of pedagogically sound design, implementing digital technologies to increase educational opportunities and, perhaps most contentiously, striving to 'prove' that technology leads to 'effective' learning outcomes. As outlined in Chapter 1, the field of educational technology is concerned primarily with questions of what *could* happen, and what *should* happen once new technologies and digital media are placed into educational settings. Yet it can be argued that the predominance of these concerns has shaped current academic understandings of schools and schooling in the digital age along rather uniform and decidedly a-critical lines – dominated by constructivist views of learning, and a pronounced tendency to focus primarily on the positive aspects of educational technology use. As David Buckingham (2007) has observed, the educational technology literature is overpopulated by in-depth investigations of 'model' schools and classrooms with enthusiastic teachers and well-resourced students basking in the glow of the 'Hawthorne effect' of the attention of researchers. With these thoughts in mind, this chapter considers alternative perspectives that could be used to frame a more socially and politically orientated understanding of schools technology.

From 'state-of-the-art' to 'state-of-the-actual'

As a profoundly forward-looking field, it is perhaps unsurprising that educational technologists are reluctant to consider the past or present realities of schools and technology. While any social scientist should remain wary of an overt historicism and 'obsessive recollection of the past' (Lefebvre 1981, p.9), it could be argued that current understandings of schools in the digital age are hampered by a curious amnesia, forgetfulness or even wilful ignorance of past phases of technology development and implementation in schools. While some educational technologists are proud of this forward-looking focus, such ahistoricism should be considered as a major weakness to any field of study. As Robert Muffoletto (2001, p.1) argued, 'those working within the field of educational technology and education in general, need to embrace a reflective historical understanding of technology and the forces that steer and maintain it within a discourse of progress, self-interests and the public good'. In particular, adopting a 'retrospective' perspective to any analysis of digital technology and education can highlight the continuities and discontinuities between different phases of digital technology use in schools – in short, identifying what is really 'new' about new technology. Thus, in trying to make sense of schools, schooling and digital technology in the 2010s there is much to be gained from looking at the educational technology literature of the 1980s and 1990s. As Caroline Bassett reasons, 'new media technologies tend to be understood (given to us) as determinant and it is only later, when they are no longer new, when the next new media technology has come along, that they are reassessed and explored in terms of their social shaping' (Bassett 2006, p.226).

Of course, the vast majority of educational technologists, researchers and commentators are well aware of the disjuncture between their forward-looking focus and the flawed past and present realities of schools technology. Yet despite a tacit acknowledgement of digital technology often 'not working' as it should in school settings, most educational technologists manage to avoid asking too many awkward questions of why digital technologies are *actually* being used in schools in the ways that they are. Of course, this reluctance to 'rock the boat' by asking deeper systematic questions is by no means a trait unique to the academic study of educational technology. There has long been a tendency among policy-makers and practitioners to shy away from what is seen as 'over-researching' and therefore over-scrutinising important issues of contention or controversy in education. This common sense assumption of 'we know what works' is a dangerous precedent to set in any sphere of life, but has increasingly become a stock response in debates surrounding the use of digital technology in education.

In the case of educational technology it could be argued that such assumption and received wisdom has come to occupy too privileged a position, and that there is a need to strive to reclaim some rigour, perspective and personal distance to the debate. Generalising one's personal experiences and presuming digital technology to be an essentially 'good thing' before setting foot in a classroom runs the risk of obscuring many of the important questions that need to be asked about technology in schools. Any educational technologist who only looks for examples of technology 'working' is likely to overlook the difficult-to-detect side effects and unexpected consequences of technology use. As Berker *et al.* (2006, p.3) warn, when technology becomes treated in an ordinary, common-sensical manner then 'it risks escaping attention, not only from researchers and academics but also from policy-makers'.

Thus despite its forward-looking focus, the field of educational technology is in a position to learn from the more critical analyses of technology which have come to prominence in other social science and humanities disciplines. These 'other' analyses and perspectives do not tend to approach digital technology as a neutral blank canvas but rather as a site of negotiation and conflict. In light of the depth and elegance of much of this work it seems appropriate that the use of digital technology in schools is also subject to what could be termed as being 'state-of-the-actual' questions – i.e. questions concerning what is *actually* taking place when digital technology meets classroom. Indeed, it is this book's contention that questions which explore digital technologies in schools from the lived experiences of those using (and those *not* using) them should be at the forefront of any educational technologist's mind, alongside questions challenging the wider shaping influences on schools and technology *outside* of the classroom walls. As such, there is a need to reconsider the theoretical frameworks through which schools and schooling in the digital age can be viewed and understood.

The need to escape 'soft' technological determinism

Choosing a theoretical perspective or stance is, of course, largely a matter of personal conviction and belief – there is no one 'correct' reading of technology and society. Yet it would seen reasonable to contend that anyone seeking to explore 'state-of-the-actual' questions about schools and digital technologies should consider taking as broad an approach as possible to thinking about technology and education. There would seem to be little sense in dismissing alternative perspectives out of hand simply because they do not chime with one's own experiences, opinions or intellectual standpoints. Against this background there is a clear need for any academic analysis of digital technology and schools to take a theoretically sophisticated and considered approach towards thinking about the technological and the social. As has been implied from the outset of this book, the careful use of social theory is an essential component of developing rich understandings of the structures, actions, processes and relations that constitute uses of digital technology in the social setting of the school. If nothing else, social theory should be seen as a prerequisite to 'building better questions that can reveal aspects of the world that have hitherto been neglected or unimagined' (Amin and Thrift 2005, p.222). Thus it would seem vital that time is taken to reflect upon the full range of theoretical options applicable to an analysis of schools and schooling in the digital age. While not decrying the value of psychological, developmental and learning theory approaches, this chapter now goes on to outline the various theoretical approaches which focus on the socially constructed, or 'socially shaped', nature of digital technologies and education.

Looking back on the past three decades of academic work on schools and technology, it could be argued that technology has been decidedly under-theorised in contrast to the sophisticated theories of teaching and learning that have been utilised during the same time. While the tendency to approach technology-based processes as a closed 'black box' is not unique to education, it is certainly more prevalent in educational studies than in most other areas of the social sciences. Throughout the 1980s and 1990s the majority of academic writing on the subject was content to imbue technologies such as the computer and internet with a range of inherent qualities.

These qualities were then seen to 'impact' (for better or worse) on learners, teachers and schools in ways that were consistent regardless of circumstance or context. The crude but compelling 'technologically determinist' perspective that 'social progress is driven by technological innovation, which in turn follows an 'inevitable' course' (Smith 1994, p.38) has a long lineage in academic research – not least in terms of widely held assumptions about 'media effects'. As David Nye (2007, p.27) explains, such technological determinist thinking tends to be externalist in nature, 'treating new technologies as autonomous forces that compel society to change'. For example, a determinist way of thinking underpins the range of claims that video games *cause* violent behaviour, or that online tuition *improves* learning. In this respect one can easily understand how a technological determinist view of schools and technology became established during the 1980s and 1990s.

Of course, these explanations of games causing violence or websites improving learning appeal to many people by offering a simplistic view of otherwise complex socio-technological situations. Recourse to the identification of causal relationships also fits well with the epistemological origins of educational technology as a field of academic study in disciplines such as engineering, natural sciences, mathematics and psychology. It could be argued that the ways of thinking associated with these disciplines persist in current approaches to the study of current educational technology – in particular the desire of many educational technologists to reduce 'uncertainly from the schooling process . . . to provide a systematic, scientifically-based, controllable process, a technology for the identification and solution of instructional problems' (Muffoletto 2001, p.2). From this perspective, a technological determinist mindset is both appealing and necessary to constructing such 'scientific' models of the use of technology in education settings.

Despite the commonsensical appeal of 'technological progress' and 'educational change' there has long been unease among more critical scholars concerned with the descriptive limitations of such determinist analyses of technology and society. The general case against the orthodoxy of technological determinism was perhaps most succinctly put by Raymond Williams (1974). Building upon the earlier work of the theorist Thorstein Veblen among others, Williams made a compelling case for understanding technological innovations as taking place within specific social and economic contexts, instead of new technologies somehow having inevitable internal logics of development. Following this line of argument there can be no pre-determined outcome to the development and implementation of technologies. Instead technologies are subjected continually to a series of complex interactions and negotiations with the social, economic, political and cultural contexts into which they emerge. Indeed, following Williams' lead, overt notions of technological determinism are now dismissed routinely by many social scientists who take great care to approach questions of technology and society in more nuanced ways that transcend simple 'cause and effect' agendas. Increasing numbers of social science writers and researchers are keen to insert disavowals of technological determinism into their opening paragraphs. Particular care is taken to avoid any inference of cause, effect or impact; instead softer phrasings are employed which portray the 'influence' and 'bearing' of technology.

Yet however carefully words are chosen, thinking about digital technology and schools without recourse to some form of technological determinism remains a difficult task. This is due, in part, to the common sense ways that 'technology' is talked about in the real (as opposed to academic) world. Although it is rare to find anyone proclaiming herself to be technologically determinist, the view persists in many contemporary popular accounts of digital technology. Current political understandings of the internet's profound effects on the 'shrinking' of the world and undermining of national boundaries are classic examples of technological determinism. Commercial marketing is continually selling the notion of '*vorsprung durch technik*', while news media warn of technology-related dangers such as how mobile phone messaging is limiting the vocabulary of young people. Such interpretations can appear as 'natural' common sense and certainly appeal to those whose job it is to make sense of the apparently fast-changing nature of new technologies. The belief that 'technology determines history' (Williams 1994, p. 218) is hard to shake.

Aside from the content of news reports and advertising slogans, it can be argued that the endurance of technological determinism in popular discourse has had a subtle bearing on academic conceptualisations of digital technology and education. Whereas most social scientists are able to resist a 'hard' or 'strong' determinist view of technology developing in complete isolation from social concerns, what can be termed a more passive form of 'soft' or 'diluted' determinist view persists throughout the literature on schools and technology. This soft determinist view sees technology impacting on social situations such as individual classrooms or whole schools in ways that are, to a degree, malleable and controllable. Rather than the internet improving learning, it can be said that the internet can *help* improve learning – acknowledging the possible existence of other contextual influences, while retaining the notion of a technological effect. As was evident in Chapter 2, this way of thinking usually reaches conclusions that recommend the overcoming of any constraining or negative contextual influences (usually reduced to the pejorative status of 'barriers') so that the inherent beneficial effect of technology may be more fully felt.

As well as rationalising any lack of change in terms of structural barriers and individual deficiencies, the promises of inevitable educational improvement through technology also coalesce into powerful and persuasive grounds for educational change with technology. As was outlined in Chapters 1 and 2, the logic of this perceived imperative for change is often presented by commentators around the world in simple but stark terms. First, it is argued that digital technologies have initiated a series of practices among current generations of learners that cannot now be ignored or abandoned. Second, it follows that educational systems are therefore left facing the challenge of how best to include digital technologies and practices within learning and teaching (see Abbott and Adler 2009). This fatalistic sense of social institutions having to react to technological change is perhaps best summed up by Clay Shirky's (2008, p.307) observation that

> our control over [digital] tools is much more like steering a kayak. We are being pushed rapidly down a route largely determined by the technological environment. We have a small degree of control over the spread of these tools, but that

control does not extend to being able to reverse, or even radically alter, the direction we're moving in.

While many educational technologists, writers and researchers appear comfortable with this soft determinist position, the arguments raised in this book so far would suggest that ascribing any degree of agency to the technological artefact rather than the non-technological processes which shape its development and implementation will result only in a narrow and reductionist understanding of schools and digital technology. In particular, anyone willing to assume an inevitability of effect when it comes to schools and digital technologies puts themselves at risk of under-playing (or even ignoring) the crucial 'contingencies, particularities, oppositions, dis-junctures and variabilities' (Martin 1996) that underlie technological change. Put bluntly, then, any critique of the social and political aspects of schools and schooling in the digital age requires a more sophisticated understanding of the social and the technological that acknowledges, as David Nye puts it, that 'devices and machines are not things 'out there' that invade life' (Nye 2007, p. ix).

From anti-essentialism to anti-determinism

Perhaps the most comprehensive corrective to soft technological determinism is the view that technology has absolutely *no* inherent qualities. In this sense technology can be seen as open completely to interpretation and capable of determining nothing. This 'anti-essentialist' approach was advanced throughout the 1980s and 1990s within the science and technology studies (STS) literature, offering the perspective that technologies lack any properties outside of the interpretive work that humans engage in to establish what these artefacts 'actually are' (see Grint and Woolgar 1992; Woolgar and Cooper 1999). Studies in the STS tradition are now an established way of challenging the single linear narrative of socio-technological change, with a more sceptical relationship between humans and machines being proposed (Latour 1987; Williams and Sørensen 2002). From this perspective, what is encountered as 'technology' can be understood as simply the outcome of interpretive accounts – some more persuasive and influential than others.

To illustrate this argument, Grint and Woolgar (1997) propose the notion of 'technology as text', where technologies can be seen as open texts which are 'written' (configured) in certain ways by those social groups involved in stages of development, production and marketing. After some time, technologies are then 'read' (interpreted) by other social groups such as consumers and users with recursive 'feedback loops' between the different stages. Although technologies can have preferred readings built into them by dominant interests, these writing and reading processes are seen to be open and negotiable processes. The metaphor of treating 'technology as text' elegantly draws attention to the often unseen work by designers, financiers, marketers and others in crafting the materiality *and* the interpretations of devices. It also acknowledges the opportunities that exist for alternative appropriations and uses of technology. In short, seeing technology as text highlights the interpretive flexibility of the rhetorical *and* material nature of technologies and, crucially, acts as a reminder that technologies are never completely closed however established or advanced their development and use may be. Indeed, Grint and Woolgar playfully propose an 'onion model' of technology, where technologies are seen to consist solely of layers of social and cultural factors without any 'hard' technical core at all. In this sense it is only the increasing difficulty of removing successive layers of interpretation that 'sustains the illusion that there is anything at the centre' (Grint and Woolgar 1997, p.155).

While the onion model of technology is a wilfully extreme extension of the anti-essentialist perspective, such accounts of technology offer a logical response to what Grint and Woolgar see as the 'residual technicism' of all other theoretical takes on technology. In this sense, the value of the anti-essentialist stance is the same as that highlighted in Ruth Finnegan's defence in the 1970s of technological determinism, i.e. that

> it is both illuminating and stimulating to have the counter-view stated forcibly. The strong case is perhaps stated over-extremely – but its very extremeness helps to jolt us out of our complacency and draw our attention to a range of facts and possible causal connections previously neglected. As a suggestive model of look-ing at social development it may well have value, despite its factual inadequacies' (Finnegan 1975, cited in Chandler 1995, n.p.).

Anti-essentialism therefore acts as a reminder that it is difficult to maintain a soft technological determinist view in the face of the apparent malleability and interpret-ability of technology. Yet technological determinism should not be set up as a 'con-ceptual straw-man' (Winner 1993) that forces any analysis of technology and society into a viewpoint where nothing can be said to be influenced by anything else. Indeed, as Raymond Williams (1981, p.102) warned, anyone resolutely attempting not to be deterministic faces 'a kind of madness'. To ascribe complete interpretability to any technology can be seen as an equally constraining and reductionist form of 'social determinism' where only social factors are granted any importance. Of course, all but the most committed anti-essentialist would concede that not every technology is *completely* open to *any* reading by *any* person at *any* time. As critics of the technol-ogy-as-text metaphor have reasoned, if so one could just as successfully interpret a fruit machine to be a means of transatlantic communication as a telephone (Hutchby 2001), or interpret a rose as an equally effective means of shattering skin and bone as a gun (Kling 1992). Anyone attempting to develop a more socially sophisticated theoretical take on the technological, therefore, is faced with deciding how best 'to introduce elements of the social into explanations of the technical rather than grant-ing the social an all-important standing' (Rappert 2003, p.568).

At best then, anti-essentialism is most useful in pointing any analysis of digital technology and schools towards a mutual shaping approach where technology both is shaped and shaping in a number of enabling and constraining ways. The anti-essen-tialist position therefore highlights the relevance of wider theoretical debates in the social sciences, not least those between realism and constructivism. It also serves to illustrate the need to reconcile long-standing issues in social theory about structure and actor agency. Above all, the extreme nature of the anti-essentialist position is perhaps most useful in moving the theoretical focus of this book towards a range of theoretical 'middle ways' (Hutchby 2001) which seek, as Bijker *et al.* (1987) put it, to 'open up the back box of technology'.

An overview of anti-determinist approaches to understanding technology

Moving away from the radical position of anti-essentialism there are a number of anti-determinist approaches to technology and schools that are worthy of consideration. These approaches are often grouped under the umbrella term proposed by MacKenzie and Wajcman (1985, p.18) of the social shaping of technology (SST). In essence the SST tradition is concerned with exploring the material consequences of different technical choices. Most proponents of SST would concur that the development of technology is best seen, to appropriate a phrase from Jorge Luis Borges, as a 'garden of forking paths' where different routes are negotiable and all leading potentially to different technological outcomes (Williams and Edge 1996). SST studies tend to consider the organisational, political, economic and cultural factors which pattern the design *and* implementation of a technological artefact. Crucially, SST researchers are interested in the relative bearing of different social groups on the technological pathways that are taken, and how these influences relate to the social consequences of technology use *in situ*. There is a particular interest in how technological innovations generate unintended consequences and unanticipated (and often contradictory) effects. As Judy Wajcman (2008, p.67) concludes, digital technologies 'themselves are conceived of as culturally and socially situated artefacts and systems, then there is nothing inevitable about the way they evolve and are used'.

Perhaps most well-known of these approaches is the social construction of technology (SCOT). SCOT studies start from the premise that the form and meaning of a technology is shaped socially rather than being a clearly defined product of a particular innovator. SCOT researchers seek to demonstrate the 'design flexibility' and 'interpretative flexibility' of a given technology, recognising that a technological artefact has different meanings and interpretations for various 'relevant social groups' (Pinch and Bijker 1984; Bijker and Law 1992). These relevant groups are not only the initial designers and producers of the technology, but competing producers, journalists, politicians, users, non-users and other interest groups. Crucially, these groups will often have diverging interpretations of the technology in question. Against this background a SCOT analysis will usually seek to first reconstruct the alternative interpretations of the technology, analyse the problems these interpretations give rise to, identify the conflicts that arise from any differences in interpretation, and then connect them to the design features of the technological artefacts. SCOT analyses then attempt to identify the point where socio-technological systems can be said to have reached a state of 'closure' where the ability for alternative interpretations of a technology diminishes. Reflecting the premise of Grint and Woolgar's onion model, SCOT studies often highlight the notion of 'obduracy' – i.e. the fact that some devices and systems are harder to alter than others based on their materiality.

One further, but less often reached, stage of the SCOT methodology relates to the shaping of the content of the technological artefact by the wider socio-political milieu. That said, many writers ostensibly working outside of the SCOT tradition have provided illuminating accounts of what can be termed the political economy of technology. The political economy approach tends to focus on the interpretations of technologies at the level of politics, policy-making and the economic and commercial activities of firms and governments. The political economy perspective therefore examines how political institutions, political environments, and the economic system intersect and influence each other at the point of technology. Although specific approaches vary, a political economy perspective will focus primarily on the relationships between the capitalist modes of production and technology use in a social setting such as a school in order to uncover the underlying power relations (Greener and Perriton 2005). This approach thereby allows examination of how persons and groups with common economic and/or political intentions appropriate technology development to engineer changes that are beneficial to their interest(s). Writers interested in the political economy of technology are concerned principally in the ways that technologies are appropriated and re-appropriated by political and economic interest groups in ways that diverge from the intentions and claims of designers (see Pfaffenberger 1992). Prominent examples of the political economy approach to technology include Edwards' (1996) work on the relations between the political discourse of the Cold War and the attendant computer designs of the era, as well as Herb Schiller's (1995) work on the role of the nexus between military, scientific and transnational corporate interests in the development of various new technologies such as the internet.

Another prominent example of the social shaping approach is that of the 'domestication' of digital technologies, which seeks to document the consumption rather than production stages of the development of a technology – what Ruth Schwartz Cowan (1987) terms 'the consumption junction'. A host of sociology, media and communications researchers over the last two decades have explored the ways in which digital technologies are appropriated and incorporated into households and domestic settings (see Berker *et al.* 2006). This work has detailed how technologies are appropriated into the domestic sphere through ongoing processes of gaining possession and negotiating 'ownership', 'objectification' within the spatial and aesthetic environment of the home and 'incorporation' into the routines of daily life (Silverstone *et al.* 1992, Silverstone and Hirsch 1992). In contrast to other SST studies that focus on the design and production processes, the domestication approach offers a focus on how new technologies are interwoven with the everyday life of households, workplaces and other social settings (Silverstone 1993). This approach has allowed researchers to examine 'how objects move from anonymous and alien commodities to become powerfully integrated into the lives of their users' (Lally 2002, p.1) as well as asking questions of how people 'make sense of, give meaning to, and accomplish functions through technical objects' (Caron and Caronia 2001, p.39).

Besides the domestication approach it can be argued that SST studies have a tendency to focus on producer-related rather than user-related aspects of the shaping of technologies. Of late, growing numbers of social researchers have therefore asserted the need to recognise the enabling (as well as the constraining) importance of materiality at the level of the individual user. In particular, growing interest has been shown in requisitioning the evolutionary psychological notion of 'affordances' (Gibson 1979) as a means of reconciling the opposing poles of pure realism and pure constructivism at the heart of the (anti)determinism debate. Adopting a position distinct from the 'technology as text' metaphor, it has been argued that acknowledgment should be given to affordances which constrain the ways in which technologies can be interpreted, and thereby frame the possibilities that they offer for action (e.g. Norman 1999). As Ian Hutchby (2001, p.44) reasons, 'affordances are functional and relational aspects which frame, while not determining, the possibilities for agentic action in relation to an object'.

It should be noted that Hutchby's use of the notion of affordances is distinct from the commonplace socio-psychological driven use of the term in educational technology research where tools and/or environments are seen to have concrete technological 'affordances' located within them for certain performances. This particular use of the concept of affordance ignores the self-referential and subjective nature of these opportunities. Instead, in the anti-determinist sense, affordances are perceived possibilities for action, referring to what people perceive and signify during their actual interaction with a technological artefact (Vyas *et al.* 2006). Used in this way the notion of affordances allows consideration of the obvious material enablements and constraints of technologies, without recourse to an essentialist analysis. It is argued that using the notion of affordances in this way allows social researchers to move beyond the known 'big issues' of representation, interpretation and negotiation that typify SST studies and, instead, allows closer examination of those actions and interactions between humans and technologies that are rather more mundane, occasional and local. As Hutchby (2003, p.582) reasons, using the notion of affordances in this manner refocuses attention towards 'the empirical question of embodied human practices in real time situated interaction involving technologies'.

Another theoretical tradition that can be located within the SST approach is the family of feminist approaches to addressing technology and society. Here writers have sought to highlight the ideologies imbued in technologies and thereby identify the potential for the development of new technologies to allow women to control and (re)construct their bodies, identities and political positions. Such feminist theories focus in particular on the apparent marginalisation of women from high status technological development and use. For many feminists, digital technology is just another aspect of the social world that is organised fundamentally along lines of gender and dominated by male participants. In particular it has long been argued that gender 'profoundly affect[s] the design, development, diffusion and use of technologies' (Wajcman 2004, p. vi), although many feminist writers also take care to point towards the mutual shaping of digital technology and gender (van Zoonen 2002; Wajcman 2010). Against this male-dominated background a range of feminist responses to information technologies have emerged since the 1970s. A 'liberal feminist' perspective, for example, argues that digital technology is an opportunity for women to 'catch up' with men. Liberal feminists therefore see a need to encourage women to use digital technology above and beyond the levels that men are using them. Conversely, an 'eco-feminist' perspective argues that digital technology is yet another male attempt to control women and nature via technology. This school of feminism therefore urges women to 'reject' digital technology as a masculine oppressive technology and seek to develop new and alternative technologies.

During the 1990, and 2000s another wave of feminist thinkers sought to build upon these established viewpoints – contending that the 'beat them at their own game' stance of the liberal feminists restricts women and technology to conforming to male modes of technology use, whereas the eco-feminist argument is limited in its out-right rejection of new technologies. This school of 'cyber-feminist' thinkers took the alternate view that instead of being something to either acquiesce to or reject, digital technology is something that women can challenge, change and ultimately control for themselves. In particular, cyberfeminists are interested in the potential for digital technology to allow women to control and (re)construct their identities, bodies and political positions. Cyberfeminism, then, can be seen as a provocative reconceptualisation of gender and technology – portraying new technologies as something that subordinate groups can reclaim, control and be empowered by.

As the cursory nature of these latter synopses suggest, there are countless theoretical approaches that could be adopted for the remainder of this book's analysis of technology and schools. Indeed, aside from these examples, a number of other theoretical approaches can be located within the SST family of social theories of technology and society – not least Actor Network Theory (Law 1987; Latour 1987; Latour 2005) and systems theory (Luhmann 2000). The remaining task of this chapter is to outline the theoretical approach that will be taken to inform the subsequent chapters' analysis of schools and schooling in the digital age.

Taking a different perspective on schools and technology

Hopefully this chapter's consideration of the many available theoretical perspectives has made a strong case for taking both the technological *and* the social seriously. It makes little sense to lapse into a determinist approach either where digital technologies are shaped exclusively by stakeholders and end-users *or* are seen as autonomous shaping forces in their own right. On the basis of the discussion so far, it should be clear that any sensible analysis of schools and digital technology should strive to 'analyse the exchanges between everyday practices and the encompassing cultural and societal structures . . . not los[ing] track of the bigger picture while allowing deep explorations into micro-practices of everyday life' (Berker *et al.* 2006). Yet while maintaining a theoretical awareness it is worth remaining mindful of Manuel Castells' lead in 'wearing one's theoretical clothes lightly' when approaching technology and society rather than displaying a dogmatic persistence to one viewpoint or approach. Indeed, Castells (2000) talks of 'disposable theory' – recognising theory as an essential tool, but also acknowledging it is something to be discarded when it outlives its usefulness in illuminating the substantive world. In these terms this book's proceeding analysis of schools and digital technology is best arranged around an assemblage of theoretical perspectives as, and when, they best fit. As Amin and Thrift (2005, p.222) reason:

theory has taken on a different style which has a lighter touch than of old. For a start, few now believe that one theory can cover the world (or save the world, for that matter). No particular theoretical approach, even in combination with others, can be used to gain a total grip on what's going on. Theory-making is a hybrid assemblage of testable propositions and probable explanations derived from sensings of the world, the world's persistent ways of talking back, and the effort of abstraction.

While this chapter has displayed an obvious preference for theories of social shaping it is important to recognise that there is no one 'correct' theoretical stance to adopt when looking at schools and digital technology. Indeed, the individual theories presented above can all be criticised and challenged on particular points and are in no way consistent with one another in their portrayal of technology and society (see Silverstone 2006). As such, each of the theories of social shaping and social construction are best suited to different forms and levels of questioning the technological. For example, all these approaches differ in their characterisation of the malleability of technology and the significance attached to the relative importance of large-scale social and economic structures as opposed to the activities of individuals and groups. Thus, while resisting the temptation to align this book's approach to one specific theoretical perspective it *does* seem highly appropriate to align this book's analysis with the general issues raised by the anti-determinist take on technology and, in particular, give some thought to the increasingly complex social settings within which digital technologies are produced and implemented. This chapter therefore concludes with a brief consideration of what such an approach entails.

As a whole, the anti-determinist approaches presented in this chapter appeal particularly in their ability to highlight the importance of a deep understanding of the social – not least in terms of interactional circumstances in which digital technologies exist, and through which they attain their meanings. Perhaps the most useful aspect of these theoretical approaches therefore lies in the 'big questions' they allow to be asked about schools technology – not least how individual digital technologies fit into wider technological systems and networks, as well as the connections that can be made with wider social concerns of globalisation, the knowledge economy and late modernity. These grand concerns aside, social shaping approaches also are significant in providing an easy 'way in' to understanding the often unseen, mundane, prosaic and perfunctory social processes which underpin the use of digital tools and applications in school settings. As such, then, the analysis for the remainder of the book will be led by a desire to uncover the critical – and hence political – dimension of the shaping of schools and digital technology. This critical take on schools and schooling in the digital age will be informed by a number of values, perhaps best summarised by Amin and Thrift's (2005, p.221) brief agenda for critical scholarship:

First, a powerful sense of engagement with politics and the political. Second, and following on, a consistent belief that there must be better ways of doing things than are currently found in the world. Third, a necessary orientation to a critique of power and exploitation that both blight people's current lives and stop better ways of doing things from coming into existence. Fourth, a constant and unremitting critical reflexivity towards our own practices: no one is allowed to claim that they have the one and only answer or the one and only privileged vantage point. Indeed, to make such a claim is to become a part of the problem.

As suggested at the very beginning of Chapter 1, the remainder of this book will therefore seek to construct a critical take on the political dimension of schools and schooling in the digital age concerned primarily with issues of equality, social justice, mutuality and social responsibility. As such, the remaining six chapters are informed by the belief that it would be foolhardy to approach the digital age as anything less than a site of intense social conflict. In this sense, there is a need to develop a socially-grounded understanding of the complex and compromised realities of digital technology and schools. Thus rather than simply taking the ineffectual approach of asking whether or not digital technology 'works' in schools, educational technologists should be seeking to imbue discourses of schools and digital technology with questions of how these technologies (re)produce social relations and in whose interests they serve (see Apple 2004). As the remaining six chapters of this book will go on to show, many of these issues are not questions about technology *per se*, but are broader educational questions about the nature and form of teaching, learning, pedagogy, epistemology and the nature of organisations and institutions.

As such it makes sense to move beyond the curiously context-free and abstracted readings of learning that underpin many of the claims surrounding digital education. As Charles Crook (2008) has argued, current debates over technology and education are predicated upon presumed 'spontaneous appropriations' of digital technologies by individual learners, independent of other commitments to learning through formal educational provision. As was argued in Chapter 1, the educational 'promise' of digital technologies is often imagined in terms of autonomous technology-based activities taking place within benign, context-free environments. Instead, it makes sense to examine schools, schooling and digital technologies from the perspectives of all of the various contexts that shape and define schools technology. While many writers and commentators on educational technology privilege the micro-level context of the individual learner and technological artefact at the expense of all others, or at best consider the use of digital technologies with one particular group of learners or in one particular context, this book will instead focus on all levels of possible shaping – from the concerns of government and industry, to the concerns of the classroom and the home. If the meaning of schools technology is inseparable from the conditions under which it is generated and experienced, then the use of digital technologies within schools is best understood as being situated within all of the social interests, relationships and restrictions that are associated with schools and schooling.

In this spirit, the next six chapters of this book are based around three different levels of description. Of course, the micro-level of the individual teacher and student is undeniably important and merits sustained consideration – not least in terms of the continued importance of immediate 'local' contexts in framing learning processes and practices. In this sense, it would be erroneous to perceive technology-based learning as somehow 'detached from the spatial condition of common locality' (Thompson 1995, p.32). Yet these micro-level concerns can only be understood fully after having considered what could be termed 'the bigger picture' of educational technology – i.e. the meso-level of the institutional structures and goals of schools, and the macro-level of wider and larger cultural, societal, political and economic values. Making these distinctions is not to argue that one level of analysis is necessarily superior to the others. Indeed, only by making sense of *all* these levels of descriptions can this book hope to develop an understanding of what Frank Webster (2005, p.453) calls 'the intimate connectedness' between 'wider contexts and conceptualisations' and the 'merely particular'.

Conclusions

This approach leads inevitably to the posing of some awkward and challenging questions about digital technology and schools – in stark contrast to the celebratory accounts usually produced about educational technology. It is perhaps important to reiterate the fact that this analytic stance is not intended to be wilfully negative about technology, or lend support to the current 'counter-orthodoxy of pessimism' among some critical scholars, 'where nothing good can be said about information technology' (Wresch 2004, p.71). This book is not attempting to promote an anti-technology perspective that is 'motivated more by fear than insight' as Behr (2009, p.22) puts it. As was made clear in Chapter 1, digital technologies and digital media undeniably matter in modern society, and it is no longer possible (if it ever was) to 'reject' educational technology or argue for an 'outsider' position. Thus in pursuing a critical line of analysis this book is not dismissing all of the 'promises' and potentials outlined in Chapter 1 outright. Neither is the proceeding analysis driven by a nostalgic longing for a long-lost 'golden age' when the mechanics of schooling were less complicated and more efficient.

Instead the remaining six chapters of this book set out to question the nature of the digital transformations and changes that many commentators anticipate whole-heartedly and uncritically with regards to contemporary forms of schools and schooling. As Henri Lefebvre (1981, p.1) reasons, 'that new changes are in store, on the way, is incontestable. Whether, as is universally claimed, they will be radical . . . is another question'. Thus this chapter has proposed taking a stance on schools and technology that certainly involves asking critical questions which are perhaps less forward-looking, often less obvious and certainly less fashionable than is usually found in academic writing and research on educational technology. As Boody (2001, p.19) reasons, 'technology is happening in society and in schools. We cannot avoid being part of it. But we need to understand that each technology offers certain possibilities that interact with already existing cultural attributes to change things when a technology is introduced'. Thus it is hoped that focusing attention on the problematic nature of digital technology and schools can provide a counterbalance to some of the more hyperbolic elements of current discourse, and therefore move educational discussions and debates towards more refined understandings of the 'intellectual, political, economic and technology dynamics that make the information technology a reality' (Hassan 2008, p.xi). While they may be construed as provocative, the remaining six chapters of this book are therefore offered as a genuine attempt to guide future implementations of digital technology in schools along more realistic, and ultimately successful, lines.

This chapter's intention in highlighting the advantages to be gained from taking an anti-essentialist, critical stance on schools and digital technology is not one of academic one-upmanship or believing one particular view to be more perceptive than any other. This chapter has simply advanced the case that an understanding of the socially shaped nature of the technological needs to be brought to the fore of analyses of schools and digital technology – offering a much-needed corrective to the view of educational technology as a closed black box whose 'effects' cannot be easily controlled. Thus, while elements of the argument developed over the next six chapters could be characterised in Lefebvre's (1981, p.26) words as a 'hypercritical' reading of schools technology, it is hoped that any criticism has been employed carefully as a corrective to the mainstream eulogising of technology in education. Above all it is hoped that the book's criticism is taken in a constructive manner. Indeed, as Wiebe Bijker (1995) reasons, only by exploring and exposing the social roots of technology can academic writers and researchers hope to make the technological amenable to democratic interpretation and intervention. With this challenge in mind the remaining chapters of this book can now go on to consider the many different levels of social shaping of schools and digital technologies – starting with the macro-level concerns of policy-makers, governments and the state.

Part II

Making sense of schools, schooling and digital technology

4 Digital technology and education policy-making

Introduction

This chapter considers the shaping of schools, schooling and the digital age at a macro-level of analysis. As outlined in Chapter 3, the social shaping of technology can involve a wide number of influences. It therefore follows that the use of digital technology in schools is influenced by a variety of stakeholders and interests long before it enters the classroom setting. This chapter examines the influence of state policy-making and policy institutions on schools technology. In particular, it explores the construction of digital technology use within recent state policy programmes and initiatives. Of course, the topic of technology use has long been a focus for public sector policy-making. The 1960s and 1970s saw the governments of many (over)developed industrialised nations react to concerns over the 'white heat' of technological development with a range of 'high tech' public policy drives – especially in areas of public life such as energy, transport, health and education. With the rise of 'micro-electronics', countries such as the UK and US saw the launch and re-launch of often indistinguishable national educational technology policies and local initiatives throughout the 1980s, with governments and politicians of all political persuasions keen to capitalise on the kudos of being seen to 'do something' about new information technologies. While continuing to be a comparatively high-profile area of state policy-making throughout the 1980s, educational technology gained a heightened importance with the emergence in the mid-1990s of the internet into mainstream societal use (as compared to previous relatively niche application in scientific and military domains). From that time onwards the field of educational technology (and schools technology in particular) has attracted the sustained attention of policy-makers, figuring ever more prominently in the education policy agendas of countries around the world. This chapter considers what role this high-profile policy-making activity has played in the shaping of schools and schooling in the digital age – not least in terms of setting an agenda for what schools technology is and what values are associated with it.

The significance of education policy to schools' use of digital technology

Although not apparent immediately in the day-to-day activities within a classroom, the influence of state policy-making is a crucial component of making sense of contemporary schools and schooling. At a basic level, education policies represent the courses of action taken by governments and other agencies of the state with respect to their obligations to deliver and regulate education provision. State policies therefore set out the official 'bottom line' on a wide range of educational issues – from what schools are obliged legally to provide to their students, to the amounts and types of funding that are attributed to different aspects and components of the school system. In this respect, policies are formalised expressions of the various engagements that take place between state and citizen. Education technology policy can therefore be seen as a formalisation of state intent to guide the implementation of digital technologies throughout national school systems. Such policies tend to take one of three main forms – interventions based on legal regulation, interventions based on the distribution of resources, and intervention designed to achieve normative change. In all these guises, education policy matters in as much as it sets the 'rules of engagement' and 'whose games we play' (Considine 2005, p.2), although not necessarily setting out how the game is played or for what purposes.

It is important to note at this point that state policies are formulated to achieve a range of explicit and specific objectives as well as fulfilling wider exhortative functions – in other words education technology policies seek to both direct and to influence the nature of digital technology use in schools. In this sense education policies cannot be said to always have homogenous and predictable 'effects'. Rather, policies have sets of intended consequences and, perhaps more importantly, sets of unintended consequences that are often apparent only at a localised level when policies enter schools and are enacted upon by managers, administrators, teachers and students. From this perspective it is worth being mindful of the capacity of state policies to produce as well as address problems – especially in the medium and long term as 'the second, third or fourth generation of effects produced by previous policy actions and instruments' (Considine 2005, p.21) become apparent. In this sense, the unintended as well as intended consequences of education technology policy-making tend to be cumulative and not wholly under state control.

One of the most influential (although usually not unintended) aspects of policy-making is its role in shaping wider understandings and expectations of education – with states using education policies to play an important legitimising and normalising role. What is said about digital technology and schools within education policy-making, and how these messages and stories are received, interpreted and acted upon, is therefore of importance in explaining some of the educational 'failures' of digital technology as outlined in Chapter 2. The contested and contestable nature of education policy is reflected in Stephen Ball's notion of 'policy as text' – where state policies are seen as being 'written' (textual) interventions into education practice, which are then read and re-written by various macro-, meso- and micro-level actors as the policy is passed down. The parallels here with the anti-essentialist notion of 'technology as text' outlined in Chapter 3 are clear, and allow a reading of schools technology policy that accounts for the flexibility and fluidity of how the initial intentions of governments are re-configured by those 'on the ground'. As Ball (1993, p.11) describes:

we can see policies as representations which are encoded in complex ways (via struggles, compromises, authoritative public interpretations and reinterpretations) and decoded in complex ways (via actors' interpretations and meanings in relation to their history, experiences, skills, resources and context). A policy is both contested and changing, always in a state of 'becoming', of 'was' and 'never was' and 'not quite' . . . Now this conception is not simply one which privileges the significance of readings of policy by its subjects. While that is important – authors cannot control the meanings of their texts – policy authors do make concerted efforts to assert such control by the means at their disposal. We need to understand those efforts and their effects on readers.

In a more subtle but no less significant way education policies also function as discursive devices. The discursive role of policy refers to the meanings, intentions, values and beliefs that lie behind these formalised expressions of state intent. State policies can therefore be seen as symbolic systems of values, acting as a means of representing, accounting for and legitimating political decisions. In this discursive sense, education policies are formulated both to achieve material effects and to manufacture support for those effects (Ball 1998). As Stephen Ball again distinguishes:

we need to appreciate the way in which policy ensembles, collections of related policies, exercise power through a *production* of 'truth' and 'knowledge', as discourses . . . Discourses are about what can be said, and thought, but also about who can speak, when, where and with what authority. Discourses embody the meaning and use of propositions and words. Thus, certain possibilities for thought are constructed. Words are ordered and combined in particular ways and other combinations are displaced or excluded (Ball 1993, p.14).

This reading of education policy draws attention to the need to examine the ideological dimensions of what is being said about digital technology within educational policy discourses – highlighting what those responsible for the production of policy think about (and what they do not think about) when striving to direct the nature and form of technology use in schools. Any overview of digital education policy-making should therefore remain mindful of the role of policy in shaping, enacting and legitimising the social arrangements and power relationships that constitute schools technology (Mulderrig 2007). Viewed from this perspective, then, it is not enough to merely attempt to identify the 'impact' or 'effect' of education policy on education practice – instead, state policy should be seen both in terms of structural mechanisms and in a wider discursive role. It is therefore important to remember that policy-making is an iterative and negotiated process. The writing and reading processes associated with the formulation and implementation of an education policy involve the writing of formal coercive laws, as well as the reforming of previously negotiated commitments and the continuation of implicit habitual conduct (Considine 2005). From this perspective, the mediated nature of state policy-making means that public policy is perhaps best understood as an effort to stimulate change or maintain the *status quo*, rather than a direct means of alteration and adjustment. With all these complexities in mind, it is perhaps most appropriate now to pay close attention to the ways in which digital technologies are imagined and 'written into' state education policies, and then consider the ideological values and implications that these policies set out to convey.

The worldwide turn towards schools technology policy-making

The implementation of digital technology in school systems has become an increasingly prominent feature of state education policy-making over the past two decades. As implied at the beginning of this chapter, the 1990s and 2000s witnessed a relentless development of ambitious national educational technology policy drives – initiated by the Clinton–Gore administration's National Information Infrastructure in 1993 and soon replicated by governments the world over. From Berlin to Buenos Aires, legislation was passed from the mid-1990s onwards to increase vastly the technological resourcing of schools in terms of hardware, software and network infrastructure. Policy drives during the late 1990s such as the UK National Grid for Learning, German Schulen ans Netz and the Singaporean ICT Masterplan for Schools saw nationwide programmes of teacher training and support for indigenous IT industries being introduced by nation states keen to ensure that the circumstances existed for the effective educational use of the new breed of internet-based digital technologies.

Nearly twenty years later, schools technology can now be said to constitute a major policy concern throughout the developed and developing world. Whereas state policy-making during the 1980s and 1990s took place mainly in (over)developed countries such as the UK, USA, Germany, Japan, Korea, Singapore, Australia and New Zealand, the 2000s saw educational technology emerge as what Lingard *et al.* (2005) describe as a 'global field' of educational policy. Technology is now one of the common 'global trends' in education policy-making (Lee and Caldwell 2010). Nearly every country in the world – regardless of geopolitical, economic or social circumstance – has formulated and implemented an educational technology strategy. In Ethiopia, for example, an ICT in Education Implementation Strategy and National SchoolNet Initiative are pillars of the country's 'ICT for Development' plan, as well as forming part of a wider state commitment to invest ten per cent of the country's overall gross domestic product into ICT projects. In Saudi Arabia the Crown Prince's Watani (My Nation) schools' ICT policy is predicated upon notions of nation building and state-craft, whereas China's 'Eleventh Five Year Plan for Education' sets out a comprehensive developmental agenda of 'educational informationalisation'. Perhaps the most pronounced and enthusiastic educational technology policy agendas have been developed in countries on the geographical and political periphery of the world stage, with the governments of such countries often seeing schools technology as a ready means of national 'cyber-boosterism'. As Zhao *et al.* (2005, p.673) note, 'the unchecked fear of missing the fast ICT train to global prominence' resulted in a 'global chase after e-learning' during the 2000s. The ever-growing levels of funding being directed towards schools technology offers ample proof of the reconstitution of educational technology over the past twenty years as a high-status and high-profile global policy endeavour.

Besides a shared sense of ambition, all these policies are notable in their general homogeneity of content – all appearing to follow a broadly similar line rather than being influenced by peculiarly local concerns. Indeed, some policy researchers have seized upon the 'unusual commonality' between countries' educational technology strategies (Zhao *et al.* 2005), a trend exacerbated by considerable policy-borrowing between countries (see, for example, Xuereb 2006). While it may be over-stating the case to argue that the educational technology policies of Saudi Arabia, Ethiopia and China are wholly interchangeable and indistinguishable from each other, there is certainly a strong 'family resemblance' between state policies the world over. For instance, most countries' early initiatives sought to insert computer equipment and internet connectivity into classrooms and establish some form of teacher training and development. These initial attempts tended to be preceded by policies seeking to address issues of pedagogic practice and stimulate a 'bottom-up' demand among teachers, parents and school administrators for technology-based learning and teaching. In both these forms, most of the school technology initiatives that emerged during the 1990s and 2000s shared the traits of being well-funded, focused on increasing the availability of digital technologies in schools and being carefully targeted at measurable outcomes. More often than not, they also involved the amendment of the school curriculum to require teaching and learning through technology accompanied by sets of measures to ensure that new and serving teachers had the knowledge and skills to make use of digital technologies in their classrooms. As Mee (2007b, n.p.) concludes, 'all of the above has led to what could at best be described as incremental accommodation of educational technologies within existing organisational frameworks'.

Accounting for the economic capture of schools technology policy-making

As was outlined in Chapter 2, much of this policy-making has been criticised in hindsight as being fundamentally at odds with the structure of the school organisations it is meant to be located within. Of course, no national policy could be said to 'fit' with the realities of schools and classrooms in a wholly satisfactory way and, as discussed above, the notion of policy 'impacting' directly on schools is a reductionist mis-reading of the policy process. Instead of attributing blame on the deficiencies of policy visions it is more useful to pay attention to the role of policy-making and policy discourses in shaping the discursive construction of schools technology. As such it could be argued that the apparent 'clash' between educational technology policy and educational technology practice does not necessarily represent a failure of policy-makers to 'understand' schools and digital technology. Rather, policy-makers may well not have developed such policies and initiatives with purely 'educational' intentions in mind. As such, schools technology policy-making could also be seen as an ideological concept whose internal contradictions and 'fuzziness' serve to mask the social, political and economic agendas it is used to propagate. That the homogenised, idealised and extrapolated versions of technology-based schooling prompted by national school technology drives and agendas have proved to jar repeatedly with the realities of classrooms and schools should not come as a surprise. Indeed, it could be argued that if digital technology has not been introduced into school systems primarily for educational reasons, then it cannot be expected to have ended up being used in educationally effective ways.

Recently a number of studies have examined the shaping of education technology policy drives around the world, all attempting to unpack the contribution of the many actors involved in the processes of policy formulation and implementation. So far much of this work has focused on the macro-economic shaping of policies, and therefore has spent much time detailing the ways in which schools technology appears to have been driven relentlessly by a number of narrow political and economic motivations. In fact, these studies suggest that once some local variation is accounted for then the driving forces of schools technology can be seen to be an essentially homogenous and well-worn set of mandates pertaining to deal with the vagaries of political and economic control in the globalised 'knowledge economy'. Perhaps most dominant of these mandates has been the notion that schools technology constitutes a delayed means of increasing a nation's economic competitiveness, with many countries perceiving a close relationship between success in global economic markets and the increased use of technology in educational institutions. Zhao, Conway and colleagues have detailed 'tremendous' and 'remarkable' similarities between developed and developing countries alike which they see as reflecting 'a techno-centric, utopian and economic driven mindset towards e-learning' (Zhao *et al.* 2005, p.674).

The linkages between schools technology and concerns of the global economy are evident throughout the recent history of educational technology policy-making. For example, as the 1990s lurch towards post-industrialism began to take shape, it was noticeable how investment in education and technology became a major prop in the theatre of economic conflict between nations – especially in terms of wider prevailing concerns over enhancing competitiveness in a globalising economy and creating lifelong learning systems fit for a successful knowledge economy. Indeed, the framing of schools digital technology in terms of economic rationales was explicitly laid out in official political pronouncements in Europe at the end of the 1990s of the combination of education and technology being 'the best economic policy we have' (Blair in DfEE 1998, p.9) and as a crucial element in making 'the individual and business fit for the knowledge-based economy of the future' (Blair and Schroeder 1999, p.2). Similarly, US policy-making throughout the Clinton, Bush and Obama administrations has espoused similar aspirations – exemplified in President Clinton's framing of telecommunications technology in terms of 'winning' the twenty-first century (Information Infrastructure Task Force 1993) or Secretary Of Education Rod Paige's later justification that 'computers have changed the way the world works. And we need to make sure our children have the skills to compete in this new global economy' (Paige 2005, n.p.). In the eyes of these policy-makers and others like them, the economic rather than pedagogic significance of schools technology continues to drive and shape its implementation in the classroom.

Within the broad motivations of gaining a comparative economic advantage, school technology policies can be seen to satisfy at least three specific economic and political criteria (see Ball 2007a) – the economics of education (i.e. technology contributing to the efficient logistics of educational provision); education and the economy (i.e. technology contributing to countries' economic competitiveness and efficiency of labour and knowledge production); the economy and education (i.e. technology contributing to the profitability and commoditisation of education). In particular, most schools technology policies are imbued with a belief that digital technology can act as a means of increasing a nation's economic competitiveness in the knowledge-driven economies of the post-industrialised world. As such, it can be argued strongly that national educational technology agendas have been conceived and perpetuated by states as a concerted attempt to change the economic 'mindset' of future workers towards a technologically-based global competition, upgrade the skills base of emerging generations of young people and create the 'workforce flexibility' to counter the threat of a global labour market. Aside from these rationales, schools are seen to offer a benign test-bed for the development of indigenous IT industries free from the more unforgiving realities of the open marketplace and critical consumers. Finally, as Lefebvre (1976) notes, one of the primary pressures facing the state in the modern world is the relatively autonomous nature of technological and economic growth. In this sense, the totemic value of schools technology for states should not be overlooked, with governments using school technology agendas as a high-profile means of being seen to be actually 'doing something' about the information age.

As all these examples highlight, the association between schools technology and economic values and concerns appears to run deep. In many ways the economic-led nature of schools technology policy is not surprising given the general economic-led nature of public sector policy-making. As Mark Considine (2005, p.26) reasons, 'policy interventions must be understood within the social and economic conditions through which resources are identified and conflicts arise [. . .] Questions of social and economic structure not only shape the work of policy makers, they may themselves be the subject matter of policy interventions'. Thus, as Brown and Murray (2005, p.84) conclude resignedly, the notion of schools technology is almost inevitably 'intertwined deeply with globalisation, the rise of neo-liberalism, the celebration of technology consumption, and ecologically destructive cultural patterns . . . new digital technology is part of a wider political, economic and ideological agenda'. This is not to suggest that educational technology is the only instance of there being a strong linkage between technology and global economic concerns. Indeed, the specific relationship between global economic markets, digital technology and nation states has also always been close (Schiller 1995). In particular, computers and the internet have long been positioned as vital drivers of economic competitiveness in the knowledge-driven economies of the post-industrialised world. As long as information processing, e-commerce and virtual networking of individuals and companies continue to remould the nature of business then this perception looks set to persist. As Manuel Castells (1996, p.16) noted at the end of the twentieth century, 'in the new, informational mode of development the source of productivity lies in the technology of knowledge generation, information processing, and symbolic communication'.

These wider linkages notwithstanding, growing numbers of critical commentators have been led to bemoan the increasingly monolithic definition of schools technology which appears to prevail in education policy-making around the world. As already implied in Chapter 2, there are obvious limitations in conceptualising the classroom use of digital technology in ways that appear to be imbued with 'no values other than economic' (Robertson 2003, p.323). Although the notion of education policies being transferred directly into school settings is an overly simplistic reading of the policy implementation process, it is important to consider the bearing of these different political and economic influences on what is experienced as 'digital technology' in the classroom. For example, within the narrow but highly influential construction of educational technology as an economic good, it can be argued that schools are positioned as little more than the knowledge factories and diploma mills of the contemporary knowledge economy in a similar way to Noble's (2002) analysis of the role of the university in the knowledge economy. Education technology policies act in a way as to frame the primary functions of schools not in terms of fostering learning or ensuring equality of opportunity but in terms of supporting the reconstruction of the individual worker-citizen and, in particular, ensuring the emergence of a 'high-skills' workforce. If educational processes are considered at all, then it is often in restricted terms of a human capital approach towards economic success and efficiency. This often leaves schools technology positioned firmly within wider economic projects of standardising curricula, improving educational 'standards', widening participation rates in post-compulsory education and increasing levels of 'lifelong learning'. Given the top-down nature of this conceptualisation of education it can be of little surprise that technology-based teaching ends up being constructed in terms of delivery rather than discovery, and that technology-based students end up in the position of being recipients of pre-packaged curricula. Perhaps most importantly, the trend of presenting digital technology as a 'technical fix' for society and education could be seen to limit the opportunities for the educational application of technology in schools. Thus as Markus Nivala (2009, p.445) outlines, this mode of policy-making can be criticised as

> not tak[ing] into consideration the agency of teachers or pupils, on whom the information society narrative is imposed, but 'forces' them to use ICT whether they find it useful or not. The spirit of the discourse, its economic and technological determinism, leaves no space for a critical and rational approach to ICT or its educational use. Second, the halo of omnipotence often attributed to ICT lessens the chances of a successful implementation of ICT in education. Unrealistic expectations could lead to a big disappointment if teachers come to perceive ICT as just another 'faddish educational innovation of the moment'. Furthermore, if ICT is believed to be a panacea for all educational and societal ills, other more effective measures to ameliorate these ills might be overlooked.

Recognising the performative aspects of schools technology policy-making

It should, by now, be clear that the introduction of school technology agendas are predicated upon a number of wider state concerns that stretch beyond the immediate interests of students and teachers. While this critical analysis of educational technology policy-making highlights the complex social, political and economic relations imbued in the construction of schools technology it would be fair to conclude that there is a need to develop an understanding of schools technology policies that goes beyond pointing out the deficiencies of the policy formation process. To return to the issues outlined at the beginning of this chapter, education policy-making should be seen as being significant for how it is interpreted and re-enacted, as much as for how and why it is initially produced. As Hamilton and Feenberg (2005, p.106) argue, at present, much critical analysis of educational technology policy-making is hidebound by its presentation of technology-based education as 'a *fait accompli* with which the [school] must comply or which it must reject out of hand in defence of traditional academic values and priorities'.

One possible means of extending this chapter's analysis of schools technology beyond the 'education/economy clash' has been explored by the Danish policy analysts Casper Bruun Jensen and Peter Lauritsen. These authors argue that most critical work on technology and policy-making has been content with merely reading *against* policy texts from a 'representational' point of view – i.e. identifying, discussing and problematising the assumptions inherent in policy reports and initiatives. As much of this chapter's discussion has so far shown, this approach largely confirms that school technology policy texts, like public sector technology policies in general, are characterised by their 'narrow definitions' and 'simple-minded goals' predicated upon economic success (Jensen and Lauritsen 2005, p.353). Yet while it is important to identify and discuss the flawed assumptions inherent in the global rush towards developing and implementing systems of digitally-enhanced schooling, Jensen and Lauritsen argue that critical scholars should also examine where these assumptions become situated and, crucially, begin to ask questions of the relations that such policies forge with various existing practices. In other words it is also useful to approach schools technology policy from a 'performative' point of view – i.e. to travel with the policies to some of the places where they have settled and taken effect. From this perspective, as well as paying attention to what policy texts says about schools and digital technology *per se*, it is important to consider the effect and influences that such discourses may (or may not) have on the subsequent 'performance' of schools technology in a country's school system.

If the focus of analysis moves from reading against the text of school technology policies to reading *with* the text, then a fuller understanding can be developed of how such policies and discourses feed into the practice of digital technology use in schools. In this way it makes sense to read with the text of schools technology policy and consider 'the effects on the environment that exceed or bypass discussions of content and intentionality' (Jensen and Lauritsen 2005, p.353), not least the actions that such policies initiate and can be connected to after their initial production. This involves a detailed critical reading of subsequent practices and programmes arising from a policy document, rather than just a static critique of its discourse. From this perspective, the argument can be made that a schools technology policy that is ostensibly focused on economic matters has a number of subsequent political, ideological and practical consequences. This is perhaps most obvious in how a schools technology policy is 'performed' in public, political and academic debate – i.e. how the notion of the policy is used to guide understandings of what educational technology is, and what it should be. In practical policy-making terms, for instance, schools technology policies are continued into other education policies and initiatives. Perhaps most noticeable, of course, is the influence of these policies on educational practice. As was implied in

Chapter 2, in many ways any reading 'with the text' of a schools technology initiative finds the performance of most initiatives to be more of a *non*-performance, or at best an unchanged performance from earlier phases of schools technology policy-making. As such, relatively little change is apparent in the ongoing performance of schools technology except in terms of the increased standing of digital technology use in political discourse and, of course, the increased levels of funding and resourcing of digital technology in a country's schools. The translation of the lofty ideals of policy documents into practical activities is usually less dynamic and certainly less transformative than may be expected from their initial tone and substance.

In all, the history of schools technology policy programmes in most countries is perhaps best characterised as a case of 'business as usual' rather than marking a transformation of national education systems. When scrutinised beyond their initial 'writing', many national policies appear to function primarily as a mechanism for various stakeholders in schools technology to continue acting as they have always done, albeit with increased prominence and resourcing. Thus government agencies provide funding and resourcing which school leaders and administrators then spend and 'implement' in classrooms alongside funding of their own. Politicians continue to talk about schools and technology in societal-level aspirational terms, academics continue to pursue their agendas of researching how best to integrate technology into education systems, and journalists and teacher groups also continue to pursue their own wider concerns (be it critiquing the lack of central government support for school principals or raising concerns over declining academic standards). To revisit Harrison and Feenberg's earlier contention, it would seem that schools, academics, journalists, unionists and the like do not so much reject educational technology policies out of hand or even comply with them wholly – rather they simply enrol these policies into their established practices, discourses and ways-of-being. Thus most of the national policy drives outlined at the beginning of this chapter have tended to be subjugated into wider concerns and ongoing practices of education and politics in their respective countries. In very few instances – if at all – could the performance of these policies be said to involve the significant disruption of pre-existing ways of 'doing' educational technology in schools.

That these policies assume a high-profile but largely symbolic role should not be cause for surprise. The apparent mismatch between policy rhetoric and policy performance that runs throughout schools technology policy-making around the world shows how policy documents like the national strategies outlined at the beginning of this chapter are not direct attempts to alter educational practice *per se*. Instead, as Jensen and Lauritsen (2005, p.365) note, state technology policies tend to work 'rather like a relay between certain administrative and political practices and a diversity of local initiatives'. The overriding observation in the case of recent schools technology policy-making is that it lacks the substance and forcefulness to establish meaningful connections between the many different actors involved in a country's educational technology community – thus allowing schools, teachers, IT vendors, technologists, journalists and the like to continue much as they always have done. It is notable how most state policy-making appears to conform to (or at least fails to challenge directly) the educational technology consensus – with a noticeable preference for addressing 'safe' or unthreatening issues of resourcing, training and connectivity rather than more controversial areas of reform.

It would be erroneous, however, to imply that the architects of national technology agendas are necessarily seeking to encourage inertia when formulating schools technology policy. It can be taken as read that policy-makers are seeking to engineer *some* change through the development of policy, albeit in an indirect and aspiring manner. In many ways, then, school technology policies are intended to be a tentative step of releasing some ideas into the educational domain in the hope that they may stimulate or provoke change. As Jensen and Lauritsen (2005, p.368) observe:

> there is a package, shiny in its vagueness, of ideas – balls thrown in the air, in the hope that someone will catch them – and formulations that are yet unfulfilled with any practical or even ideal content.

These good intentions notwithstanding, it could be argued that the gulf between the lofty global ideals often found in government reports and policy statements (such as creating 'innovative thriving knowledge societies') and the resulting mundane local actions on the ground (such as forming professional development clusters or developing 'internet-safety' tools) are simply too great to add any real power or durable connections to the existing networks and communities of educational technology stakeholders. At most, then, the 'game' of educational technology (to borrow Mark Considine's earlier analogy) is allowed to continue as before, albeit with slightly more funding and a higher political profile. The performance of the initial all-inclusive aims and objectives of a national technology policy agenda sees such initiatives being subsumed into prosaic issues of funding, local politics and wider educational debates – thus becoming ever 'more mundane and compromised' in contrast to the 'grand ideas' of the initial policy documents (Jensen and Lauritsen 2005, p.364).

Reading schools technology policy-making in this 'performative' manner highlights the need to acknowledge the ideological nature of such initiatives and policy programmes. This observation relates back to Goodson and Mangan's (1996) critique of the ideological underpinnings of the 'computer literacy' programmes and initiatives that were then being implemented by policy-makers into school curricula throughout the 1980s and 1990s. Here it was often argued by some commentators of the time that computer literacy was a poorly defined and delineated concept, lacking clarity of educational purpose or outcome. Yet Goodson and Mangan contended that the vagueness surrounding the concept of computer literacy was not entirely accidental nor the mere result of confusion among its proponents. Instead they argued that 'computer literacy' was a largely ideological concept, whose fuzziness and internal contradictions served to mask the social, political and economic agendas it was being used to propagate. In this sense it can be argued that most state policy-making of the 2000s and early 2010s continues to function as a means of establishing the use of digital technologies as a form of consensual discourse in educational arenas – positioning the use of digital technologies in schools as an all-pervasive and widely accepted issue that is backed by hitherto unseen levels of official authority (see Apple 1979). As has been argued throughout the latter half of this chapter, this pervasive digital 'world-view' and its continual commonsensical recourse to vague notions of the 'effectiveness' and 'impact' of digital technologies in the classroom belies the lack of real transformation of nation school systems along the lines anticipated in Chapter 1.

Conclusions

This chapter has laid out briefly the different ways in which schools technology is shaped by state policy-making. While it is unwise to ascribe any particular direct effect or impact, it is clear that schools technology policy drives and agendas have done much to articulate and formalise the link between digital technology use in schools and the interests of state, economy, industry and other economic stakeholders. Perhaps the most prominent manifestation of this relationship has been the political use of digital technologies such as the internet as a policy device to align schools and schooling with a number of significant contemporary societal issues – not least global economic concerns of national competiveness, the up-skilling of workforces, performative logic of the labour market, the dynamics of global capitalism and the intensification of the economic function of knowledge. In all these instances, state policy-making in the area of schools technology feeds into and reflects wider societal issues and global political concerns, bringing them to bear on the structural processes of contemporary schooling. As Mark Considine (2005, p.1) observes, state policies 'contain and express the conflicts and tensions of contemporary societies . . . Questions of policy are therefore always also questions of institutional design. Official gestures, rules, counter-rules and each new act of political imagination bring to light the structures holding society together and driving them apart'.

In many ways, then, education technology policies are not intended to lead to re-stratification or significant realignment of school systems along digital lines. Instead, technology policy drives can be understood primarily as symbolic interventions on the part of state – offering a ready means for governments to maintain legitimacy as an economic state and act as a high-profile way of keeping 'on message' with a number of broad political themes. This is not to say that these policies are intended to fulfil no purpose at all – rather that the intended outcomes are broader than may first appear to the case. For example, state interest in schools technology can be seen as playing an emblematic role in terms of wider ambitions towards the 'transformation' of countries' public sector organisations along lines fit for a globally competitive economy. In this sense schools technology policy-making since the 1990s is testament to the general nature of public sector policy-making during the last twenty years, where economic concerns have tended to prevail. As Stephen Ball argues:

> Generally speaking, within this new episteme, education is increasingly, indeed perhaps almost exclusively, spoken of within policy in terms of its economic value and its contribution to international market competitiveness. Even policies which are concerned to achieve greater social inclusion are edited, modified and co-opted by the requirements of economic participation and the labour markets and the values, principles and relations of trade/exchange . . . Education is

increasingly subject to the normative assumptions and prescriptions of economism and the kind of culture the school can be is articulated in its terms. Within
policy this economism is articulated and enacted very generally in the joining up
of schooling to the project of competitiveness and to the demands of globalisation and very specifically through the curriculum of enterprise and entrepreneurship (Ball 2007a, p.185).

Perhaps most significantly, understanding schools technology policy as discourse
focuses attention on the ideological aspects of what is *not* being said about schools
and schooling in the digital age – where there is inaction rather than action, where
there is silence rather than noise. While a number of silences are obvious, perhaps
most significant are the ways in which much state policy-making serves to obscure the
structures of power and real shaping concerns behind the ostensibly bland, neutral
face of schools technology. Many of the school technology policies highlighted in this
chapter could be said to construct a consensual but deliberately vague social identity
for the state and other powerful stakeholders involved in the formulation and implementation of schools technology – not least private interests and commercial actors
(see Mulderrig 2007). As such, particular attention needs to be paid to the commercial
and non-state issues underlying what can be termed the increasing 'privatisations' of
schools technology (see Ball 2007a). The role of schools and digital technology as a
nexus for economic, commercial and educational concerns therefore provides the
focus for the next chapter in this book. Perhaps more so than in other areas of education, digital technology is an area of schools and schooling where the state cannot
claim to have overall governance. The role of other 'significant' actors in the shaping
of schools technology will now be considered in Chapter 5.

5   Digital technology and
the privatisations of schooling

Introduction

Chapter 4 made the case for understanding the policies of schools technology as doing political work. These issues already extend any analysis of schools technology far beyond the usual concerns of the academic study of educational technology. In particular, the last chapter highlighted the importance of the politics of the state in influencing how and why digital technologies are used (and not used) in the ways that they are in schools. Of course the arguments covered in Chapter 4 provide a powerful but not complete picture of schools and technology – especially given the often weakened power of the state to affect change in the public sector. Indeed, the past twenty years or so has shown the need to move beyond a state-driven 'institutional' perspective in order to understand schools and schooling in contemporary society. As Meyer and Rowan (2006, p.3) argue, schools can no longer be seen as being 'fully controlled by government and the profession and thus beyond the grip of market forces . . . schools are no longer shielded from the pressures of accountability and efficiency; the once airtight government monopoly of schooling has been invaded by private providers; the dominant institutional forms of schooling no longer serve as unrivalled models for emulation'.

While schooling could be said over much of the latter half of the twentieth century to have been a largely state-driven activity, the influence of non-state interests on the development and implementation of technology throughout this time is well accepted. A wide range of industrial, scientific and commercial interests have been involved centrally in the genesis and development of most of the major technologies of recent times – from the automobile to the contraceptive pill. The production of most digital technologies has long been a profoundly commercial affair. Put simply, nation states do not have the technical capacity or technological expertise to produce most of the technologies that underpin the digital age. There are very few examples of state-produced laptops or mobile phones – even in the most dirigiste and authoritative of countries. As was implied in Chapter 3, it is important to recognise the role of commercial and private actors in the social construction of digital technology in schools. Indeed, the literature on the social-shaping and social construction of technology is concerned primarily with the fact that the development and implementation of digital technology will involve a pathway of different commercial actors from initial producers to end-users. Thus any aspect of schools technology – from a managed learning system to an interactive whiteboard – is not a neutral, homogenous product but a socially constructed set of practices stemming back to when it was first conceived of. As Oushoorn and Pinch (2003, p.24) put it, any digital technology should be seen as

> a culturally contested zone where users, advocacy groups, consumer organisations, designers, producers, salespeople, policy makers and intermediary groups create, negotiate, and give differing and sometimes conflicting forms, meanings and uses to technologies.

With these thoughts in mind, the remainder of this chapter will detail and explore the influence that these non-state interests have on schools technology, focusing in particular on the shifting notions of public good and private interests. What bearing do private interests and values have on what is ostensibly a public concern?

Digital technology and the privatisations of contemporary schools and schooling

It is now acknowledged widely that state-provided education in most capitalist societies has been party to a series of 'privatisations' over the last thirty years or so. While digital technologies certainly represent one of the significant recent privatisations of education this is by no means the only area where private interests have come to play a key role in the day-to-day running of schools and schooling. The role of the private sector in the provision of education 'resources', 'administration' and 'support' is now considerable – with schools being serviced by a set of autonomous, contracted, satellite industries concerned with everything from the production of textbooks and testing programmes to catering, cleaning and clerical arrangements. While these auxiliary activities have intensified over the last thirty years, attention should also be paid to the growing role of private interests in the overall governance and provision of schooling – what Ball (2007a, p.13) terms 'the fundamental re-design of the public sector [where] the state is increasingly re-positioned as the guarantor, not necessarily the provider . . . the state is very much a market-maker or broker'. One of the most high-profile instances of the privatised governance of education over the last thirty years has been the state introduction of for-profit organisations into the education arena under the banner of 'standards-driven reform', thus rendering public education first and foremost a profit-making business. So-called 'education management organisations' have been created precisely for this purpose in the US and the UK making visible in their subsequent activities the extent of the ongoing privatisation of public education. It is now estimated that in the US alone, education management organisations are operating in twenty-eight states managing over 500 schools with over 250,000 students, including sixty internet-based 'virtual schools' (Molnar *et al.* 2008)

As will be argued throughout this chapter, digital technologies lie at the heart of the contemporary privatisations of schools and schooling, with private sector interests responsible for providing a range of digitally based or digitally-enhanced products and services to education systems and schools. Indeed, digital technology is implicit in many aspects of what Dale (2009) distinguishes as the dominant forms of private sector interest in the 'schools market' – i.e. the 'school improvement industry' and the 'student improvement industry'. As such, the bearing of private sector interests and concerns with school-related digital technology use demands close scrutiny. Of course, the design, production and sale of digital technology hardware and software to schools is almost wholly dependent on commercial interests, most notably in the form of the many multi-national, national and local IT companies responsible for supplying computer hardware, software, connectivity and 'content'. Private interests also sell a range of technology-based services to schools – from the management of schools' IT infrastructures, information management and payroll systems to a range of monitoring and surveillance technologies. The for-profit sector also plays a key role in the subtler 'selling' of the concept of in-school and outside-school technology use in order to sustain demand for educational use of digital technologies. In a more detached sense, business and industry interests also enjoy privileged roles in shaping the formation of the state technology policies outlined in the previous chapter. In all these instances, the nature, form and governance of digital technology use in schools are predicated upon the involvement of commercial firms and other non-state interests. The overriding question that follows, therefore, is to what extent and in what ways do these private interests exert a shaping influence on schools technology?

Mapping the extent of private sector involvement in schools technology

In the most immediate sense, private interests play a key role in the selling and supplying of digital resources to schools – not least computer hardware, internet connectivity and the plethora of 'content' such as learning materials software, online content and broadcast services. As such, schools' use of digital technology constitutes a thriving marketplace where thousands of commercial providers in any country are concerned with selling tens of thousands of products to schools, school districts and their advisers. The procurement of schools technology is literally big business – representing a significant and potentially lucrative market within which the IT industry operates. Schools technology also allows private firms to sell technology to consumers other than schools, not least parents and households with school-aged children. For example, technology-based 'edutainment' now forms a substantial part of what has been termed the 'para-education' or 'shadow-education' market. As Plowman *et al.* (2010) observe, the last twenty years have seen a proliferation of toys and other 'edutainment' products aimed at children as soon as they enter the school system that combine digital and physical opportunities for play and learning. Perhaps the most noteworthy shift here over recent years is the growing commercial mass provision of home-based online education for students of all ages by what Hinchey (2008) terms 'media-giant producers' such as Pearson, Mattel, Lego and Disney.

The full range of commercial involvement in selling digital technology to the schools' marketplace is made clear in the enormous educational technology trade fairs that take place annually around the world, where new products are launched and contracts negotiated. From the EduTech educational technology and services fair in the Middle East, to the annual BETT and Learntec shows in Europe, the full extent of commercial involvement in schools technology can be seen at such events. Hardware manufacturers promote the latest classroom friendly laptops and desktop computers, as well as peripherals and 'add-ons' such as smart-boards and clickers. Software producers and vendors promote their wares alongside a range of associated products and services – from technology-friendly furniture to training manuals and 'how-to' books. The overall effect of such events is one of a high-octane, high-technology bazaar. As David Buckingham (2007, p.1) reflected, such fairs 'provide a startling indication of the growing importance of technology companies within the education marketplace'.

In this sense private sector involvement in schools technology is not simply a case of a few large technology companies such as Dell and Microsoft selling products directly to schools. Beneath each digital technology device or application that can be found in a classroom lies a network of other private-sector interests that meet attendant needs such as maintenance, training, technical support, the provision of peripheral products and so on. The complex nature of private sector involvement in schools technology is illustrated by the firms associated with the use of interactive whiteboards in UK schools. As Stephen Ball observes:

> Interactive whiteboards are another example of a multi-faceted policy opportunity for business from infrastructural developments which as a new pedagogical technology has received considerable encouragement from government. There is the sale of boards, technical support contracts, training (pedagogical and operational), installation, software sales (EasyTech, BoardWorks) and work for freelance trainers. The whiteboard companies (Cleverboard, Clevertouch, GTCO, SMART, Hitachi, RM Classboard, Promethean), market their goods to LEAs (the London Challenge has provided at least one whiteboard to every secondary school in London). The interactive whiteboard software bites deep into the pedagogical core of classroom work (Ball 2007a, p.49).

As the example of the interactive whiteboard suggests, much of the private sector involvement in schools technology involves the provision of services and support rather than actual products. Indeed, commercial interests are implicit in schools technology use in a number of pervasive ways above and beyond equipping classrooms with computers and cabling. Perhaps most directly, private sector management of schools' digital technology infrastructures has emerged as a prominent site for the 'public–private' partnerships that have come to characterise education provision in many developed countries. In the UK, for example, the state puts contracts out to tender for the supply of 'locally managed services' under which private sector organisations bid for the supply of infrastructure and supporting services (such as servers, routers, browsers and software packages) to groups of schools. Aside from the direct control of technological infrastructure and procurement in schools, private sector firms are also responsible for the production and provision of a range of technology-based administrative and managerial services, such as student information management systems, managed learning environments, 'dataveillance' and other management and administration tools. The provision of such services is highly lucrative. Blackboard – the company responsible for the sale of one of the most popular virtual learning environments used in schools and universities – develops and licenses software applications and related services to education institutions in more than 60 countries, reporting revenues of over US$ 340 million in 2009 having bought out their main rival competitor in 2006. Yet, as the earlier example of the home-based edutainment market suggests, firms do not solely sell digital products to schools. In terms of the direct selling of products, many schools allow private firms to broker schemes with individual students, allowing students to either purchase or lease their own personal laptop computers at subsidised rates. Similarly, most software and hardware vendors provide 'student' versions of their products to be sold to individual learners or teachers through schools as well as offering other school-based discounts at subsidised prices.

As these latter examples suggest, firms would like to project a distinct philanthropic air to some of the commercial involvement in schools' technology use, with digital technology seen as a ready focus for what Ball views as the 'import of American-style corporate philanthropy and the use of 'positional investments' by business organisations and the 'acting out' of corporate social responsibility' (Ball 2007a, p.122). This philanthropic involvement takes a variety of forms – from the 'donation' (or some would argue disposal) of 'pre-used' computer equipment from private sector organisations to local schools, to the commercially sponsored equipping of whole school systems. A notable instance of this latter activity over the 1990s and 2000s was the involvement of supermarket retailers in some countries in providing digital technology resources to local schools. Tesco – the biggest retailer in Britain and the third biggest retailer in the world with annual sales of nearly £40 billion – provided over £100 million worth of computer equipment to UK schools through its annual 'Computers for Schools' scheme where shoppers received vouchers in return for their purchases. As Joanna Blythman observed at the time, such schemes were seen to benefit both the retail company and the communities they operated in:

> Tesco's favourite community service badge of honour is reserved for its annual Computers For Schools scheme . . . the scheme is a striking example of how a supermarket chain can help the community, yet still extract several pounds of retail flesh. Tesco shoppers feel they are benefiting their local schools each time they shop there [even though] the sums behind it didn't stack up (Blythman 2004, p.246).

Similarly, in many developing countries the use of digital technologies in schools and schooling is now a well established focus for philanthropic activity and quasi-developmental aid from organisations in the US and elsewhere in the developed world. This is perhaps most apparent in initiatives such as 'One Laptop Per Child' where developing nations are encouraged to invest in US-produced laptop computers to 'create educational opportunities for the world's poorest children by providing each child with a rugged, low-cost, low-power, connected laptop with content and software designed for collaborative, joyful, self-empowered learning' (OLPC 2008, n.p.). The initial One Laptop Per Child scheme (set up by the Massachusetts Institute of Technology and originally labelled the '$100 laptop' programme) prompted other computer companies and development organisations to follow suit in producing low-specification and low-cost laptop and netbook computers for the developing world. The intentions of these private sector actors were multi-faceted, with these new products constituting what Michael Dell (of the eponymous computer manufacturers) termed 'the perfect device[s] for the next billion internet users'. As the Intel chief executive Paul Otellini put it, providing his company's 'Classmate' laptop product was 'hyper expansive to the existing market' (cited in BBC News 2008). This blend of educational and marketplace expansion illustrates ably the politics of private sector involvement in schools technology – in this case prompting an obvious comparison with what Ball (2007a, p.125) terms the 'Victorian, colonial philanthropic tradition [of] outsiders behaving as if they were missionaries'.

The significance of private sector involvement in schools technology

Of course, these privatisations of schools technology can be justified as a wholly necessary and largely beneficial feature of schooling in the digital age. In neo-liberal terms at least, the blend of public/private interests underpinning school-related use of digital technologies can be argued to work well for all parties concerned. On the one hand education policy-makers, school leaders and administrators appear to get the digitally infused school settings that they desire. Conversely, a strong relationship with the schools sector appears to make sound commercial sense for the IT firms concerned. Given that profits in the IT industry are to be found mostly in adding value to existing products and chasing the high-margin, high-profit upper ends of the market, school students and their parents represent a convenient and captive cluster of burgeoning consumers. It could even be argued that students themselves benefit from subsidised exposure to the commercially produced tools they will encounter and the skills they will require in the world of further education and employment. Market forces can be argued to have the ability to achieve all these aims far more efficiently than any alternative models of procurement – such as the centralist state-directed production of technology resources mooted at the beginning of this chapter. Yet these beneficial issues notwithstanding, there are a number of reasons to question and challenge the growing influence of private interests in shaping the schools technology agenda in these ways. Perhaps most significant is the concern that the 'realpolitik' of business means that IT producers and vendors may lack a sustained commitment to the public good of educational technology above and beyond matters of profit and market share.

The profitability of schools technology

Concerns over the role of profit-driven interventions in education have been voiced long before the mass introduction of digital technologies in schools. Michael Apple, for example, drew attention to the extent to which education had been turned into a 'business' by capitalist enterprise pursuing profits via the creation and sale of curriculum and testing materials (Apple 1979). Subsequently, it has been regularly argued by critical commentators that industry has consistently misunderstood the nature and needs of education-sector marketplaces. As David Noble (1997, p.1321) has argued:

> from the start to the present Big Business has never really known what it was doing in this area. Again and again, major firms have exploited political opportunities to break into the education market and have flailed wildly trying to make the killing they had convinced themselves was there for the taking.

Not surprisingly, the growing influence of business and industry in determining educational agendas has been treated with caution within the academic educational community, even with regards to apparently altruistic gestures by private interests towards state education. In particular, critics have questioned the interest that industrial actors profess to have in matters of 'social responsibility' and the 'public good' above and beyond their driving motivation of profit (Bennett 1995). Put simply, it has been reasoned that the world of business is focused first and foremost on generating profit for private gain, usually in competition with other companies. Thus even when the stated aims of a commercial involvement with education are ostensibly 'not-for-profit', it can be argued that many private actors simply do not understand the profoundly non-commercial nature of the markets that they are dealing with. For instance, as Larry Cuban has argued, many of the guiding philosophies behind the 'One Laptop Per Child' initiative can be considered to be 'naïve and innocent about the reality of formal schooling' in developing countries (cited in Markoff 2006). While the generated profit may or may not benefit schools, many commentators remain suspicious that the concept of public good can ever be central to industry's concerns (Tasker and Packham 1993). At best, as Daniel Menchik (2004, p.197) reasons, 'there are numerous business interests represented in the [new] arenas of education, making the line that separates benevolent, authentic concern for student learning enrichment from self-interested entrepreneurship difficult to ascertain'.

While the ambiguity of any stated 'social responsibility' motivations by firms involved in selling products and services to educational markets is to be expected, there is a sense that digital technology amplifies and intensifies these concerns. Indeed, some sceptical academic commentators have raised the suspicion that educational institutions are often used as little more than testing grounds for second-rate or embryonic technology products (what the IT industry themselves refer to as 'vapourware'), with 'tax-payer subsidy . . . thereby partially offsetting their losses and the absence of any real market demand' (Noble 2002, p.83). Yet the notion that the involvement of private interests in the schools marketplace is based primarily around the general *modus operandi* of chasing the 'possibility of super profits' (Dean 2002, p.3) is a problematic one, and there is a danger that such discussions over-simplify the profitability of educational technology. Indeed, schools technology cannot be said to represent an especially lucrative marketplace for large, multi-national corporations accustomed to dealing with multi-billion dollar profit margins rather than the millions of dollars or less associated with most educational technology contracts. As Bromley

(2001, p.43) points out, while schools do constitute a ready customer-base for IT firms 'the challenge has been mobilising that market, rousing a historically slow-to-change institution to invest energetically in a new technology'.

If anything, then, the main commercial benefits of schools technology for most major IT firms are indirect and long term – based around the establishment of 'brand awareness' and loyalty among young, future customers, as well as the symbolic benefits of being seen to be involved in what can be construed as a socially responsible activity. These guiding motives are apparent in many of the privatisations outlined above, from the production of cheap, low-specification educational products to the philanthropic use of schools technology. As the commercial responses to the 'One Laptop Per Child' initiative illustrated, many IT companies are open in their acknowledgement of these motivations. Google's recent forays into the provision of online services on behalf of education institutions were justified by the company's spokespeople in terms of the underlying goal of capturing young consumers 'for life' (Paton 2007, p.11). Similarly, as Jodi Dean observes, 'computer companies' donations of computers to schools [. . .] are clearly implicated in the production of new users, consumers, and markets' (Dean 2002, p.143).

From this perspective, a primary concern for critical scholars of educational technology is the lack of sustainability that can be associated with commercial involvement in schools technology. Unlike the state, private interests have little or no obligation to remain involved in schools technology beyond the terms of their latest contract. The precarious nature of private sector involvement in technology services can be seen in the current difficulties that commercial interests are finding in solving the 'conundrum of due moneterisation' associated with the current lack of profitability of social media (Preston 2009, p.10). The precarious commercial foundations of digital technology is perhaps best illustrated by Rupert Murdoch's News Corporation Group purchase of MySpace (and thirty less high-profile online applications) in 2005 for $580 million. Four years later News International's new media unit tasked with developing MySpace was reported as contributing only $7 million to News International's profits of $818 million in the second quarter of 2008, prompting Murdoch to comment 'I think we have to find new ways to monetise our huge audiences' (cited in Preston 2009, p.10). While many News International shareholders would judge this attitude to be pragmatic and sensible with regards to a commercial venture such as MySpace, its logic sits less easily with similar investments in technology use in state schooling.

As the changing corporate nature of Google and MySpace illustrate, commercial concerns have a distinct bearing on the nature of the technologies that are used and often taken for granted by computer users. It is therefore important to remain mindful that the shape and form of much of the computer hardware, software and online content that presently is used in schools is 'ultimately shaped by commercial needs' (Cox 2008, p.508). In this sense, the IT industry's concern with matters of profit above more educationally-focused matters could also be said to restrict the nature and form of technology-based teaching and learning, with much computer-based teaching and learning in schools following limited, business-orientated lines of word processing, slide-show presentations, spreadsheet and database use. This relates back to the notion outlined in Chapter 3 concerning the notion that technologies can be seen as open texts which are 'written' (configured) in certain ways by those social groups involved in stages of development, production and marketing. Some of the most influential groups in this sense obviously include IT industry actors such as designers, developers and programmers who ensure that preferred readings are built into commercially produced hardware and software products. Keith Grint and Steve Woolgar (1997) identify the many social processes that take place throughout the commercial development and production of a technological artefact in 'configuring the user' – i.e. the processes of making explicit and implicit assumptions about how imagined end-users would accept, reject, or modify the technology. As Nelly Oudshorn and colleagues (2004, p.37) also observe, 'configuring the user of technologies is a complex process. Design practices are usually characterised by the construction of a wide variety of, sometimes conflicting, user representations that are intentionally, or unintentionally, produced by a variety of actors, including policy-makers, designers, producers, marketeers, journalists, and test users'.

In the case of educational technologies – or at least the technologies that are used in educational settings – there is often little sense of explicitly educational perspective informing the configuration process. This is perhaps most apparent in the educational promotion of 'Office' applications that have been developed for the business sector where the configured user for such products is clearly not seen to be located in a classroom but in an office environment. This leaves software applications such as 'Word' and 'PowerPoint' understandably 'overloaded with the material-semiotic infrastructure of business' (Fuller 2003, p.160), and therefore demanding and dictating decidedly hierarchical and linear modes of technology use based around the (re)presentation and one-way distribution of information rather than any more creative or empowering use of technology for learning. As Clegg *et al.* (2003, p.49) conclude, much technology-based 'learning' that uses such software packages therefore 'merely mirror[s] simple information giving functions' valued in the business world for their efficiency and clarity. Thus it could be argued that students' exposure to digital technologies throughout their school careers rarely progresses beyond the 'PowerPointlessness' of Office applications which reduce scholarship to 'being taught how to formulate client pitches and infomercials' (Tufte 2003, n.p.) in ways that 'routinely disrupt, dominate, and trivialise [the] content' of teaching and learning (Guernsey 2001, p.1).

Similar concerns can be raised with regards to how commercial demands contribute to the compromised configuration of internet use in schools – whether in the guise of the intervention and censoring of user content by providers (often under the guise of 'acceptable use policies') or else the manipulation of increasingly commercialised relationships between the individual user, online content and other users. From this perspective any critical analyses of school-based use of digital technologies should remain aware of what Torin Monahan (2005) terms the 'built pedagogies' and configured forms of 'learner' designed into the structures and systems of online technologies. Recently, for example, critical commentators have pointed in particular to the expected and encouraged commodification of creativity that many 'social media' applications engender – pushing users to concentrate on a commoditised promotion of self and exchange of what can be considered to be personal 'micro-details' in pursuit of competitive advantage in the 'attention economy' of an internet based around the collection of 'friends' and other such measures of popularity. As Cox (2008, p.506) observes:

> Users' behaviour combines quite conscious altruistic appearing behaviour whose purpose is gaining attention with a cloying language of community and positivity. In this way, the users' consumption of [online applications] leads them to commodify their own behaviour, in ways that coincide with commercial purposes. Much of this behaviour . . . seems quite solipsistic.

The corporate capture of educational technology governance

Many of the concerns expressed above centre on private actors' understandings of – and commitments towards – what is essentially a very public concern. Beyond immediate matters of the production and sale of technological products, such issues are also manifest in the growing control and authority that private interests are able to exert over the management and implementation of schools technology. In other words, the increasing corporate capture of governance is perhaps the most significant but least acknowledged privatisation of educational technology in recent years. The growing privatisation of authority and governance over schools technology can be seen in a number of senses. Most immediately – and perhaps most obviously – is the role of private interests in 'managing' and 'maintaining' technology services within schools. This succession of control and direction represents a substantial shift in authority and status, with the role of the private actor shifting from one of provider to one of controller. While some schools are content to accede responsibility for the technically complex 'problem' of managing their technology infrastructures, such arrangements can be said to often result in compromised and unsatisfactory configurations of technology use within the school (such as the filtered and restricted internet access highlighted in Chapter 2). The increased role of private interests in the governance of schools technology also extends more substantially to the configuration and articulation of state policy-making in the area of schools and technology. Indeed, many of the policy processes outlined in Chapter 4 are decidedly 'public/private' affairs, with multinational corporations such as Cisco, Microsoft and Sun involved heavily in the schools technology agendas and plans of countries around the world – from China to Chile.

The involvement of private sector interests in the governance of schools technology is therefore extensive and multi-faceted, with IT industry interests gaining an increasing influence throughout the education sector. While concerns are raised regularly in public debate over the involvement of multinational corporations such as Google and Facebook in national technology policies and strategies, often the influence of the commercial sector in the governance of public sector technology is more parochial and subtle, especially in the case of education. This was illustrated in Stephen Ball's (2007a) examination of the example of Tony Cann – the founder and vice-chairman of a UK interactive whiteboard company with a turnover in 2009 in excess of £38 million. At various stages throughout the 1990s and 2000s as interactive whiteboards were being implemented throughout the UK schools sector, Cann assumed a number of influential positions in the UK education sector – from being chairman and board member of a number of government education organisations and advisory councils in the area of education and training (including the UK government's influential University for Industry body), sitting on college and university boards as well as being a key founder and financier of the University of York's 'Institute for Effective Education' research department.

Of course, private interests have a deep involvement in all sectors of public policy-making, with business and industry concerns long playing a powerful lobbying role in the state formulation of policy. Yet there is a sense that digital technology has provided a ready platform for private interests to adopt a set of far deeper and more extensive roles in education policy-making along 'neo-Corporative' lines – where the business class can be seen as wielding disproportionate influence over public policy through the state's structural dependence on corporate investment in technology (see Lindblom 1977). In this sense, the inherently commercial nature of digital technology development and production can be seen as allowing business and industry to assume a 'privileged position' within the education policy-making process – both in an informative and advisory capacity, and in a more influential and leading role. Indeed, schools technology proved to be a key site throughout the 1990s and 2000s for the 'public/private partnership' model of public policy-making adopted in Europe, America and Japan, with the role of the state positioned firmly as one of facilitator and the private sector as the generator of change (Downey 1999). As Henri Lefebvre observed thirty years ago, state pragmatism in the policy-making process is an established tactic of governing in contemporary society – 'the state will accept not being the exclusive or dominant actor in the social game, withdrawing in favour of other, well-informed actors' (Lefebvre 1981, p.138). In this way, an enhanced degree of private sector involvement in education technology policy-making is an understandable and strategic response on the part of the state.

Indeed, digital technology can be argued to have seen the notion of public/private partnership move beyond notions of the state entering into a 'purchaser-provider' relationship with the IT industry. Instead schools technology could be seen as a ready example of what Jane Kenway and colleagues (1994) identified as a 'markets/education/technology' triad, with digital technology allowing private interests to be involved in the initial formulations and reconfigurations of policy ideas and imperatives, and then playing a key guiding role in their eventual promotion and implementation. Thus, although sponsored initially by the state, the school technology policies outlined in Chapter 4 should be seen as also largely reliant on commercial interests and private expertise. In this sense, schools' use of digital technology is informed overtly both by educational and market values – thereby encapsulating the growing influence of market and technological forces in education over the last thirty years.

The involvement of 'significant others' in digital schooling

So far this chapter has made a strong case for recognising the increased influence of private-sector commercial interests in the resourcing and governance of schools and schooling in the digital age. Molnar (2005) identifies three types of commercialism in schools – the process of the selling *of* education, the process of selling *to* education, and the process of selling *in* educational institutions. As the examples provided so far in this chapter have illustrated, digital technologies are implicated in all three of these aspects. Yet it should be remembered that a number of actors other than IT industry interests are involved in the shaping of schools technology. This chapter now goes on to review a powerful but little discussed influence on schools technology – what has been termed by David Buckingham (2007) as the 'educational-technology complex'. This can be seen as an amalgam of 'other' stakeholders in schools' use of digital technologies that represent a range of vested interests in educational technology. As was alluded to briefly in Chapters 2, 3 and 4, these actors include journalists, educational technologists, advisory services, teacher groups and parental advocates, researchers, marketers, non IT-related commercial interests and the extensive local and central quasi-government bureaucracy which exists to oversee and steer policies and initiatives. As a field of policy and provision, therefore, the area of schools technology should be seen as involving a complicated variety of actors and interests. Digital technology therefore provides a ready example of what is recognised as an increasingly common feature of general education provision:

> the context of policy production involves an educational policy field, consisting of a site of contest between bureaucrats, policy advisors, politicians and 'spin doctors' and now stretched to varying extents beyond the nation, but the process also implies the involvement of other social fields in which to communicate the implications or message of these policies to principals/heads, teachers, parents and the broader public. This process is, of course, often contested by teacher unions, parent groups and so on. There are structural links both to the fields of education and the fields of journalism (Lingard *et al.* 2005, p.768).

While rarely discussed, it is worthwhile taking time to map out the main constituency groups in the context of schools technology, and consider their contribution to the shaping of digital technology use in schools. Ostensibly these actors and groups can be categorised as seeking either to promote the idea of educational technology, to use technology as a focus for influencing the nature of education, or else to use technology as a means of providing alternative forms of education. As will be argued, despite their apparent diversity these actors can be seen as pursuing broadly similar sets of goals based around two specific versions of digital schooling – one that seeks to transform educational practices and processes along socio-constructivist lines, and the other that seeks to maintain traditional educational forms and structures of power. As shall be discussed in further detail, these agendas are often articulated through concerns of 'benefit' or 'risk' over the intellectual, moral and technical development of 'the child'. Above all, many of these actors exercise a considerable influence over the schools technology agenda above and beyond the levels that may be expected in other areas of education. Thus, while not immediately apparent, these 'other' interests play a significant shaping role in influencing schools' use of digital technologies.

Groups seeking to promote digital technology in schools

Perhaps the most obvious group of 'others' involved in the shaping of schools technology is also the most nebulous and ill-defined – what can be termed the 'educational technology community'. This is a loose grouping of actors responsible for much of the technical expertise and enthusiasm underpinning the implementation of digital technologies in schools. Elements of the educational technology community can be found at all levels of the education system, most notably the cadre of specialist school teachers who remain responsible for the day-to-day co-ordination and governance of technology in schools (see Davidson 2003). These teachers are supported in their endeavours by school district and local authority technology advisers, as well as advisers and product 'evangelists' working on behalf of IT firms. Advice is also offered by powerful advocacy groups and lobbyists existing to further the standing of technology in education. These groups engage in the active promotion of educational technology in a number of ways. For example, the US EdTechActionNetwork takes an overt lobbying role, seeking in its own words to provide 'a forum for educators and others to engage in the political process and project a unified voice in support of a common cause – improving teaching and learning through the systemic use of technology' (EdTechActionNetwork 2009, n.p.). Similarly, the UK British Educational Suppliers Association exists as an influential trade association purporting to promote the interests of UK educational technology firms. Conversely, the British Computer Society's recent attempts to present digital technology to school students as 'really exciting' (Thompson 2007) included a range of strategies such as a schools technology training programme, webpage design competitions for school students, and even a Boy Scouts badge awarded for information technology aptitude.

Expert opinions on educational technology are also provided by educational technology specialists who work in the university teaching and research sectors – either in university departments of education and teacher training, or in specialist research 'labs' such as the MIT Medialab or the Serious Games Lab. These researchers and academics serve to legitimate and justify schools technology through the publication of specialist journals, conferences and other scholarly activities. These professional and practitioner groups have been joined of late by a number of educational technology organisations operating in a quasi-academic hinterland – described most accurately as combining elements of the work of academic researchers, policy think-tanks and commercial research and development units. The Education Services Australia (formally Education.au) organisation and the UK Futurelab outfit, for instance, fulfil roles as agent provocateurs and cheerleaders for forward-looking educational technology thinking in their countries. These groups also work alongside a number of high profile and media-savvy educational technology 'gurus', who can be best described as charismatic individuals whose work promotes the notion of digital technology use in education. While these individuals operate usually as independent consultants often working under university flags of convenience, their influence is considerable. Most notable are internationally renowned advocates for educational technology such as Nicholas Negroponte, Stephen Heppell and until recently Seymour Papert – with a number of nationally prominent figures working along similar lines around the world.

The bearing of these various representatives of the 'technological classes' on schools technology can be seen throughout the recent history of digital technology – not least in the origins of home and schools computing in the academic, scientific and 'hobbyist' communities of programmers and hackers throughout the 1960s, 1970s and 1980s. For some commentators, these interests constitute a hidden yet dominant influence on the development of technology in society – forming a kind of 'expert capture' of the field of digital technology which narrows its focus around technical rather than social concerns. Jodi Dean, for example, decries the excessive influence of the 'programmer priesthood' in the IT research and development sectors with 'access to powerful forces . . . [constituting] a select, esoteric group bound together by arcane knowledge . . . a highly trained cadre of professional men with their own particular quirks and talents' (Dean 2002, p.95–96). In the area of schools technology, the influence of such experts and advocates certainly extends far beyond their physical presence. Brown and Stratford (2007) argue that such groups of education technologists – especially when organised into professional groups and in academic institutions – fulfil a valuable role as 'public intellectuals' regarding what is understood by nonspecialist publics as educational technology.

One particularly influential group of experts and advocates can be found in the extensive official schools technology agencies and departments that have emerged in most countries. As with most areas of public policy, schools technology has seen the development of extensive bureaucracies operating at a meso-level between central government and individual schools. These actors function as 'an intermediary between the state and the community, implementing the state's policies, and providing the public with a voice in government' (Webb *et al.* 2002, p. 98). In the European Union, for example, the European Schoolnet body co-ordinates the efforts of the thirty-one national official agencies that are concerned with schools technology – from the Estonian Tiger Leap Foundation to the Portuguese Equipa de Missão Computadores, Redes e Internet na Escola. While differing in specific function and powers, all of these organisations can be described loosely as quasi-government agencies that act as fulcrums of education policy, provision and practice. Schools technology has also formed a central concern for various international organisations and intergovernmental organisations keen to encourage worldwide change along market-led lines through policy interventions and recommendations (Rutkowski 2007). Intergovernmental organisations such as the World Bank, OECD and UNESCO have all been prominent advocates of digital learning and schools technology. All these bureaucratic actors as a whole play a substantial shaping role in initiating, interpreting and modifying the educational technology arrangements of countries around the world (Lingard *et al.* 2005).

One final group involved in the promotion of technology use in schools is what in old-fashioned terms could be referred to as the fourth estate or journalist community. The growing use of digital technology in schools has been a prominent example of what Hattam *et al.* (2009) term the 'mediatisation of education policy', where governmental agendas are expressed and worked out through selected parts of the media. This use of the news media to shape public and professional expectations of schools technology, feeds into governments' 'preference for sound bites above sustained policy debate' (Hattam *et al.* 2009, p.161) and their ongoing attempts to manage and manipulate public discourse on educational change. Throughout the 1990s and 2000s the UK newspaper press, for example, had a number of regular educational technology supplements that would be published at strategic times of the school year, with many now retaining a strong online rather than print presence into the 2010s. The general news media also regularly feature recurrent stories about schools and technology – a perennial favourite story being instances of children being taught by various digital technologies to exceptional levels of expertise. Of course, this mediatisation can also lead to what Hattam *et al.* (2009) term 'backlash politics'. This was evident in the recent UK media reaction to proposed state plans to introduce an element of teaching about social media applications into the primary school curriculum. These proposals led to a generally hostile reaction from media commentators over what most saw as the trivial nature of internet applications such as Twitter (a 'micro-blogging' application) when set against the devalued importance of learning about the British Empire and World War Two – with some national newspapers rubbishing the proposals as examples of 'crackpot schemes' introduced into schools by poorly advised politicians (see Selwyn *et al.* 2010).

Groups seeking to influence education through digital technology

Most of the groups outlined above function to promote and shape the use of technology in schools as an end in itself – sharing what can be seen as a 'pro-technology' agenda. Other sets of interests also exist to lobby for the inclusion of certain types of digital technology use in schools as a means of influencing the wider nature of schooling. The groups loosely fall into Ouudshorn and Pinch's (2003) category of 'consumer organisations' – although the 'consumers' of schooling tend to be varied and not usually organised in a formal sense. This lack of definition notwithstanding, these groups seeking to influence education through digital technology can be seen as being concerned primarily with the bearing of schooling on children, on workforces and on the moral and emotional well-being of society in general. All of these interests contribute to the shaping of schools technology in a number of direct and indirect ways.

Perhaps the most prominent constituency in this respect are individual parents of school children – one of the silent 'publics' of schools technology who nevertheless exert a significant influence over the nature of their children's schools. As Sun Lim's (2006) study of Chinese urban middle-class families shows, the perceived educational allure of digital technologies such as the internet continues to be prized highly by many parents. In this sense, much of the daily prioritisation of increased digital technology use in schools stems from the personal expectations and experiences of parents around the world. Many teachers and parents make extensive use of technologies such as the internet and mobile phones in their everyday lives. Buying consumer goods, researching holidays, pursuing hobbies and interests are all now common activities for many adults. Many parents work extensively with digital technologies themselves and are therefore keen to see their children experience similar benefits at school. Moreover, most parents of school-age children were themselves the recipients of computer-based schooling as pupils throughout the 1980s and 1990s. All of these personal experiences add up to the almost unconscious connection in the minds of many parents and guardians between digital technology and the 'quality' of their child's education.

The influence of parents and families therefore acts to shape schools technology in a number of ways. Parents and grandparents will often purchase computer equipment in the hope that it will assist children with their homework and other 'worthy' informal learning activities – much as previous generations of parents would have purchased sets of encyclopaedias or employed private tutors. As outlined earlier, there is a booming market in home 'edutainment' products and online services, as parents look to boost their children's educational attainment and future employment prospects by any means possible. Many parents see school-related digital technologies as a desirable and 'pro-social' form of engagement with new media and technology. It is understandable then, that, all of these expectations from the home translate over into public expectations of what schools 'should be doing' with digital technologies. On one hand, many parents will expect to see their child's school boast the latest technology equipment as a symbol of its high quality of teaching and learning. Growing numbers of parents also expect to be able to keep in contact with their child's school via email, websites, text messaging and other forms of communication. Making extensive and efficient use of digital technology is therefore an important factor in many parents' views of what makes a 'good school'. Of course, when highlighting the role of parents in the shaping of schools technology these issues tend to refer specifically to the capture of technology use by the interests of middle-class parents and families best positioned to 'respond to the contemporary risks, anxieties and uncertainties surrounding the social reproduction of their family position' (Ball 2007b, p.157). In this sense, digital technology use in schools is of particular interest and importance to the middle-class families and parents with the cultural, economic and technological capitals that draw upon and feed into the use of digital technology for social advantage.

Many of these parental imperatives for change stem from adult rather than child concerns over what constitutes 'good' schools and schooling. Alongside the concerns of parents there is also a general sense from employers that encouraging school children to use technology will be of long-term economic benefit in a world where future workforces are increasingly expected to make use of technology in all professions and walks of life. Thus digital technology use in schools tends to be framed in deferred terms of 'employability', workforce efficiency and high-skills development. As Sarah Holloway and Gill Valentine have observed, even primary schools are seen as 'places where children as workers of the future are educated' (Holloway and Valentine 2003, p.30). While they may not appear of immediate relevance to classroom teachers, these workplace-related pressures form the most-used justifications for increasing the use of digital technology in schools. As the UK government's Chief Inspector of Schools recently reasoned:

> ICT needs to be given high status, both by the government and in individual schools, in line with its importance to young people's future economic wellbeing (Christine Gilbert, cited in BBC News 2009, n.p.).

A further set of advocacy groups can be seen to play a more restrained shaping role on schools technology, concerned largely with the wider moral and ethical aspects of digital technology use in schools. These are actors lobbying ostensibly on behalf of parents and promoting a generally conservative set of concerns over the changes to schooling that some forms of technology use are seen to bring. These concerns range from the declining levels of literacy and 'traditional' skills associated with the rise of technology use, through to a set of broadly expressed concerns over the 'risks' and dangers associated with 'inappropriate' and 'unsafe' technology use. The UK government's recent 'Safer Children in a Digital World' review involved representations from a host of such organisations, including the Children's Society, National Children's Bureau, Childnet International, Children's Charities Coalition for Internet Safety, the Family and Parenting Institute, Family Online Safety Institute, Internet Watch Foundation, Internet Education Foundation, Internet Keep Safe Coalition and Parenting UK. In the US, maintaining the wholesome nature of in-school technology use has been the focus of attention from groups as disparate as the 'Christian Department of Education' to the 'Progress and Freedom Foundation'. The publicity material for this latter organisation describes it as 'a market-oriented think tank that studies the digital revolution and its implications for public policy . . . combin[ing] an appreciation for the positive impacts of technology with a classically conservative view of the proper role of government' (Progress and Freedom Foundation 2010, n.p.). These groups, and many others like them, play significant but often submerged roles in influencing the nature of schools' uses of digital technologies along rather more restricted and 'traditional' lines than many of the other interests outlined in this chapter.

Groups seeking alternative provision of education

A final set of actors that should also be considered as having a growing influence on the shaping of schools technology are those groups seeking to use digital technology to provide additional or alternative forms of education provision. In one sense, some of these actors are using digital technologies in a complementary manner – with digital technology providing educationally-related public sector organisations an opportunity to extend their provision. For example, the educational activities of museums, libraries, arts and cultural institutions and other public-sector organisations have been extended significantly into schools of late through the provision of no-cost or low-cost online content and services. In the UK, for example, one of the most significant non-private providers of schools-focused online content has proved to be the BBC state broadcasting corporation, as well as the quasi-commercial broadcaster Channel Four. At the beginning of the 2000s the UK government announced its intentions to subsidise the BBC's production of an official 'digital curriculum' of resources to schools, building upon the corporation's public service remit and long-standing educational interests. As the director-general of the BBC argued at the time:

> there is no-one on the market who wishes to do the complete digital curriculum.
> . . . nobody wants to do some of the less popular subjects because they might

not be marketable . . . We have done this because we think it is an initiative that has real value in this society: it is one of the things the BBC should be doing. The BBC has a long history in education and in terms of the digital curriculum, we saw that as the logical next stage (Greg Dyke in Hansard 2002a, col. 28).

The proposals for the so-called 'BBC Jam' service were eventually discontinued after intensive criticism and lobbying from other IT industry actors opposed to what was seen as unacceptable levels of government control and intervention in the machinations of the free-market. Nevertheless, the BBC continues to produce a range of technology-based schools resources alongside many other broadcast, media and entertainment producers. Aside from organisations with existing educational remits, digital technologies such as the internet are supporting a variety of other reconstructions of school provision – ranging from the fast food chain McDonald's provision of subsidised online 'McMaths' tutoring programmes to secondary school pupils in Australia (Curtis 2009), to similar corporate sponsored online 'resource provision' in many other developed countries. While the commercial agendas of companies such as McDonald's are relatively straightforward, particular concern has been raised of late with regards to the use of the internet and other digital technologies by a complex alliance of forces pursing an amalgam of neoliberal, neoconservative and authoritarian populist religious goals. This is especially the case with technology-based home-schooling by neo-conservative and fundamentalist religious groups in the US to support alternative forms of schooling outside of state control (Apple 2004; Peters and McDonough 2008). Instances such as these highlight the fact that digital technologies serve to connect school systems – as well as the individuals and institutions within – to a wide range of interests and agendas that they may have previously been less directly connected with.

Conclusions

This chapter has highlighted the role of a number of influences on schools technology use that are little discussed or acknowledged. While the influence of state policy-making is clear, the role of 'other' interests from across the private, commercial and public sectors of society are often more hidden and less obvious. Yet few people could deny that schools are tied to other social institutions such as families, higher education, the economy and the wider public sector. As such it is perhaps unsurprising that digital technology in schools has emerged as a ready focus for the legitimating of a variety of external publics with differing aims and objectives. Much of this chapter has illustrated the wider point that state education is no longer the sole preserve of the state – if indeed it ever was. As Held and McGrew (2002, p.123) reason, 'the locus of effective political power can no longer be assumed to be simply national governments – effective power is shared and bartered by diverse forces and agencies at national, regional and international levels'. While this chapter has taken time to highlight the problematic aspects of this diversification of definition and governance, it would be easy to over-emphasise the extent of the 'producer capture' and the influence of all these 'other' interests on schools' use of digital technologies. While it may be tempting to decry the 'Faustian bargain' that technology engenders between public and private interests (Wilhelm 2004) this chapter is not arguing for 'dire visions of hegemonic corporate control by means of computers' (Nye 2007, p.217). Indeed, as Sarah Bragg observes, care should be taken not to demonise the IT industry as a 'monolithic bloc that has a conspiratorial purpose beneath the surface' (Bragg 2003 p.524). All the actors discussed in this chapter are just one facet of the wider shaping of schools and schooling in the digital age.

While acknowledging this need for restraint, it is clear that any discussion of schools and schooling in the digital age must take account of the wider interests that digital technologies serve to link schools with. As described in the last two chapters the development of schools technology is testament to the fact that 'our current digital landscape has been broadly shaped by the informational needs of capitalism' (Gere 2008, p.202). Indeed, educational technology has quickly become a mainstream public/private element of most education systems around the world and therefore co-opted into the high-profile 'conflict of interests between those answerable to shareholders and those answerable to stakeholders' (Potter 2005, p.142). All these issues will be considered in further detail in Chapters 8 and 9. For the time being however, it should be clear from this chapter's discussion that issues of social responsibility and governance require careful consideration if more equitable forms of technology use are to be enabled in the school setting. As the examples in this chapter all illustrate, while some commentators may wish to imagine a degree of 'corporate social responsibility . . . in the new media world' (Withers with Sheldon 2008, p.7) there are plenty of reasons to assume otherwise. In this sense, the involvement of IT firms and other interest groups in schools technology demands continued scrutiny.

6 Digital technology and the organisational concerns of schools

Introduction

Having considered a range of macro-level actors and interests it now makes sense to consider the immediate social context of technology use in schools – i.e. the school itself. As reasoned in Chapter 1, schools become such a familiar and conditioned experience for those who attend them as children that the nature and form of the school is rarely later reflected upon or challenged by adults. Yet for even the most detached observer, it is obvious that schooling is a profoundly organised and structured process. From this perspective much can be gained from understanding schools in an organisational sense – i.e. as sites where labour is divided and different activities carried out in various parts that are connected to each other. Although schools are diverse organisations, their core business can be described as taking place largely in classrooms run by teachers. Outside of the classroom these teachers are sub-divided into subject departments and year groups, central management and administrative duties are conducted by senior management teachers, all overseen by a central administration in the form of school districts and local authorities. In this manner there are many aspects of 'the school' organisation that can influence the use of digital technology.

One aspect of the school that differs from many other non-educational organisations is the sheer range of ways that its practices and processes are arranged explicitly (rather than implicitly) into hierarchical configurations according to relations of authority and power. The timetabling of school activities remains highly complex – with school days divided into lesson-times and break-times, and school years divided into terms, semesters and holidays. Some schools run dual-track or split timetables to allow greater numbers of students to be processed using the same amount of resources. Once in school, pupils and teachers are often placed within age-based, ability-based and subject-based systems of grades and year groups. Student attendance, behaviour and performance is monitored and assessed on a daily basis through systems of registers, report cards, tests and inspections. A range of recurrent sanctions and rewards exists – from detentions, suspensions and expulsions to commendations, certification and other forms of prize-giving. A multitude of internal school hierarchies and relationships exist between and within teacher and student groups – from teachers acting as heads of departments and year groups, to students acting as prefects, monitors and captains. Schools are also ordered by what could be termed the materialities of schooling – i.e. the array of objects that can be found in schools which taken together constitute the sites of schooling. Many of these objects are rendered almost invisible by their sheer ordinariness and overly familiar nature – for example, walls, fences and other boundaries, the location and physical layout of classrooms and offices, the use of school desks, the presentation and exhibition of work on walls, the imposition of uniforms and vestimentary codes. As Lawn and Grosvenor (2005) reason, even these apparently invisible materialities contribute to the ways that schools work and, it follows, the ways that digital technologies are used in schools.

As these brief examples suggest, many of the mechanisms and structures that constitute the school as an organisation are a combination of material artefacts and social relations – all sharing a common trait of being 'designed to instruct, socialise and discipline pupils' and therefore underpinning 'the structural framework of pedagogical practice' (Brehony 2002, p.178). David Tyack and William Tobin (1995, p.454) refer to all these mechanisms as constituting the basic 'grammar' of schooling – i.e. 'the regular structures and rules that organise the work of instruction. Here we have in mind, for example, standardised organisational practices in dividing time and space, classifying students and allocating them to classrooms, and splintering knowledge into 'subjects'. This notion of the 'grammar' of schooling is a powerful analogy – echoing Noam Chomsky's classifications for generative grammars where grammar can be seen as 'a system of many hundreds of rules of several different types, organised in accordance with certain fixed principles of ordering and applicability and containing a certain fixed substructure which, along with the general principles of organisation, is common to all languages' (Chomsky, 1968, pp. 87–88). In this sense, the particular notion of the grammar of schooling echoes the almost subconscious way that rules and approved 'ways-of-being' are internalised, adhered to, sometimes transgressed, and often reproduced by those who work within the school setting. In many ways, then, the grammar of schooling is well understood, but rarely commented on in explicit terms:

> Practices like graded classrooms structure schools in a manner analogous to the way grammar organises meaning in a language. Neither the grammar of schooling nor the grammar of speech needs to be consciously understood to operate smoothly. Indeed, much of the grammar of speech needs to be consciously understood to operate smoothly. Indeed, much of the grammar of schooling has become so well established that it is typically taken for granted as just the way schools are. It is the *departure* from customary practice in schooling or speaking that attracts attention (Tyack and Tobin 1995, p.454).

Most developed countries have seen the enduring arrangement and organisation of the school around the principles of standardisation, order and hierarchisation. Although it would be foolhardy to claim that schools have not changed *at all* over the last 100 years, a set of very strong reference points have certainly endured and remained intact over this time. What Tyack and Tobin identify as the grammar of schooling has continued in one form or the other since at least the late nineteenth century. While the material artefacts of the school may have changed, many of the social relations out-lined above have remained far more stable and intransient. These social arrangements are not pre-determined *per se*, but arise from what Collins (1975, cited in Barton and Walker 1985, p.193) calls 'the real behaviour of everyday life, primarily in repetitive encounters'. Therefore the enduring social structures of the school arise from the behaviour of people within the school (teachers, leaders, students, administrative and support staff) towards one another. In simple terms, then, the enduring structures of schooling derive from what people have repetitively done – and continue to do – within the school context.

From this perspective, understanding any activity that takes place within the school setting requires an understanding of issues of power and control. The organisational structure of a school is perhaps best understood in terms of the social relationships that are arranged (or at least permitted) by those with the power to do so – usually school leaders and teachers (King 1983). Schools embody tightly controlled structures and processes, often perpetuated but also restricted by those within them. Schools are subject to large-scale administrative organisation – or bureaucracy – with centralised and unambiguous patterns of authority with hierarchical levels, elaborate divisions of labour and extensive specialisation of services, as well as elaborate systems of rules and actions. As such, issues of power, authority and control are central to understanding how schools work.

Of course, many of these descriptions of the school derive from academic literature produced during the 1970s and 1980s – yet anyone with even a passing acquaintance with contemporary schooling would concur that the schools of the 2010s remain remarkably similar to the schools of the 1970s that were described by the likes of Tyack, Tobin, Lortie and others. Indeed, many people would argue that the bounded relations and structures described in the 1970s and 1980s have intensified over the past three decades. Kupchik and Monahan (2006) talk now, for instance, of the 'New American School' which functions to link students to the needs of post-industrial society and the new logic of global capital based around issues of labour intensification, just-in-time production, decentralisation, computerised automation, temporary employment, and a continued emphasis on passivity, precision and subordination. Thus making sense of the school as an organisation is a crucial element of developing a critical understanding of schools, schooling and digital technologies. While a digital technology of today (e.g. the interactive whiteboard) is physically and technologically distinct from a comparable educational technology of the past (e.g. a chalkboard), the social relations that surround the use of these technologies still merit close scrutiny and attention. This is certainly reflected in Tyack and Tobin's (1995, p.454) observation that continuity in the grammar of instruction has remained remarkably stable over the decades in ways that have 'frustrated generations of reformers who have sought to change these standardised organisational forms'.

The remainder of this chapter therefore goes on to develop the argument that digital technologies tend to be enrolled into the grammar of schooling, rather than undermining and redefining it as many educational technologists would wish to believe. Indeed, it is argued that digital technologies are now an integral means through which schools organise and achieve their main 'batch processing' functions – i.e. the monitoring and control of students, assignment of tasks to students and ensuring that students complete these tasks. Of course, it is important to acknowledge both the explicit and implicit aspects of school organisation. Steven Brint (1998), for example, distinguishes between the 'formal logic' and the 'underside' of school organisation, as well as the mostly tacit 'moral organisation' of the school. From these perspectives, then, the enrolment of digital technologies into the organisational machinations of the school can be seen through a series of different readings of school use of digital technology – i.e. technology use and the organisational culture of schools; the place of digital technology in the administrative and academic sub-cultures of schooling; and digital technologies and the disciplinary structures of schools.

Digital technologies and the organisational culture of schools

In one sense, schools can be seen as being organisations that are based around a set of stable and well-defined goals, including the preservation and transmission of information and authority, as well as the inculcation of certain values and practices at the expense of others. As such the institutional values of schools can be seen to coalesce into a general 'organisational culture' based around a respect for hierarchy, competitive individualisation, division of knowledge into segments that are susceptible to mastery, and receptivity to being ranked and judged. This is not to suggest that schools necessarily operate as rational actors in the pursuit of these goals. As Steven Hodas (1996, p.198) argues, schools are 'first and foremost, organisations, and as such seek nothing so much as their own perpetuity'. This, Hodas continues, leads to an 'innate conservatism' and 'natural resistance to change' within schools when it comes to the use and non-use of digital technologies (1996, p.198). In this sense, the use of digital technology in the school needs to be contextualised against the fact that schools are 'socially constructed mechanisms intended to produce and reproduce positions from which to understand the world, in ways that are controlled, catego-rised, proposed, unequally distributed and so on . . . [the school is] an institution – a social organism with its own needs for self-preservation, growth, reproduction and change. As the school has evolved over the past century, it has become an institu-tional site of sedimented values and practices' (Goodson *et al.* 2002, p.6).

For authors such as Hodas and Goodson, the organisational culture of schools con-tinues to be predicated around strong and self-perpetuating 'norms and procedures of entrenched bureaucratic organisations' (Hodas 1996, p.217). These norms and pro-cedures are most often based around the maintenance of status and authority that derives from control over, and access to, the form and flow of information. From this perspective, most procedures and processes within the school can be understood in terms of the exercise of power – be it coercive power to inflict punishment, the power to reward or withhold, the expert power that derives from superior skill or compe-tence, or legitimate power that uses institutionally-sanctioned position and authority. Schools therefore seek to implement and use digital technologies in ways that maintain these various forms of power and control over information and people.

For Hodas, then, the use of digital technologies in schools should be seen in terms of assisting the school organisation rather than the individual learner or teacher *per se* – in contrast to the rhetoric of improved individualised learning outlined in Chapter 1. School technology use can therefore be seen as primarily taking the form of 'the uses of machines in support of highly normative, value-laden institutional and social systems' (p.213). Digital technologies therefore tend to be used in ways that contribute to – rather than conflict with – the 'strengthening of administrative priority and control over teachers' (p.211). The appropriation of digital technologies in schools often assumes forms that 'instantiate and enforce only one model of organisation, of pedagogy, of relationships between people and machines. They are biased, and their easy acceptance into schools is indicative of the extent to which that bias is shared by those who work there' (p.212). According to this analysis at least, the most used digital technologies in schools are those that can be seen as fitting with the 'social purposes [that schools] serve, the manner in which they serve them, or the principles of socially-developed cognition from which they operate' (p.214). Evidence for this viewpoint can be found in the ways in which any number of contemporary digital technologies are used in schools, echoing Eraut's (1991, p.37) resigned conclusion that, 'the insertion of a computer rarely affects either the curriculum or normal classroom practice: its use is assimilated to existing pedagogic assumptions'.

These arguments are perhaps best illustrated by the linear progression of 'old' and 'new' learning technologies that have found a place within the school – not least the progression from the chalkboard to the interactive whiteboard, the progression of the overhead projector to the combination of PowerPoint and data projector, or the progression from the print encyclopaedia to online information resources such as Wikipedia. This notion of limited progression can also be seen in the continued temporal and spatial organisation of digital technology use within school settings. For instance, digital technologies are often only able to be used in schools at designated times, in designated places and in designated places – as evident in the continued popularity of dedicated computer rooms and virtual learning environments. Chapter 2's portrayal of the types of digital technology use that tend to figure most prominently in schools technology use hinted at the ways in which these technologies tend to be enrolled into the dominant 'data processing regimes' of the school – not least the 'scheduling, grading, communication and tracking' activities that constitute schools' administrative uses of digital technology (Hodas 1996, p.211). Indeed, educational technologists are increasingly making the distinction between the uses of such 'institutional technologies' in schools, as opposed to the classroom focused use of 'learning technologies'. As Griffith and Andre-Bechely (2008, p.40) describe, much of what digital technology is used for in schools can most accurately be described as based around activities of reporting, measuring, monitoring, assessing and accounting – 'rationalised procedures for producing knowledge of what is happening' rather than supporting teaching or learning. In all these instances, the organisational logic and interests of the school can be seen as prevailing over any other qualities that may be seen to be associated with the technology itself.

Of course, it is important not to over-ascribe the influence of a homogenous and omnipotent organisational culture on schools' use and non-use of digital technologies. In its purest form, Hodas's thesis can be seen as being a socially determinist account of schools and technology. It makes little sense to argue that the organisational culture of school determines *completely* the use of technology by students and teachers, although its influence must be seen as considerable. In this sense it is best to understand Hodas's arguments as highlighting just one aspect of the social shaping of schools technology. The organisational culture of the school is not monolithic, but part of wider, ongoing struggles that characterise the day-to-day operations of the school. It is therefore worthwhile remembering that schools are also formulated by a series of informal relationships, interactions and ongoing playing-out of 'micro-politics'. Indeed, as Ball (1987) argues, schools are intense 'arenas of struggle' that involve the interests of individual actors as well as the wider maintenance of organisational control and conflict over policy. In this sense, then, digital technologies are not co-opted automatically and unproblematically into the bureaucratic organisation of the school – instead technology should be seen as representing a new site for largely old struggles and conflict. As Ivor Goodson argues, 'educational innovation comes to represent a new arena for the contestation of educational goals and purposes, in which stakeholders attempt to redraw the borders of institutional control' (Goodson *et al.* 2002, p.6).

Digital technologies and the sub-cultures of schooling

This analysis of the organisational culture of the school having a profound shaping influence on the ways that digital technologies are enrolled, appropriated and objectified within schools is a compelling one. Yet as just discussed, school culture should not be conceptualised as a holistic concept (i.e. the notion of one prevailing 'school culture'). It is important to recognise the diversity of interests and perspectives that exist within a school – a fact acknowledged in Hodas's assertion that

> since schools are complex organisations not all their component members or constituencies have identical interests at all times; that a technology that is favourable to one faction at a given moment may be resisted by another which might favour it for different reasons under different circumstances (Hodas 1996, p.213).

It makes sense therefore to consider the influence of various 'sub-cultures' and 'micro-cultures' that can also be said to influence the processes and practices of schooling. There has been much interest in academic studies of work, employment and society in the potential existence and formation of subcultures in organisations. There is now agreement among scholars of work and employment that a variety of cultural sub-groupings will exist within any organisation in regard to different kinds of cultural knowledge and understandings (Yinger 1960; Sackman 1992). In this sense, the notion of subculture reflects the wide diversity of norms to be found within many societies, institutions or organisations, and the normative aspects of behaviour that arise as a result. In thinking about digital technologies and schooling in this way, two main sub-cultures can be seen to come to the fore – i.e. the administrative and the academic subcultures that can be found within the different groupings of managers, administrators, teachers and students. It is worthwhile taking the time to consider each of these groups in more detail.

Digital technology and the administrative subculture of schools

As it should already be clear from the last three chapters, digital technology use in schools is shaped at different times by different actors with different motives and rationales. It therefore makes sense to contextualise school technology use in terms of the mounting administrative and managerial pressures that many people at all levels of the school organisation face in relation to increasingly 'intensified' forms of education. Indeed, the increasing use of digital technology in schools over the past thirty years is entwined with a parallel transformation of the general *modus operandi* of schools. Since the 1980s, schools in many developed countries have found themselves having to respond to state concerns over global economic competitiveness, the need for expanded numbers of well-qualified 'knowledge workers' and a general desire to see the 'modernisation' and 'incentivisation' of public sector services along economic-led lines of 'New Public Management'.

These issues have had far-reaching effects on the day-to-day operation of many schools, as education systems in most countries face increasing accountability and pressure to perform efficiently and profitably. There has, for example, been a noticeable shift in countries such as the US and UK towards the evaluation of schools in terms of 'through-put' and 'out-put' criteria such as student placement in higher education or employment, number of qualifications awarded and student retention rates. Schools are now subject to 'audit cultures' of standardised content, assessment, official inspections and target-led performativity. All told, the guiding concerns of school leaders and administrators have been recast substantially along the lines of 'new managerialism' – i.e. discourses of management derived from the for-profit sector based around issues of efficiency, effectiveness, modernisation, rationalisation and the reduction of spending costs (Deem 2004). This has given rise to schools having to become more 'entrepreneurial' in their approach (Clark 1998), not least in terms of 'finding effective ways of dealing with larger student numbers and running more complex organisations' (Deem 2004, p.292).

New managerialism can be seen as first and foremost a political process – involving 'a decisive reconstitution of power relations . . . outcomes remain the focus but they are now constituted as targets and benchmarks rather than comparisons with other institutions' (Ball 2007a, p.25). From this perspective, it is notable that much of the focus for digital technology use within school systems has been in terms of technologies that support school administration processes – not least the collation and communication of information flows required to keep schools working and to enhance school performativity. Indeed, digital technologies have been welcomed as a ready solution to many of the new managerial issues faced by school administrations. In its most immediate sense, digital technologies have been readily used as a means of reducing expenditure – as Hank Bromley puts it, offering school administrations 'the ability to 'produce' more efficiently, to yield a higher level of measurable student performance with little or no increase in funding . . . enabl[ing] more learning to happen without hiring more teachers' (Bromley 2001, p.41). For example, the Californian state government's plan in 2009 for the state-wide replacement of textbooks with 'digital textbooks' (or 'Flexbooks' as they are commercially marketed) was based not only on a benevolent concern to 'ensure every California student has access to a world-class education' (Schwarzenegger 2009), but also on reducing the annual bill for $350 million on textbooks from the state's $24 billion budget deficit. As the Californian Office of the Governor (2009, n.p.) stated at the time:

> This initiative has the potential to save California's schools millions of dollars. The average textbook costs about $75 to $100 per student. For a school district with about 10,000 high school students, the use of free digital textbooks in just science and math classes could save up to $2 million dollars [. . .] With a deep recession and a deep deficit, Governor Schwarzenegger is doing everything possible to help schools do more with less.

This administrative logic of digital technology use is not based solely on matters of reducing expenditure. In the increasingly competitive market-driven climate of school choice and diversity, digital technologies became a vital element during the 1990s of the market 'branding' of education institutions, bestowing a high-tech veneer onto schools' practices. As Noble (2002, p.29) observed, digital technologies therefore lent educational institutions 'a fashionable forward-looking image [while] reducing their direct labour and plant maintenance costs'. Digital technologies are now also an integral element of the entrepreneurial pursuits of some schools (especially those operating in the for-profit sector), not least in reaching hitherto physically inaccessible but potentially lucrative markets of overseas students. In a similarly entrepreneurial vein, the digitalisation of teaching leaves schools with a legacy of electronic resources which are replicable, scalable and saleable – with any semblance of intellectual property rights transferred from the teacher to their employers.

For some critically-minded commentators, these shifts towards a technology-enhanced effectiveness and rationality mark a further stage in the movement of education away from its traditional ideological functions of promoting reason, culture and enlightenment (see Readings 1996). One could argue, for example, that the new managerial application of digital technology has little concern with enhancing the quality of school education. A model of technology use based on student throughput and market reach could be seen as part of the wider 'dumbing down' and a lowering of standards in contemporary education with 'only secondary consideration given to the pedagogical and professional concerns that guided early experimentation and innovation' (Hamilton and Feenberg 2005, p.304). The argument has also been made by some critics that the appropriation of technology along new managerial lines leads to depersonalised and dehumanised forms of teaching and learning, and an overall 'factory model' of school education that runs the risk of atrophying learning opportunities while dehumanising instructors and students (Cooley 1999). As Kupchik and Monahan (2006, p.626) reason, such uses of technology serve primarily to 'reinforce accountability regimes and 'audit cultures' that privilege the production of documents (whether video recordings, spreadsheets or test scores) over all other activities or outcomes. This results in a state of 'fragmented centralisation'.

Digital technology and the academic subcultures of schools

Aside from these shared administrative concerns and understandings, it should be remembered that schools are also places of teaching, learning and scholarship. In particular another significant manifestation of schools as cultures is what has been referred to in the educational literature as 'departmental' and 'subject' subcultures. The notion of subject specialisation is such a well-established feature of schooling (especially at secondary level) that it is often taken for granted when making sense of schools and schooling. Many of the studies that have been carried out in this area indicate that subject subculture has a strong defining presence on school organisation and practice. As Louis and Firestone (1997) reason, subjects and departments provide a clear disciplinary base for teachers who as individuals identify themselves, and are identified as, subject specialists. Academic subject areas, as focal points for interaction between groups of specialists, therefore develop their own perspectives on a school's objectives and inevitably shape their own actions accordingly.

These academic subcultures can therefore have an important influence on school processes in a way that is common across schools, school districts and countries. The most obvious example would be the influence that subject cultures have on how teachers approach their work. As Stodolsky (1993, p.343) states, 'teachers of one school subject will differ from those in another in terms of assumptions about teaching and learning, institutional practices, and student placement'. This relates to what Ball and Lacey (1984) earlier termed as subject paradigms, i.e. the views of an academic subject by its participants as understood by their ideas about appropriate content. Besides these understandings of the content of learning, subject areas are also highly distinct in terms of their views of subject pedagogy – i.e. the views of teachers regarding appropriate methods for the transmission of subject knowledge and procedures for the organisation of learning (Ball and Lacey 1984).

All of these subject-related issues should be considered pertinent when considering the implementation of digital technologies in schools. Perhaps the most succinct analysis of these issues was provided by the empirical work of Goodson and Mangan (1996) regarding the effects of subject culture on classroom use of computers. These authors discuss how computer use was understood by teachers working in some subject areas as demanding a much more individualised teaching environment than they felt that their subjects would usually permit, causing an inevitable 'culture clash' between the computer and the subject area. Only certain areas of the curriculum, such as technological studies, art and design, were found to have cultures compatible with the pedagogical and organisational changes that computer use dictates. Thus, Goodson and Mangan concluded that the computer was constantly fighting a battle against pre-existing subject subcultures, occasionally succeeding but generally failing to be adopted in a meaningful manner. While referring to pre-internet forms of computer use, Goodson and Mangan's line of enquiry has been replicated throughout the 1990s and 2000s with a succession of studies highlighting the continued influence of subject-specific understanding and traditions in areas of schooling such as music studies (Gall and Breeze 2007), history (Haydn 2002) and the steady rise of what Torin Monahan (2005, p.17) identifies as the new 'occupational group of information technology specialists'. As John and La Velle (2004) observe, the traditions that give rise to these subcultures are complex and tend to be rooted in organisational practices, individual biographies, and collective experience. As such the notion of what a subject discipline is, and how it fits or clashes with digital technology is a historical construct reinforced by generations of school practice.

These arguments all suggest that digital technology use can be seen as itself constituting a distinct culture that is more congruous with some subject areas than others. Carrie Paechter's (1995) study of design and technology subjects in the 1990s highlighted how some staff (and, it would seem, students) 'retreated' into their subject subcultures when faced with another subculture to adapt to. In some subjects, therefore, digital technologies can be seen as battling with existing, deep-rooted norms and values while in other subjects they are more easily assimilated. However, it would be a mistake to see 'low' technology-using subjects as necessarily backward or deficient in any way for not adapting readily to technology use. In a historical sense, for example, digital technologies are clearly more congruous with some subjects' histories and practice than others. The historical linkages of the development of computerised technologies with fields such as mathematics, science and business studies, for example, are obvious. However, the technological traditions of use in subject areas such as religious studies or poetry are less clear. This point echoes Lave and Wenger's (1991, p.101) more general point that any practice-based group's participation involving technology 'is especially significant because the artefacts used within a cultural practice carry a substantial portion of that practice's heritage . . . Thus understanding the technology of practice is more than learning to use tools; it is a way to connect with the history of the practice and to participate more directly in its cultural life'.

Digital technologies and the disciplinary structures of schools

The above issues notwithstanding, the organisational concerns of the school stretch far beyond issues of administrative efficiency and bounding of academic knowledge and practice. A further element of schools' shaping of digital technology use that merits consideration is what can be termed the regulatory functions of the school – in particular the ways in which schools are based around institutional relations of power and domination, or as Ivor Goodson and colleagues put it, 'the extant directions and priorities of the school as a regulatory technology' (Goodson *et al.* 2002, p.146). One of the most persuasive and useful accounts of these issues can be found in the work of Michel Foucault who examined nineteenth-century schools, along with prisons, asylums and hospitals, as microcosms of the principles of power, domination and normalisation that permeate society as a whole. From this perspective the school can be seen as an institution of surveillance and control in which the bodies of students are disciplined through regimentation in time and space. In particular, Foucault detailed how the management and control exercised over students in school is achieved through processes of 'normalisation' that create a form of homogeneity through the comparison, categorisation, homogenisation and differentiation of students.

For the large part, Foucault's analysis of Victorian schooling still holds true for the schools and schooling of the early twenty-first century. As social institutions, schools can be seen to continue to be based around a range of disciplinary relations leading to the normalisation of students and teachers. In terms of the normalisation of knowledge, for example, the content and form of the school curriculum as embodied knowledge continues to be controlled tightly, even amidst efforts to afford an element of curriculum 'entitlement' and 'choice'. As Harris (1994, p.65) summarised:

> Learning is restrictive in the sense that students' development is not liberating but rather constructed in a highly ordered and differentiated way – rather than being in control of the process students are 'subjects' on the receiving end.

Foucault's description of schools' normalisation of students and teachers as subjects could also be considered to have a continued relevance in the twenty-first century, continuing to manifest itself throughout present-day practices. Schools continue, for example, to be sites where disciplinary power is employed through 'dividing practices' such as testing, examining, streaming and the use of desirable identities such as being a 'good worker' or an 'able student'. As described at the beginning of the chapter, much of the school day continues to involve the keeping of registers, filing of reports, compulsory wearing of standardised uniforms, observance of rules, use of timetables, examinations and punishments. Students' behaviour therefore continues to be defined and normalised through micro-technologies of physical and ideological control which leave them, in Foucauldian terms, as 'docile bodies' who are able to contribute to the productive patterns of schools and, it follows, capitalist society. In theory, most individual actions within schools are therefore party to regimes of self-surveillance and self-policing. The regimes of control that are in operation within a contemporary school are many, all leaving the student as 'the obedient subject, the individual subjected to habits, rules, orders; an authority that is exercised continually around him and upon him and which he must allow to function automatically in him' (Foucault 1979, p.227).

This conceptualisation of the school as a site of normalisation and domination provides a powerful framework for understanding schools' assimilation of, and relationship with, digital technology. In particular, there has been much sociological interest in the use of digital technologies in the enrolment of individuals into bureaucratic networks of surveillance. It has often been argued that the digital age is perhaps more accurately seen as a 'surveillance age' with innumerable electronic networks accumulating and aggregating information on individuals' everyday activities and transactions (see Lyon 2006). Much has been written of the digital extension of Foucault's notion of the Panopticon as disciplinary technology, with electronic networks seen to act as ready means of surveillance, observation and regulation (e.g. Poster 1995).

From this perspective, many of the ways in which digital technologies are used in schools can be seen to fit neatly with the Foucauldian notion of the school as a rigid technology of control. In other words the school acts, more often than not, to assimilate digital technologies as simply another form of disciplinary regime. This can be seen, for example, in the highly visible gate-keeping that has grown up around digital technology use in schools, with schools carefully regulating and controlling technology access and use. The ways in which digital technologies such as computers and the internet are organised and regulated in schools has altered little since the early days of the single 'school computer' being wheeled between classrooms on a trolley. It remains the case that schools' use of technology is centred around and controlled by small cliques of staff (from the lone IT co-ordinator in some smaller schools to the teams of specialist technicians and teachers in larger schools), privileged physical locations (such as computer 'labs' or 'learning resource centres) and overt and covert regulations of use – all of which act as powerful 'technological gatekeepers' in deciding when and where technologies are used (see Pettigrew 1973). Thus unlike other organisations, schools have not seen digital technologies prompt a significant decentralisation of power and control. The idealised notion of digital technologies leading to the 're-negotiation of professional knowledge, discourses and practices within organisations' (Bloomfield and Coombs 1992, p.461) has certainly not occurred to date within the vast majority of schools around the world.

Instead it could be contended that most schools are now stocked with technologies that reinforce and augment the 'panoptic gaze' described by Foucault. For instance, the use of the internet within schools can be seen as contributing to the internal surveillance of students, alongside the external surveillance of education institutions through the management of performance information. As Torin Monahan (2005) describes, much of how digital technologies are organised and used in schools – from the layout of computer labs to the network monitoring applications that run 'underneath' students' technology use – coalesces into what he terms a 'built pedagogy of surveillance and panopticonism' which reinforces an ethic of discipline and undistracted labour. Indeed, in-school use of the internet is party to a complex array of physical and virtual surveillance techniques and devices. These can include staff supervision, identification cards, the arrangement of classrooms with outward-facing computer screens, peer-surveillance and the monitoring of printer output. A range of specific 'dataveillance' techniques also abound, such as the monitoring of students' internet search histories, visited web pages and downloaded documents, as well as the use of bespoke software that allows teachers to view students' computer screens both in 'real-time' and on a retrospective basis (Hope 2005).

All of these examples highlight the increasing 'climate of distrust' that can be said to be pervading contemporary schooling – often legitimised by discourses of 'risk' and 'safety' (Kupchik and Monahan 2006, p.622). As Monahan concludes, such arrangements lead to forms of digital technology use that are based, at best, around a sense of structured discipline with students positioned as disciplined and passive users of technology who are conditioned into following a self-regulated use of digital technology:

> this socio-technical space teaches students that they, too, can gain technological (and by extension economic) power provided that they work diligently alone and refrain from the temptations of social distraction (Monahan 2005, p.59).

The reach of panoptic gaze in schools is perhaps best illustrated by one of the most prevalent but most hidden digital technologies in schools – closed-circuit television

(CCTV). Andrew Hope (2009), for instance, has detailed the increasing use of CCTV and other forms of digital security technologies that allow school locations and the people within them to be subjected to remote surveillance under the pretext of guarding against 'risks' as diverse as preventing intruders through to monitoring students' transgressive behaviours such as bullying, vandalism or smoking. The use of CCTV in schools is now commonplace. While the UK news media feigned surprise at one London school's reported use of over 100 cameras (including two cameras in each classroom and forty cameras in its playgrounds, canteens and corridors), such levels of surveillance technology have long been commonplace in North American schools (Shepherd 2009; Monahan and Torres 2010).

Now in the UK, the technology-based 'surveillance school' is also an increasingly commonplace occurrence – with the presence of CCTV in UK schools reckoned to be comparable to the levels of surveillance that can be found in prisons and airports (Taylor 2010). As Andrew Hope (2009, p.1) argues, rather than being a neutral and benign technology, CCTV plays 'an increasingly important role in social control and serve[s] to illuminate the underlying values inherent in changing disciplinary practices'. As such, CCTV provides a pertinent example of schools' use of digital technologies as part of wider 'practices of access control, conduct control and evidence gathering . . . stressing issues of visibility, self-policing, disciplinary discourse and resistance' (Hope 2009, p.2; see also McCahill and Finn 2010). While perhaps a rather extreme example, CCTV serves as an appropriate reminder of how schools operate around such 'cultures of control'. It can be argued that this disciplinary use of digital technology therefore represents 'an underlying shift in values, away from social integration to system integration, wherein disorder is perceived as mundanely inevitable and the priority becomes situational control of deviancy' (Hope 2009, p.2).

Conclusions

This chapter has considered a number of arguments concerning the shaping role of the organisational concerns of the school on the ways in which digital technologies are used – and not used – within school settings. A number of different instances in which the institutionalised adoption of digital technologies takes place have been highlighted, often in ways that do not necessarily chime with the 'promises' and 'hopes' outlined in Chapter 1. For example, while Steven Hodas' (1996, p.213) description of schools as 'grim, self-perpetuating systems of repressive mediocrity' may appear to some readers as alarmist or exaggerated, it serves to highlight many of the organisational issues that are little discussed in terms of the apparent 'failure' of digital technologies to be used to their 'full potential' in the classroom. Hodas' analysis is especially useful in highlighting the contested and often unaware nature of technology use in schools. Indeed, the ways in which technologies are used – and not used – to 'maintain organisational status quo' (1996, p.213) are easily overlooked amidst the everyday to-and-fro of the school setting.

On the whole, most of the arguments highlighted in this chapter suggest that digital technologies are assimilated into pre-existing (and often 'pre-digital') systems and structures of schools in ways that reflect and reinforce the wider grammar(s) and logic(s) of schools as organisations and the groups of people that work within them. Many of these arguments highlight the use of digital technology as a 'technical fix' to the perceived shortcomings or failures of the industrial-era school. The rising use of CCTV within schools perhaps provides the clearest example of this reasoning. As Kupchik and Monahan (2006, p.625) reason, the increased use of such surveillance technologies in schools 'illustrates the adoption of market logics that harmonise public education with the needs of a post-industrial marketplace characterised by the rise of high-tech industry and the adoption of technological solutions to complex social problems'.

In this sense, focusing on the (sub)cultural concerns of the school as an organisation points towards the ways in which digital technology use tends to mark a set of continuities – rather than radical discontinuities – with pre-digital forms of schooling. This, it could be contended, reflects the overtly political nature of schooling in (late)capitalist societies, where the logic of capitalism continues to be based around notions of homogeneity (e.g. in terms of space, times and the standardisation of daily life), fragmentation (e.g. in terms of the division of labour, social separation), and the hierarchisation of functions and objects. This, of course, stands in stark contrast to the heterogeneous, 'anything goes' celebrations of contemporary digital technology that sometimes pervade education discussion and debate.

This chapter has furthered this book's account of the importance of the politics of schooling in making sense of technology use and non-use. In particular the chapter has developed a sense of the struggles and conflicts that surround the competition for and contestations of minimal resources in school – be it in terms of time, space, grades, status, authority or knowledge. In this sense, the chapter reinforces the wider observation that 'every dimension of schooling and every form of educational practice are politically contested spaces' (Monchinski 2007, p.3). Thus it should be recognised that digital technologies are both shaped by – and themselves shape – the power relationships that constitute all aspects of schools and schooling. This is apparent at all levels of the school organisation – from the executive activities of school leaders to the daily routines of the school kitchen (see Mörtberg *et al.* 2010).

In particular, this chapter has seen how digital technologies are party to power that is authoritative (i.e. schools getting teachers and students to do what they do not want to do) and power that is influential (i.e. schools influencing, shaping or determining teachers' and students' wants). In both these respects, it would seem that the (non)use of technology within schools cannot be understood fully without some reference to the wider structures and ordering of power within the school setting. Yet, as is the case with each of the last three chapters of this book, it is important to note that the issues outlined here do not constitute an all-encompassing analysis of schools and schooling in the digital age. Any description of the organisational structuration of schools and schooling should, of course, be balanced by a corresponding consideration of individual agency. Care must be taken to avoid an overly determinist reading of the correspondence between the social relations of schools and the individual actions of students and teachers. In terms of the self-disciplining nature of students' technology use, for example, it would be remiss to assume that all students learn to discipline themselves, and that transgressive behaviours do not take place.

The next chapter therefore extends these themes by considering digital technology use from the perspective of the individual teacher and individual student. It is important to recognise that the relations of power and control outlined in preceding discussions are not fixed and unchangeable, but constantly changing and being challenged from inside and outside of the school. As Tyack and Tobin (1995, p.476) reason, 'the organisational patterns that shape instruction are not a-historical creations etched in stone. They are the historical product of particular groups with particular interests and values at particular times – hence *political* in origin.' Thus having reviewed the politics of digital technology use from an organisational perspective, the next chapter now goes on to consider the contested nature of technology use from the lived experience of the individual teacher and individual student. It is to this micro-political context that Chapter 7 now turns.

7 Digital technology and the lived experiences of teachers and students

Introduction

As many of the examples considered in Chapter 6 have illustrated, a prominent theme emerging from this book is the importance of the politics of schools technology. In particular, the past three chapters have framed the use of digital technology in schools in terms of a set of negotiations and struggles between various actors – from the organisational concerns of schools to the interests associated with state policy-making, the IT industry and other professional and technical communities. In this spirit, the present chapter now goes on to consider how these negotiations and struggles continue (and, if anything, are intensified) at the 'micro-level' of the classroom. The chapter focuses on the contested nature of digital technology use for the individual teacher and individual student – paying further attention to the issues and tensions that arise when digital technologies enter the classroom setting. As Ivor Goodson describes:

> there is an ongoing tension between what is planned, designed, created and strategised: and the play of unintended consequences, heterogeneous networks, ill-fitting financial and technological strategies and disorganised response . . . Even the most of tightly planned interventions, is always fluid, contested, disrupted, subverted and appropriated – in short diverted – to a greater or lesser extent (Goodson *et al.* 2002, p.7).

As Goodson's description of diversion, disruption and subversion suggests, any discussion of technology use in the classroom must acknowledge that digital technology is not something that is simply 'done to' teachers and students. In light of all of the shaping influences considered over the last three chapters of this book it may be tempting to assume that technology use in the classroom follows a decidedly predetermined nature – constrained by the prescribed logic of the 'grammar' of schooling and the 'neo-liberal orders' that are associated with macro- and meso-level influences. In the terms set out in Chapter 6's discussion of the organisational cultures of the school, for example, there may appear to be little space for a teacher or learner to act upon the grammar of schooling in ways that contradict the *a priori* determinism of pedagogical practices. Yet the individuals who work in school settings should be seen as social subjects rather than passive atomised functionaries. In this sense it would be foolhardy to presume a direct correspondence between the interests of school authorities, policy-makers and IT firms and the micro-level behaviours of teachers and students. As well as concentrating on the structural determinants of behaviour, this book's analysis should also pay attention to the active choices of actors. This involves developing an understanding of the capacities of individuals to appropriate and use digital technologies in surprising, subversive or unintended ways – not least to pursue actions that resist as well as conform to the impositions of constricting circumstances (see Webster 2005).

The remainder of this chapter therefore takes time to consider the role of digital technologies in teachers' and students' experiences of schooling – not least how digital technologies 'fit' with the explicit and tacit demands of their 'jobs'. In particular, the chapter seeks to highlight the critical and reflective thinking on the part of teachers and students when engaging with digital technologies in the school setting. This is not to say that teachers and students simply 'do technology' as completely free and rational agents. Rather, any sense of individual agency and action must be set against the social, cultural and technological constraints of educational institutions. From this perspective, the chapter seeks to gain an understanding of the place of digital technology within what Kevin Brehony qualifies as 'the (relative?) autonomy of classroom life', where teachers and learners negotiate the technological situations they encounter, and where local interactions are informed by broader social conditions (Brehony 2002, p.181). In this sense digital technology use can be seen as a site for interactions between and within groups of teachers and learners that are centred on issues of negotiation, meaning-making and identity formation. These issues are hopefully given some substance and clarity by first considering the role of the teacher in making sense of digital technology.

The lived experience of digital technology use for the teacher

Teaching is first and foremost an occupation, with all of the struggles, tensions and negotiations that labour and work entail. From this perspective, the (non)use of digital technologies in schools must be understood (at least in part) in terms of teachers' ongoing negotiations of their day-to-day work – a process that involves meaning-making and fitting various technologies with the 'job' of being a teacher and, conversely, fitting the 'job' of being a teacher with the demands of digital technology. As was implied in Chapter 2, these negotiations are not necessarily straightforward and can perhaps be understood best in terms of an ongoing series of struggles involving competition for scarce resources. As was seen in Chapter 6, these struggles are often constrained by the expected roles of the teacher within the organisational culture of the school. These include the expected role of the teacher as an authoritative information source and disciplinary agent, as well as their implicit role in enforcing regimes of surveillance and accountability, hierarchies of knowledge and expertise, regimes of assessment and ranking, and routines of physical and temporal confinement. All told, there is a mass of factors underlying how digital technology interacts with 'the teacher'.

Technology and teachers' strategic concerns

In all these ways, then, a teacher's use of digital technology can be seen as a strategic concern – influenced by what was termed in Chapter 6 as the 'grammar of schooling', but ultimately something that is also acted out in terms of serving the interests of the individual teacher, of their students or of their school. A teacher's use of digital technology should not be seen as a logical, rational action *per se*, but rather as a combination of tactical and habitual decisions that allow teachers, in Tyack and Tobin's words, to 'discharge their duties in a predictable fashion and to cope with the everyday tasks that school boards, principals and parents expected them to perform: controlling student behaviour, instructing heterogeneous populations, or sorting people for future roles in school and later life' (Tyack and Tobin 1995, p.476). In contrast to the discourses of deficiency and conservativeness outlined in Chapter 2, teachers could be argued to often be pragmatic, strategic users of digital technologies while in school – only utilising technologies in ways that 'fit' with the wider 'job' of being a teacher and appearing to 'resist' technology use only when it is of little direct benefit to their job. In these terms, the (non)use of digital technologies should be seen in light of teachers' primary concerns of maintaining discipline and order in their classes; of ensuring that students achieve 'good' grades in external and internal assessments of learning; that classroom activities follow set curricula and meet the varied expectations of school managers, parents and other stakeholders. Teachers' uses and non-uses of digital technology could therefore be seen in terms of being a strategic choice which is contingent on the wider 'life world' of being a teacher. As Stephen Ball reasons, teachers' choices of action in a school or classroom context can often be understood in basic terms of survival:

> School life is dominated by what is most pressing and most immediate; priorities are constructed on the basis of practical necessity, of 'survival'. In effect, routine organisational life is set within the 'negotiated order', a patterned construct of contrasted, understandings, agreements and 'rules' which provides the basis of concerted action (Ball 1987, p.20).

A theme running throughout much of the academic literature is the tendency of digital technologies to be used where there is a perceived congruence and 'good fit' with the concerns of the teacher and the job of teaching. Lankshear and Bigum (1999), for example, identify principles of 'complementarity' and 'workability' in guiding teachers' uses of technologies in the classroom. Conversely, it is argued that digital technologies tend to be used less where there is a perceived lack of 'good fit' with the immediate concerns of the teacher. The ways in which internet applications tend to be used in schools, for example, mirror potential teacher concerns over the need to maintain authority relationships between themselves and students, and avoid where possible the 'de-centring of the teacher as a voice of authority in the education of children' (Muffoletto 2001, p.3). This is not to underplay the role of digital technology products and practices in influencing and shaping the nature of teaching. Many accounts exist, for example, of how technology use may contribute to a tendency for teachers to

alter their approaches to teaching and 'to become more constructivist in their pedagogical orientation over time' (Windschitl and Sahl 2002, p.166). Conversely, technologies such as the interactive whiteboard and slideshow software such as *PowerPoint*
are seen to contribute to a growing sense of teaching being largely presentational in
nature. Gabriel Reedy's ethnographic study of teachers' uses of digital technologies
in UK secondary education observed the development of a 'PowerPoint mindset'
among teaching staff, with presentational technologies shaping subtly how teachers
approached classwork. As Reedy concluded:

> The PowerPoint mindset may be problematic to teaching and learning. The
> visual tools of the IWB, the LCD data projector, and PowerPoint combine to
> encourage a particular sort of presentational mindset that could be beginning
> to shape the classroom experience. Teachers and students alike may begin to
> think and work within the constraints of PowerPoint slides, whether or not it is
> appropriate to do so. In many cases, PowerPoint has become the tool of choice
> for teaching and learning – at [the school], many teachers think of PowerPoint as
> synonymous with ICT – even though both students and teachers recognise that
> it can potentially discourage complex thinking, reasoning, and writing, and can
> encourage pointless animation and ostentation (Reedy 2008, p.161).

Technology and teachers' performativity and resistance

While these latter points highlight the mutual shaping relationships between technology and the social, it would seem that there are many implicit issues, understandings and demands that exert a significant influence on the ways in which digital
technologies are used by teachers in schools – above and beyond the explicit 'official' roles, requirements and demands of teaching. In particular four interlinked 'hidden' aspects of teaching merit attention – issues of time, discipline, authority and
what can be termed 'performativity'. The issue of time is highlighted as a guiding
concern in studies of teachers at work. As Dan Lortie's (2002, p.xii) exhaustive study
of teaching as a labour process was led to conclude, 'time is the most scare resource
in schools'. Teacher time in schools is laden with concerns of being 'productive'
and 'effective' in terms of achieving learning and student outcomes. The politics of
a teacher's working time is therefore a central issue in understanding the ways that
schools work, and the ways that people work within schools. As is the case in other
occupations and places of work, digital technology use is often seen as offering an
intensification of teachers' work, 'chang[ing] the nature and meaning of tasks and
work activities, as well as creating new material and cultural practices' (Wajcman
2008, p.66). Digital technologies are implicit in many of the intensifications of work
that are felt to characterise contemporary teaching – not least the micro-co-ordi-
nation of the disparate demands of teachers' work schedules, and the experience
of time scarcity associated with the rigid temporal organisation of the school day.
At best, technologies are often used to merely cope with the increasing temporal
pressures of teaching – 'getting done is substituted for work well done' (Apple and
Jungck 1990, p.235).

Similarly, teachers' concerns with issues of authority and discipline can be seen to contribute to modes of technology use that mirror what McNeil (1986) calls 'defensive teaching' – i.e. processes and practices of teaching that are characterised by an over-riding concern with maintaining control. Mark Garrison and Hank Bromley's (2004, p.596) ethnographic study of digital technology use in US urban high schools identi-fied two varieties of technology-associated defensive teaching: 'First, teachers would insist, especially in the computer lab, that students wait for step-by-step instructions even when it was clear that they were capable of proceeding without constant over-sight. Second, teachers would incorporate the computer into a reward/punishment dynamic, using it for discipline and motivation as well as instruction' (Garrison and Bromley 2004, p.596). Indeed, this discipline-related use of digital technology is most often seen in the use of the 'computer-as-reward' especially with younger students – where teachers allow technology use as remuneration for finishing non-technology based work or for good behaviour.

These issues of time, intensification of work, discipline and defensiveness can all be seen to relate to the wider issue of 'performativity' – a mode of regulation where 'the performances of individual subjects or organisations serve as measures of pro-ductivity or output, or displays of 'quality', or 'moments' of promotion or inspection' (Ball 2007a, p.27). As with many contemporary professions, teachers are party to increasing numbers of targets, indicators and evaluations during the course of their work. One of the key elements of performativity in contemporary teaching is the assessment and regulation of an individual's productivity or output – often opera-tionalised in educational terms of 'quality'. As was discussed in Chapter 6, schools are characterised by a pervasive culture of assessment and accountability. This is perhaps most clearly manifest in what Hodas (1996) refers to as 'the crucial technologies of assessment' – i.e. the performance of students on high-stakes testing and examina-tions. While it would be misjudged to label all digital technology use in schools as being assessment driven, concerns over accountability, assessment and what Ball (2007a) terms 'the terrors of performativity' certainly have a significant bearing on the ways in which digital technologies are used in schools. As Garrison and Bromley (2004, p.607) observe:

> At all levels, whether it's teachers requiring evidence of student productivity, schools requiring evidence of teacher effectiveness, or state requirements for higher test scores, efforts to cope with demands for accountability end up inter-fering with the actual accomplishment of what is putatively being demanded.

Of course while some teaching staff will strive to fulfil these demands other teachers are left with feelings of inner conflict and resistance. Indeed, the notion of teacher resistance is also a key element to understanding the 'fit' of digital technology to the personal or professional concerns of teachers. From these micro-level perspectives, the apparently unsatisfactory use of digital technologies by teachers could be seen less as a case of individual deficiency and more as a case of informed choice and even 'tactic of resistance' within the constrained context of the school and classroom (see de Certeau 1984). Crucially, then, teachers' (non)use of digital technologies can also be understood in dual terms of both resistance *to*, but also resistance *through* technology-based teaching.

The notion of teacher resistance *through* technology-based teaching is little commented on, but can be observed widely throughout school systems. A number of recent ethnographic studies of classroom teaching have shown how using digital technologies with students provides some teachers with an opportunity to gain respite from the pressures and traumas of contemporary teaching. Part of Garrison and Bromley's earlier description of the defensive teaching strategies associated with digital technology use involved teachers implicitly 'striking a bargain' with their students that little meaningful technology-based work would be expected in return for a minimal amount of disruption and ill-discipline. The opportunities offered by digital technologies to allow teachers to leave students to 'fend for themselves' and for teachers themselves to 'appear busy, regardless of the subject matter' was also noted in Monahan's (2005, p.278) ethnographic study of technology use in inner-city Los Angeles high schools. As this study concluded, 'in a profession where content and responsibilities are increasingly pre-scripted, the establishment of a computer lab granted [teachers] freedom to manoeuvre in self-selected ways but resulted in the neglect of students' (Monahan 2005, p.278).

More commonly acknowledged is teachers' resistance *to* digital technology use. In particular, much has been written about the role of technology in contributing to the deprofessionalisation and even alienation of teachers as a profession – with technologies such as the computer contributing to the notion of a fragmented and atomised pedagogic 'assembly line' (Sarason 1990, p.123). Here one of the more influential readings of digital technology and the deprofessionalisation and deskilling of the teacher has been provided by Michael Apple. For Apple, teaching is a complicated labour process with digital technologies more often than not contributing to the degradation of teachers' labour. In particular, Apple and Jungck point towards the role of the computer in rationalising and standardising the job of being a teacher and contributing to 'separation of conception from execution' of teaching:

> When complicated jobs are broken down into atomistic elements, the person doing the job loses sight of the whole process and loses control over her or his own labour because someone outside the immediate situation now has greater control over both the planning and what is actually to go on (Apple and Jungck 1990, p.230).

Although over twenty years old, much of this analysis holds true in the present context of virtual learning environments, e-portfolios and shared digital learning resources. In particular, Apple and Jungck pointed to the growing use of digital technologies by school administrators and other authorities in the (over)planning and controlling of the nature and form of teaching – whether in terms of teaching content, the time, place and pace of delivery or the management of assessment. Perhaps the most obvious contemporary manifestation of this bounded use of technology is the 'virtual learning environment' – where learning takes the form of pre-packaged curriculum content and teachers are positioned as providers and supporters of students' navigation through set activities. The virtual learning environment – and other digital technologies – can be argued to depend on the deskilling of teachers and their students, engendering a 'tool' mentality where technology is used 'to yield mechanical tasks and situations of social disconnect' (Monahan 2005, p.290). Thus while recognising that some teachers may indeed still have space for manoeuvre, Apple argues that the majority of teaching staff were on the whole deadened and dulled to conform to the deskilled use of technology in their teaching – with technology-based teaching creating a 'context that makes it seem unrealistic and not in their immediate interest for many teachers to do other than participate in recreating conditions that foster continued difficulties in their own labour' (Apple and Jungck 1990, p.237).

Many of these issues of alienation and deprofessionalisation are associated with notions of teachers' professional and personal identities – not least an individual teacher's beliefs and philosophies of the purpose and form of teaching. In these terms, it has been argued that teachers may resist or subvert technology use in the classroom for a number of reasons associated with their own personal identities as teachers. Morgan *et al.* (2010) argue, for example, that the factors that motivate teachers and sustain them on a daily basis are often emotional in nature – based around issues of job satisfaction, an enthusiasm for working with young people, 'making a difference' and 'doing work that they enjoy'. These passions contrast with the many pressures that infuse technology-based schooling – 'the great pressures of reform agendas, school re-structuring, accountability, high-stakes testing and other macro-movements that translate to teachers' routine experiences' (Morgan *et al.* 2010, p.193). In this sense, teachers' resistance to technology can be seen as 'a complex anxiety' – 'a large component of institutional self-interest, since no one wants to lose their job. But the notion that it would be possible to be replaced by a machine cuts deeper, to the heart of teachers' identity and self-respect' (Hodas 1996, p.213). From this perspective, some authors have begun to note a growing technological disenchantment within the teaching profession for a number of personal and professional reasons. As Convery (2009, p.38) observes, 'the benefits of technology in classrooms can be exaggerated, leading to continuing wasteful investment, and more importantly, significant difficulties for teachers who try to fit their practice to technologists' unrealistic aspirations'. While portrayals of widespread disenchantment and disaffection may be somewhat exaggerated, it would seem fair to conclude that teachers' orientation towards digital technology is strongly influenced by the ways in which they come to understand the conditions under which they experience technology-based teaching as 'facilitating' or 'inhibiting', 'constructive' or 'destructive'.

The lived experience of digital technology for the student

All of the issues discussed above point towards teachers' uses of digital technologies being seen as 'a form of good sense' – i.e. teachers' uses and non-uses of technology are best viewed in terms of their wider understandings about their work (Gitlin and Margonis 1995). The same thesis can be applied to students' engagements with digital technologies – albeit with the proviso that students face a markedly different set of priorities, pressures and preoccupations than their teachers. Furthermore, students are more clearly party to the reproductions of social stratification that take place in schools. As Bauman (2005, p.28) argues, 'the meaning of education' is an obvious instance where 'the perceptions of the 'teaching' and the 'taught' classes diverge. And no wonder, given the difference between the frames within which their respective lives are woven, as well as between the respective life experiences on which they reflect'. In this sense, students' uses of digital technologies can be seen in similar terms of negotiation of work – i.e. meaning-making and fitting digital technology with their own 'lived' experiences of being a student. This perspective necessitates an understanding of the act of 'being a student' in social, economic, political as well as educational terms. As studies of contemporary childhood and adolescence show, it is clear that there is a lot more to the 'job' of being a student than learning with (or without) digital technology – not least students' juggling of a number of academic and non-academic demands during their school careers which place them in various conflicting roles such as learner, peer, son, daughter, socialite and (as students get older) part-time employee and prospective college student. All of these spheres of students' lifeworlds should therefore be seen as having a bearing on their use of digital technology in school.

Technology and the micro-economy of the classroom

Studies of students' in-school engagement with digital technologies suggest that students often act as 'savvy' but pressured consumers of schooling who engage with their studies – and therefore with the technology – in pragmatic and strategic ways. This strategic (non)engagement with technology can be seen in terms of a number of short, medium and longer-term issues that face school students. From a short-term perspective, students' reading of digital technology must be set against the 'consequential validity' of assessment, i.e. 'the effect of the test or other form of assessment on learning and other educational matters' (Boud 1995, p.38). For many students, especially those in school systems based around 'high stakes' testing, the peripheral role that digital technology takes in the assessment demands of their school careers (besides the word-processing of essays and cursory searching of the internet for relevant information) provides a clear strategic impetus to rarely make extensive use of technology. As Knight (1995) argued, students can often view assessment as a 'moral' activity by teaching staff, clarifying what is valued in their courses and by schooling in general. The fact that most school courses retain a focus on summative assessment and the 'culture of the grade' therefore shapes students' approaches to learning in limited 'syllabus-bound' ways (Norton *et al.* 2001). Thus the timed paper-and-pencil examination, the practical lab test and class-test all militate against extensive use of digital technologies.

Similarly, the medium-term perspectives of many students on completing their school courses and being awarded a reasonable classification could be seen as 'technology-free'. In the relatively short life of modular courses and ongoing coursework assessment there is often little time for older school students to develop new skills at the risk of jeopardising the quality of their work and, ultimately, final examination grades and grade classifications. Given the conflicting roles that digital technologies play in their lessons, many students have little medium-term incentive to continue to use technology and are compelled instead to adopt 'low-level' approaches to studying. As Sarah Mann observed of students entering higher education from the UK secondary school system:

> many learners at different times tend to adopt either a surface approach to their study, characterised by a focus on rote learning, memorisation and reproduction, a lack of reflection and a preoccupation with completing the task; or a strategic approach, characterised by a focus on assessment requirements and lecturer expectations, and a careful management of time and effort, with the aims of achieving high grades (Mann 2001, p.7).

Even in terms of many students' longer-term perspective of gaining employment or continuing into college education, digital technology could be said to play a peripheral role. As their school careers progress, students are encouraged to become 'portfolio people' (Wright *et al.* 1999), driven by building their resumes, personal development plans and the like. In contrast to the views of policy-makers and school administrators, students often see digital technology as being a basic, but not ultimately essential, element of developing their 'marketability' to college admissions tutors or prospective employers. After fifteen years in technology-saturated school environments, many students are confident in their abilities to fulfil the levels of skills expected by future colleges, universities or employers as and when required. Crucially, this ability to 'use IT' is often not seen as being contingent on sustained in-school use of digital technology during their years of school education.

All of these points highlight the need to understand technology use in light of students' ability to negotiate strategically with the micro-economy of the classroom. For instance, where digital technologies do not 'fit' well with the micro-level concerns of being a student (such as passing exams, gaining free time from studies, maintaining identity and status with peers), then less use may be made of them. These driving concerns and strategies are not always obvious to a non-student observer. Selwyn (2001) found issues of perceived utility and added value to frame even the youngest of school students' perceptions of computers in the classroom. In this study students as young as six years were found to make complex distinctions between what they considered to be valuable and useful aspects of technology use in terms of the micro-economy of their particular classrooms. In the case of six and seven year old students in UK primary schools these benefits were found to range from the 'free play' benefits of finishing work before any other student, to concerns that the amount of personal effort put into a piece of work was readily apparent to the teacher. Similarly, a 'moral' concern of originality and 'ownership' was also prevalent in some of the children's responses, as were concerns with the aesthetic value of computer-based work. All these issues point towards the ability of students of all ages to shape their use of technology at school according to their circumstances and concerns. In this sense many students have been found to display measured and sometimes sympathetic views of their schools' less-than-perfect technology provision. As such, although many students are well aware of 'digital disconnects' they are also 'school savvy' enough to work around these issues rather than choosing to disengage with school technology use altogether. The wholesale disaffection and alienation of current generations of students with in-school technology outlined in Chapter 2 would seem to be a rather simplified analysis of what is a more nuanced relationship between students, schools and technology.

Technology and reproduction of social stratification

Of course, it would be unwise to construct a wholly agentic account of students' experiences of schooling and technology. Consideration should also be given to the ways in which issues such as social class, race and gender mediate students' educational experiences with technology. On one hand there is clear evidence from the existing empirical literature of the various ways in which access to and use of digital technologies in schools differs within student populations in terms of age, social class, race and gender. Significant differences are also apparent regarding the availability of different digital technologies between schools, especially in terms of factors such as income, socio-economic status and race (see Hess and Leal 2001). Empirical studies of how digital technologies are actually used within schools suggest that these differences persist beyond initial matters of access and availability and continue into the nature and outcomes of technology use. Janet Schofield's (1995) ethnographic study of US high school computer use provided an evocative account of the 'bright, white boys' domain of the school computer room. Other studies have detailed the comparatively expansive ways that digital technologies tend to be deployed with students from relatively privileged 'high' socio-economic backgrounds in comparison to their 'lower' socio-economic counterparts (Warschauer *et al.* 2004). Overall, a consistent picture emerges of how digital technology appears to contribute to – rather than overcome – differences between and within schools, with inequalities of gender, race and class reproduced through digital technology. As such, students' digital technology use would appear to be something that is more often entwined with than opposed to the well-established internal processes of stratification within schools. As Mark Warschauer and colleagues concluded:

> We found no evidence to suggest that technology is serving to overcome or minimise educational inequities within or across the schools we examined. Rather, the evidence suggests the opposite: that the introduction of information and communication technologies in the schools serves to amplify existing forms of inequality. Differences in human support systems for technology use, homework assignment patterns, and emphases on preparation for testing all mitigated the extent to which technology could be used effectively for academic preparation in low-SES schools (Warschauer *et al.* 2004, p.584).

The reproductive function of technology in the classroom can also be seen in terms of students' identity formation. Digital technology use has long been found to offer a ready space where the 'role conflicts' that students often experience in their relationships with their peers, teaching staff, school work and so on are worked out. These issues have been used to explain, for example, the gendered nature of students' use and non-use of technology in schools. Parlo Singh's (1993) ethnographic study of computer use in Australian primary schools demonstrated how digital technologies fed into and perpetuated social constructions of gendered (technical) competence – more often reinforcing rather than subverting students' gendered identities, social positions and relations. Similarly, as Carol Reid's more recent study of Australian high schools has shown, issues of academic and gendered identities often compromise students' orientation towards in-school technology use. Put simply, school-based technology was something that only a minority of high achieving, male students in Reid's study valued in terms of skills and knowledge, and that they felt sufficiently emotionally engaged with:

> In terms of computing studies in high schools and their articulation to university courses in Australia, participation is formerly organised around a set of skills, knowledges and prerequisites. You cannot, for example, do high-level computing studies unless you have high-level mathematics and science. Many students are not interested in these subjects. Not only is there a rejection of the competitive academic curriculum by all groups except males with a high interest in computing studies, there is also a rejection by all except high-interest males of the life associated with working in IT. For those who have experienced junior level IT subjects and for those who take the senior level IT subjects there is another dynamic at work – pedagogy. There are gendered dimensions to these practices and choices [. . .] young people are rejecting [technology studies at school], not because they fear or do not understand technology but rather because their knowledge and use of technologies permits a clearer understanding of what they are rejecting – boredom, alienation and a dependence on tired old paradigms that would have them submit themselves to compromising their freedom to know and the sustainability of their futures (Reid 2009, p.300).

Technology, tactics and resistance

This is not to suggest that students are wholly compliant with the compromised and reproductive nature of in-school technology use. The past three chapters have all highlighted recurring issues of power, control, negotiation and struggle in making sense of schools and schooling in the digital age. These issues should also be seen from a student perspective, where technology offers some students a ready site for struggle and resistance. In this sense, some students' lived experiences of technology use in school can also be equated with Michel de Certeau's wider notion of the tactics that non-powerful individuals often employ throughout the practice of everyday life. De Certeau argued that while those with authority and power may be able to organise affairs in a stable and strategic fashion, the ordinary individual is often able only to resort to makeshift tactical behaviours in order to re-appropriate objects, processes and procedures in order to make them their own. Thus for de Certeau (1984, p.29) those who have power are 'cumbersome, unimaginative and over-organised', while those who do not are 'creative, nimble and flexible'. Larger forces of domination (such as schools) tend to be over-organised and utilise top-down and cumbersome strategies of control. In contrast, the oppressed (such as students) tend to be weaker and often only able to revert to tactics. This is not to say that these tactical responses are of lesser value to the individual concerned. As de Certeau (1984, p.38) described:

> tactical ruses and surprises; clever tricks of the 'weak' within the order established by the 'strong', an art of putting one over on the adversary on his own turf, hunters' tricks, manoeuvrable, polymorphic mobilities, jubilant, poetic and warlike discoveries.

From this perspective many students can be seen as being well able, for example, to resist the 'hidden curriculum' of technology use in schools where they are taught implicitly how to fit in with a social system, how to follow rules and order, respect authority, obey, compete, and achieve success within the boundaries of the system. As should be apparent from previous discussions throughout this book, much in-school use of technology involves a hidden curriculum of becoming compliant and 'productive' users of digital technology, and is one that some students will resist actively. These forms of resistance can take many forms. For example, Andrew Hope's ethnographic studies of technology use in UK secondary schools uncovered a variety of student resistance to the rules and regulatory regimes that surrounded their use of the internet in school. As Hope described:

> students obscured the view of computer screens, relied on the speed of their reactions and chose locations/times where observation was minimal . . . [others] used others' passwords, claimed someone else had used their password or accessed unsuitable sites with innocuous web addresses (Hope 2005, pp.367–369).

Other studies have shown how students will, for example, try simultaneously to resist and modify the straightforward patterns of technology use that are imposed on them. In particular, the contrasting side of the institutional use of digital technologies in a disciplinary manner outlined in Chapter 6 is the possibility – even likelihood – of resistance from those being disciplined. Indeed, as Andrew Hope (2005, p.360) concluded, while the practices and processes of education are predicated upon observation and knowledge gathering about students, 'technological developments have meant that both the capacity to carry out surveillance and the potential for resistance have grown'. These opportunities to resist and test authority range from the relatively playful ability for students to conceal their informal online activities, to the rather more challenging instances of 'sousveillance' where students (and others) seek access to proscribed online information through 'hacking' into otherwise restricted administrative systems and databases. In this sense instances of improvising, appropriating, 'making-up' and 'making-do' with digital technologies are all part of the student tactics of everyday life within the school setting – the ways in which individual students attempt to negotiate the multiple sets of rules and systems, structures and spaces that characterise the school.

As with making sense of teachers' engagements with digital technologies, it is important to also recognise students' more general resistance to schooling *through* their technology use. Garrison and Bromley highlighted the ease with which some students use technology for what could be termed 'defensive learning' – going 'off-task' and withdrawing their intellectual labour through the guise of technological incompetence or invisibility. Garrison and Bromley's ethnographic study of US high schools identified at least two varieties of technology-based 'pretending' by students – what the researchers termed as withholding (i.e. pretending inability) and superficial busyness (i.e. pretending productive engagement). Often, Garrison and Bromley (2004) reported, students acted as though they were incapable or unwilling to do work that had been set them on the computer – work that they had at other times been observed to be able and willing to do. This, the authors reasoned, was often simply a case of students responding to the similar behaviours of their teachers:

> That students focus on appearances and spend their time looking busy, that they withhold and sabotage their own work, is both a cause and an effect of defensive teaching techniques. Prompts and protocols are relied on because students, in fact, seem to need prompts and protocols to complete the most basic assignment. Yet, students will predictably respond to overbearing control by resorting to any available subterfuge to carve out some space of their own. Defensive teaching, then, both elicits and is elicited by student pretending and undermining. The circularity of these practices means that they cannot be explained by reference to each other but rather as a response to the broader context (Garrison and Bromley 2004, p.602).

In all these instances it is difficult to ascribe precise meaning or intent to such acts of resistance – often individuals are themselves unable to explain exactly why they resist. As Gitlin and Margonis (1995, p.393) reason, 'the meaning of resistant acts, therefore, is likely to remain ambiguous. On the one hand, resistance may be nothing more than laziness or an excuse of some kind; on the other hand, it can reflect important political insights'. Yet it would seem that digital technology is a growing site for resistant – and therefore political – acts that reflect students' understanding of the hidden implications of schooling and the ways that schooling acts to reproduce inequalities. As Paul Willis (1977, p.126) concluded, students 'may not know what they say, but they mean what they do'.

Conclusions

Many of the issues highlighted in this chapter have pointed towards the notion of teachers and students being 'knowing users' (and 'knowing non-users') of digital technology in schools. As such, the chapter has moved attention away from viewing technology as having an inevitable – or even consistent – 'impact' on teaching and learning. Instead, the case has been made for understanding digital technology use in terms of its concrete and practical application in the daily life of the school and the classroom. It should be now clear that there is no educational logic inherent in how digital technologies 'work' in schools. Instead, the chapter has highlighted some of the many reasons, motivations and issues that underlie teachers' and students' acceptance and rejection of the technologies that enter the classroom setting. This chapter has therefore provided a social and cultural balance to the structural accounts of teacher and student behaviour outlined in Chapter 6. As such, the notion of informed non-use has been raised – i.e. choosing not to use a technology on the basis of 'digital decision' as opposed to 'digital division'. This feeds into the wider understanding that individuals are sometimes able to refuse or reconstitute the 'changes' associated with technology for a variety of reasons and from a variety of standpoints – albeit in an often stratified way. Thus the distinction should be acknowledged, as Henri Lefebvre reasons, between 'acceptance of daily life as it is (as it develops in and through its changes); or refusal of it, a refusal that can be either heroic and ascetic; or hedonistic and sensual, or revolutionary, or anarchistic' (Lefebvre 1981, p.1).

This chapter has helped outline the importance of structure *and* agency in making sense of digital technology use in the classroom. It has highlighted the many issues that lie between the position of viewing teachers and students as being manipulated or controlled, however subtly or unsubtly, and the position of viewing technology (non)use to be an agentic and creative act. In particular, the chapter has shown how teachers' and students' 'decisions' and 'choices' need to be understood within the wider contexts of schools and schooling – not least what can be termed the 'moral economy' of the school as perceived and experienced by the students and teachers within it. Borrowing a concept from the 'domestication' studies of technology use outlined in Chapter 3, this concept of the moral economy frames the school as being in constant exchange with the informal and formal economies that surround it, thus operating within and constituting a transactional system (Berker *et al.* 2006). Just like households, workplaces and other organisations, the school can be seen to 'domesticate' certain digital technologies into the pre-existing transactional system of classroom. As Berker *et al.* (2006, p.2) observe, 'we can observe a domestication process when users, in a variety of environments, are confronted with new technologies. These 'strange' and 'wild' technologies have to be 'house-trained'; they have to be integrated into the structures, daily routines and values of users and their environments'.

This notion of 'taming' otherwise 'wild' technologies conveys neatly the sense of struggle and conflict that can be said to surround many of the negotiations over technology use in schools. In this sense, the use of digital technology in school can be seen as part of wider issues of power and control that inform and underlie what goes on in school settings – i.e. 'the distribution of power to organise behaviours, the interests of those who possess that power, and the compliance or consent of those subject to the exercise of that power' (Friedkin 1985, p.208). In this way the symbiotic nature of much digital technology use in schools must be recognised – i.e. where different interests are able to gain from the same arrangements. This is perhaps most apparent in the often mutually beneficial arrangements between students and teachers when using technology in the classroom. Although this chapter has considered the social dynamics surrounding technology use separately for teachers and students, these behaviours are perhaps better understood when taken together as a whole, and in relation to the school and classroom context where teachers and students use technology in collaborative as well as oppositional ways. Digital technologies can therefore be seen as a ready site for the formation of alliances and constituencies between teachers and students in the pursuit of mutual interests and independent goals (see Webb 2008). For example, as Mark Garrison and Hank Bromley observed of the defensive teaching and defensive learning arrangements in their technology-using classrooms, (non)use of technology can be a mutually beneficial arrangement for teachers *and* their students:

> So what is to be made of students whose work is simply to look busy? Again, we have an arrangement that works for all involved, at least in the short term: As long as students looked busy and caused no trouble, they could have their autonomy and carve out some scarce private space in the generally intrusive school routine (albeit a space filled with pointless activities), and teachers could devote their attention to more urgent matters. Indeed, teachers who kept their classes looking busy and productively engaged in the lab were avoiding scrutiny in much the same manner as students who kept themselves looking busy to avoid the teacher's gaze. Both coped with somewhat unrealistic demands by controlling appearances – at the expense, of course, of substance, although unavoidably so under the circumstances (Garrison and Bromley 2004, p.606).

All of the issues highlighted in this chapter add to the developing sense over the last four chapters that digital technology use in schools is best understood as being a highly contested and uncertain practice. As such, the last four chapters have advanced a critical perspective on the present state of schools, schooling and technology – highlighting the social, cultural political and economic complexities that are often lacking from mainstream academic accounts of contemporary educational technology. Having developed this understanding of the intensely political nature of schools and schooling in the digital age, the final two chapters of the book now go on to consider how best to address the problems, tensions and shortcomings that have been identified. Given all of the issues that have arisen from the preceding analyses, what is now to be done with schools in the digital age?

Part III

What to do with schools in the digital age?

8 Reconstructing schools and schooling in the digital age

Introduction

The last seven chapters have seen this book develop a wide-ranging analysis of schools, schooling and digital technology. In short, it has been argued that the use of digital technology in schools can be best understood in terms of a number of linkages – i.e. to the needs of the state and to the needs of commercial and quasi-commercial interests; to the global flows of information and capital that constitute the economy; and to the local flows of power and authority that constitute the actions of individuals within the structures of the school. In other words, schools technology is a knot that is 'tangled up' in a web of practices that stretch into complex systems beginning and ending outside of the school (Nespor 1997). Any understanding of how digital technologies are used – and not used – within a school must therefore take account of local school district politics, (inter)national economic policies, popular cultures, corporate agendas and all of the other 'webs of social relations' that embed schools in neighbourhoods, cities, regions and nation-states (see Nespor 1997). As such, this book has produced a joined-up account of schools and schooling in the digital age that can serve as a ready basis for suggesting possible areas of change, adjustment and improvement. The final two chapters, therefore, conclude the book by confronting as well as analysing the dominant patterning of power and politics within the school – refocusing attention, in Michael Apple's (1986) words, towards the possibility of thinking 'otherwise' about schools and digital technology.

Making critical sense of schools and schooling in the digital age

The last seven chapters have constructed a case for making sense of the shaping of digital technology use in schools along a number of different lines. It is clear, for example, that the implementation and integration of digital technology in the school setting cannot be understood solely from the perspective of the teacher/learner interface. Drawing on all of the evidence presented so far, the last four chapters have shown how the undoubted educational *potential* of digital technology appears to have been curtailed in *practice* by the sometimes conflicting political, economic, cultural and social agendas pursued by the many actors with a vested interest in schools technology. As has been discussed, these interests range from the individual student's tactics of survival and resistance within the micro-politics of the classroom to the profit-seeking motives of the trans-national corporation. As such, anyone seeking to gain a clear understanding of schools in the digital age must be able to focus their attention on the network of social relations that surrounds and envelops the use of digital technologies in schools.

It follows that any 'failure' of schools to make use of digital technologies in a 'proper' or 'efficient' manner cannot be attributed to any of the individual or organisational deficiencies outlined in Chapter 2. The paucity of digital technology use in schools is not due simply to logistical deficiencies such as a lack of resourcing, whole-school 'vision', technical support or time. Neither are these 'problems' caused by deficiencies on the part of individuals working within schools. It is not the case that teachers and school leaders simply 'do not get' digital technologies or lack the necessary skills, aptitudes or ambitions to make the best of technology in their work. Rather, the last four chapters have detailed how digital technology in schools is the preserve of a wide-ranging complex of interests – from state policy-makers, IT firms and advocacy groups to schools, teachers, parents and (of course) the students themselves. All of these actors appropriate and utilise technology in different ways for different ends, all playing a key part in determining what comes to be seen as the relative 'success' or 'failure' of educational technology.

Looking back to the theoretical perspectives on schools and technology that were discussed in Chapter 3, it is clear that any analysis of schools and digital technology requires a rich understanding of the contexts that shape and construct it. In this sense the last four chapters have illustrated how the use of digital technologies in schools continues to be socially shaped in a number of ways and by a number of influences that may not be immediately apparent to many students or teachers. Whether readily apparent or not, these influences have a profound and long-lasting bearing on what is experienced as 'educational technology' within school settings. Chapters 6 and 7, for example, gave a clear sense of how digital technologies are embedded and imbued deeply within the micro-politics of schools and schooling. In this sense, the (non)use of digital technologies in the classroom must be seen within the context of individuals 'getting on with the job' demanded of the role of being 'a teacher' or 'a student'. Indeed, digital technology is entwined with all aspects of contemporary reformations of teaching and the 'new lives of teachers' – not least notions of professionalism, collegiality and 'effectiveness' (see Day and Gu 2010). Non-use of digital technologies must therefore also be seen within the context of school leaders and authorities responding to the pressures of new managerialism and rationalisation and, not least, of the pressures for schools to function as technologies of control and regulation. Chapters 4 and 5, on the other hand, offered a picture of some of the macro-political contexts of technology use in schools – not least the ideological agendas that underpin the educational technology community, the commercial concerns of the IT industry, and the legitimising concerns of most governments and policy-makers towards global economic success and nation-building.

It would seem that all of these social constructions of school digital technology use are understandably very different from the visions of technology use that tend to be promoted within much of the educational technology literature. Rather than encouraging more individualised and 'freer' forms of learning, this book has shown how many of the dominant shaping interests and agendas outlined above coalesce to enrol the use of digital technologies in schools into decidedly narrower projects of standardisation, rationalisation and institutional control. One can see, for example, how technology-based teaching and learning in a country such as the UK with its standardised curricula and testing regimes ends up being constructed along rather different lines than the technology-assisted voyages of individual discovery that some academics and educational technologists are keen to promote. From this perspective technology can be as much a focus for the expansion of authoritarian forms of education as it can be used for the extension of intellective and individual freedoms (see Saltman and Gabbard 2010). As such, it is perhaps not surprising that the many constructivist and socio-cultural promises of individually-centred, technology-enhanced learning outlined in Chapter 1 are not being borne out on a widespread and sustained scale. In fact it would appear that the apparent digitisation of schools and schooling can be associated with far *less* change and alteration than might be assumed. Beneath their high-tech veneer, the current state of schools and schooling in the digital age would appear to be very much a case of 'business as usual' – or as Ivor Goodson puts it 'doing the same old business by different means ... change leading to sameness, and the future pointing to the past' (Goodson *et al.* 2002, p.147).

In this sense, schooling in the digital age can be best described as marked by a set of continuities, rather than a set of radical discontinuities, from schooling in preceding ages. While associated clearly with some readjustments and re-alignments to the organisation of education and learning within schools, digital technologies could not be said to have transformed the core power relations between individual students and formal institutions. Instead, it would seem that the use of digital technologies in schools is associated most readily with a perpetuation of long-standing issues of production, reproduction and domination – and all the problems, inequalities and injustices that lie therein. In this respect, digital technology use in schools would appear to be no different to any other aspect of society. As Henri Lefebvre concluded, 'information technology can neither resolve nor cancel contradictions: it can only express them – or disguise them' (Lefebvre 1981, p.145).

Digital technologies and the wider politics of schools and schooling

This analysis suggests that many of the tensions and controversies that surround schools and digital technology have little to do with matters of technology *per se*. Instead they feed directly into wider controversies and tensions surrounding the forms and functions of schooling in contemporary society. As such, the specific debates over the need to use digital technologies in schools and the imperative to develop digital forms of schooling are actually concerned with more fundamental questions of what functions schools should play in contemporary society and what purpose systems of mass schooling may have in the early twenty-first century. Any debate over the future of schooling in the digital age, in other words, is highly political and ideological in nature. These are not benign debates over neutral technical adjustments to the provision of education to children and young people. These are highly charged debates over the politics of schools and schooling in the twenty-first century.

As has been implied throughout this book, the politics of education can be understood as a practice of everyday life in schools, as pedagogic practice, as policy formation and governance *and* as individual and collective activism (Youdell 2010). For instance, much of the shaping of digital technology use within schools is linked to the wider function of schooling in maintaining and furthering a range of social, political, economic and commercial interests associated with contemporary capitalist society. From a macro-economic perspective, for example, much of what goes on within schools in the digital age continues to be justified in terms of meeting the 'needs of the economy' – not least producing skilled workforces and boosting economic performance in light of all the changes associated with globalisation and modernisation. In these terms at least, it makes sound sense that technology-based schooling remains centred on an ethos of credentialism and target-setting, homogenisation and hierarchical organisation. It makes sense that globally competitive economies draw strength from systems of schooling that are based around what could be termed 'education as outcomes' where teaching and learning remains orientated towards the setting, assessing and attaining of targets and the preparing of students for tests and examinations (Young 2007). It also makes sense that the dominant forms of schooling in (late)modern society continue to be the highly regulated, ordered, sorted and institutionalised processes that have persisted since the late nineteenth century. As such, digital technology practices and processes within the school setting are shaped by a dominant mode of formal learning that is concerned essentially with the instrumentalist 'consuming of massive amounts of symbolic information' (Monke 2008, p.4).

In these terms it is not surprising to see the enrolment of digital technology into the wider political, economic, social and cultural roles that schools continue to play in contemporary society. While it may be overly simplistic to assume that the logic of digital technology in schools follows rigidly what Murdock (2004, p.19) terms 'the globalisation of capitalist imperatives and its shifting relations to state logics', digital technologies would certainly seem to retain a close association with a number of political concerns. These factors could go some way to explaining why schools technology appears to be distant from the 'fluid' and 'free' forms of digital technology use that remain close to the hearts of middle-class, well-educated, adult technology enthusiasts. In particular, these commentators often fail to acknowledge that schools continue to function as places where many of students' local knowledges are discarded in favour of received wisdoms. Instead schools should be seen as sites where students are socialised into very particular and formalised ways of 'doing' digital technology, almost inevitably at odds with how many of them engage with digital technologies outside of the classroom.

Digital technologies and the realpolitik of schools and schooling

All of these issues go some way to explaining why digital technologies tend to be used within the institutional confines of schools in the ways that they do. Yet within this broad macro-level understanding of the social relations of contemporary capitalist society it is important to remember that digital technology use in schools is party to a range of more specific localised struggles. For example, within the school itself it would seem that most actors are at least tacitly aware of the over-riding structuration of the school as a technology of social control, and are often able to operate within (and sometimes around) these confines to meet their own needs. This was apparent, for instance, in Chapter 7's description of the tactics of survival and resistance often displayed by teachers and learners when engaging with digital technologies. Chapter 5 described the similar strategic manoeuvrings (albeit on a larger scale) of various non-state actors and interests. Such machinations were even evident in Chapter 4's description of the construction of educational technology through state policy-making. All these instances highlight the need to remain mindful of the real-politik of contemporary school education that is played out inside and outside of the immediate school setting. In this sense, schools technology can be approximated to a strategic and positional 'game' for many of the individual actors concerned. From this perspective, it is perhaps unsurprising that the manifestations of schools technology 'on the ground' are far removed from the 'promises' and 'hopes' for digital technology outlined in Chapter 1.

This is not to deny that the use of digital technologies in schools is currently very important for learners, teachers, school leaders, policy-makers and the IT industry alike. Yet it could be argued that in the longer term much of what constitutes schools technology is of very little sustained practical consequence at all. In this respect, a lot of what is *said* about schools technology by anyone other than the students and teachers currently charged with using it is not to be taken at face value – and it is in this discursive sense that schools technology is perhaps most obviously a 'game' that is currently being played by all in education. It could be argued that, in the long term, educational technology is perhaps not as important at the 'chalkface' as its supporters would like to believe. Few people appear more than superficially concerned over the lack of evidence that digital technology use leads to sustained and widespread 'gains' in learning or increased educational 'standards' (however one chooses to define these nebulous terms). Few people appear more than superficially concerned that 'ground-breaking' and 'innovative' state policy initiatives of the 2010s seem to cover much of the same ground as previous technological initiatives and programmes from the last two decades. At best, most of what is said about digital technology at a macro- and meso-level should only be seen as seeking to engineer educational change in an indirect and aspirational manner.

This is not to say that this indifference or lack of real expectation exists only at the 'macro' level of analysis. It could be argued that, despite the widespread bemoaning of schools' underwhelming use of digital technologies outlined in Chapter 2, there is a lack of real concern or concerted effort by most actors to force change. Few people appear more than superficially concerned that digital technologies remain just another 'tick in the box' for many learners and teachers in a long line of 'core' activities and imperatives that dominate the current educational landscapes of the (over)developed world. Few people appear concerned beyond the point of mild disapproval that the multinational and national IT firms that are currently so visible in the schools marketplace are displaying a less-than public spirited approach to selling their products to learners, parents and school administrators – even less acting in a manner that suggests a long-term commitment to educational technology. Few people appear more than superficially concerned that computers in the classroom continue – to reuse Larry Cuban's (2001) phrase – to be 'over-sold and under-used'.

It could therefore be argued that despite the paucity of *real* impact or change on the ground, many (if not most) of the involved stakeholders, actors and interests are happy with playing the 'game' of digital technology use in schools on their own terms and with little obligation or accountability. The key point here is that this is a game that is being played out in the most part in a knowing, informed and deliberate manner. Indeed, it would be wrong to judge any of the positions outlined above as 'better informed' than others – none of the actors involved in schools technology should be assumed to be stupid or naïve. As Dean (2002, p.5) reflects, 'people know very well what they are doing, but they do it nevertheless'. Of course, some actors stand to gain a lot more from their actions than others, yet it would be unwise to characterise anyone's actions within this game analogy as unthinking or irrational. As Lefebvre (1981) also observed:

> There is no such thing as false consciousness – everyone has an intellectualised understanding of what they are doing, but these understandings are shaped by the material conditions in which they operate and live. As such we can only make judgement over what is good sense and what is bad sense – in my case from a socially concerned perspective. Every position has an element of good sense, even among the dominant and oppressive groups.

In this sense, the relative lack of substantial change to the practice and processes of schools technology over the past forty years of the 'information revolution' is perhaps easier to understand if it is accepted that school change is not necessarily the goal or priority for many concerned. Thus it is wholly unsurprising that schools have proved to be sites of considerable continuity despite the apparent technological revolution over the forty years. As Dan Lortie (2002, p.vii) reflected at the beginning of the 2000s, 'education does not change at a rapid pace – the major structures in public education are much the same today as [thirty years ago]'. Having reached the 2010s, there remains little reason to disagree with this sentiment.

Giving up on the school as it currently stands

While providing a realistic analysis of the continuing complexities of schools technology this prognosis can be criticised as offering little hope of change or a 'better' future. The structures and social relations that underpin the 'game' of schools technology look set to endure for many years to come. It could be argued that there is little reason for any of the actors described in Chapters 4, 5, 6 and 7 to challenge or question the *status quo* as long as their own interests continue to be met (be it in terms of making a profit, gaining electoral favour or just surviving the school day). It could be that change is most likely to be initiated from within the constituency group that has been relatively absent from this chapter's discussion so far – what can be termed loosely as the educational technology community. As was outlined in Chapter 5, this is the loose configuration of actors with a primary interest in the technology itself rather than the machinations of the business of schools and schooling. As was briefly discussed in Chapter 5 these actors can be seen as professional hobbyists, charged with exploring the future of technology enhanced learning. If other elements of the educational establishment or IT industry are unlikely to drive changes in schools' use of digital technologies along necessarily educational lines, what then of learning technologists, academic researchers and other technological enthusiasts?

Of course, whether they openly acknowledge it or not, most people arguing for the technological transformation of schooling are well aware of the intransient nature of schools as political organisations. As this chapter's portrayal of schools technology as a 'game' implies, this state of inertia actually serves many of these actors and interest groups well – not least providing the continued existence of a 'big problem' for them to address and overcome. It could be argued that if even half the predictions and prophecies outlined in Chapter 1 came to fruition then a lot of academics, educational technologists, consultants and advisers would be struggling to justify their professional positions. From this perspective, it perhaps makes some sense for these people to continue to retain a faith in the long-term transformative promises and hopes for digital technologies in schools in the knowledge that these changes are unlikely to come to fruition in the short term. Yet while maintaining support for schools technology continues to serve elements of the educational technology community well, there has been a creeping sense over the last ten years or so of a shift in emphasis in the stance of many people towards schools. Growing numbers of educational technologists – especially those working in the academic and commercial sectors – are beginning to see the school as it currently exists to be increasingly irrelevant to, and incompatible with, the needs and demands of the digital age.

Indeed, irrespective of the wider social and political issues outlined above, the long-standing apparent disconnect between schools and technology is now prompting a burgeoning number of academic commentators to 'give up' on the notion of the industrial-era school as it currently exists. This renouncement of the industrial-era school as a viable site of digital technology use is evident across the ideological spectrum of academic writing on educational technology, from the most techno-centric of authors such as Seymour Papert through to economically and socially concerned commentators working from otherwise incompatible neo-liberal *and* libertarian positions. If the impetus for meaningful change to schools in the digital age is to come from the academic educational technology community, then this current thinking should be considered in more detail – especially the two main lines of argument that characterise such discussions and debates at present, i.e. (i) arguments for the complete abandonment of the school, or else (ii) arguments for the radical reconstruction of the school.

Arguments for the abandonment of the school in the digital age

In the minds of some educational technologists and other concerned academic commentators the seriousness of the 'school problem' has now passed a point of no return, leaving little choice but to renounce completely the school as a viable site for technology use. Thus the idea that technology-based learning could replace the idea of school altogether is becoming a proposition that is being taken increasingly seriously by certain proponents. Growing numbers of academic writers and educational technologists are now content to conclude that the school is a 'dead' site for meaningful use of digital technology and will never be able to adapt sufficiently to the challenge and disruption of the computer, internet and other digital technologies. In this sense the school is derided as an outmoded technology from a past industrial age that should be dismantled. As was discussed in Chapter 2, a range of reasoned arguments are now being promoted that all of the structural impediments and challenges to technology (including the school) must be removed in order to facilitate the realisation of the digital transformation of education.

From this perspective, powerful arguments are being advanced that children and young people may well be better off learning among themselves through the support of digital technologies. Internet technologies are now seen as capable of providing a ready basis for young people's circumvention of the traditional structures of their schools and generally 'finding something online that schools are not providing them' as Henry Jenkins (2004, n.p.) has put it. For example, social media tools such as wikis, social networking and 'folksonomy' applications have been discussed in terms of being able to move education away from being 'a special activity that takes place in special places at special times, in which children are instructed in subjects for reasons they little understand' (Leadbeater 2008a, p.149). As Nicole Johnson concluded from her study of teenage 'expert' technology users, home use of digital technologies was felt to allow students a greater freedom and autonomy of learning in spite (rather than because) of their school-based education:

> The [students] were able to choose what they learned and when they learned. They viewed the medium in which they did it as a form of leisure. They were also able to choose who and what they learned from – not just what has been set up as exclusive and privileged. They were able to both learn and receive pleasure from their engagement and not have to be concerned about the hierarchisation and failure in relation to how traditional schooling determines competence. They were in fact designing and engaging in their own learning. (Johnson 2009, p.70).

This synopsis is typical of excitement within the academic community for the capacity of digital technologies to make education a more fluid arrangement where learning can involve a variety of people and places throughout a community for a variety of reasons. In this respect, much faith continues to be vested in digital technologies as a catalyst for the total substitution of twentieth-century modes of teaching, learning and schooling.

In particular, there is a distinct groundswell of support within the educational technology community for non-school based technology enhanced learning. From James Gee's (2006, 2008) sustained celebration of the learning potential of computer games through to MIT Medialab's 'Lifelong Kindergarten' agenda, some influential elements of the educational technology community appear to be quite happy to see the industrial-age school wither away as a site of learning and instruction. Indeed, a spirit of using digital technologies to bypass traditional education institutions is evident in online services such as the School of Everything – a popular online space designed to put teachers in contact with learners and therefore aiming to be 'an eBay for stuff that does not get taught in school' (Leadbeater 2008b, p.26). Similarly, online services such as NotSchool.Net are well established and officially endorsed online platforms that aim to re-engage young people otherwise excluded from the formal education system with learning and the pursuit of qualifications. Yet rather than being cursory additions to traditional schooling, these examples and others like them are seen to mark the first steps in a radical rethinking and reorganisation of existing structures and organisation of education provision. As Leadbeater (2008b, p.26) reasons, the imperative of digitally-based education provision

> require[s] us to see learning as something more like a computer game, something that is done peer-to-peer, without a traditional teacher . . . We are just at the start of exploring how we can be organised without the hierarchy of top-down organisations. There will be many false turns and failures. But there is also huge potential to create new stores of knowledge to the benefit of all, innovate more effectively, strengthen democracy and give more people the opportunity to make the most of their creativity.

Arguments for reconstructing the school in the digital age

Attention should also be paid to the more conciliatory (but no less radical) proposals for the substantial reconstruction of the school along digital lines – retaining the notion of the school as institution but as a reconfigured set of relations. For example, it is now received wisdom among many academic commentators, educational technologists and even some practitioners that the educational potentials of new technology will only be realised through a radical rethinking of the processes and practices of contemporary schooling – as evident in present calls for the development of 'school 2.0' (e.g. Wang and Chern 2008). Such 'reschooling' arguments are advanced most commonly via proposals for the development of digitally aligned modes of schooling that are built around the active communal creation of knowledge (rather than passive individual consumption and a 'one-size-fits all' mentality), and imbued with a sense of play, expression, reflection and exploration (e.g. Williams 2008). As Collins and Halverson (2009, p.129) put it, this involves not only 'rethinking what is important to learn' but also 'rethinking learning'.

  This need to reconfigure the structures and processes of formal schools has perhaps been explored most thoroughly in terms of curriculum and pedagogy, as evidenced in the rash of recent proposals from enthusiastic academics and practitioners for the development of 'pedagogical mash-ups' and new pedagogies of social interaction (e.g. Fisher and Baird 2009; Code and Zaparyniuk 2009). All of these curricular reconfigurations are predicated upon the notions outlined in Chapter 1 that digital technologies are leading to different types of information and knowledge production that are based around fast-changing, non-textual forms that require new forms of more critical and reflexive information skills and literacies (Buschman 2009). In this sense, arguments are increasingly being made that it no longer makes sense to retain 'pre-digital' models of curricular organisation focused on the rigidly hierarchic organisation of static content under the control of the teacher. Instead, questions are now being asked in relation to how to best develop twenty-first century curricula that can be negotiated rather than prescribed, that are driven by learner needs and based on providing learners with skills in managing and accessing knowledge and thereby taking control of their own learning pathways and choices (Facer and Green 2007). Thus growing numbers of authors are now discussing the likely nature and form of 'curriculum 2.0' – what Edson (2007) terms as 'user-driven education' allowing learners to take an active role in what they learn as well as how and when they learn it. Of course, this 'pick and mix approach' to curricular content and form presents a fundamental challenge to the professional roles and cultures of educators (Swain 2009). As McLoughlin and Lee (2008, p.647) conclude, all of these proposals therefore centre on the need for teachers to

> expand our vision of pedagogy, where learners are active participants or co-producers of knowledge rather than passive consumers of content and learning is seen as a participatory, social process supporting personal life goals and needs.

Following this line of thinking the argument has emerged from the recent academic educational technology literature that technology-based practices of collaboration, publication and inquiry should be foregrounded within schools' approaches to teaching and learning. Thus many current discussions in the field of educational technology conclude with proposals and manifestos for various models of 'peer e-assessment' and 'remix curricula', as well as ongoing debates over the refocusing of the teacher's role and the need to physically rebuild schools to accommodate the spatial and technical requirements of twenty-first century technology use (e.g. Fisher and Baird 2009; Prensky 2008). For instance, calls continue to be made for a grandiose over-hauling of the school system – not least the remodelling of schools to fit with the needs and demands of modern technology. From William Mitchell's (1995) suggestions for a 'recombinant architecture' in schools, to proposals for the re-design of the school environment into 'collaboration-friendly', 'really cool spaces' (e.g. Dittoe 2006) the notion of redesigning and rebuilding the physical environment of the school continues to gain popularity and support.

In particular, the mass collaboration seen to be at the heart of social media and web 2.0 applications has been touted by some commentators as having the potential to 'change everything' (Tapscott and Williams 2008), even to the point of students (re)writing and (re)editing their school textbooks. Underpinning many of these suggestions is the belief that children and young people should be given increased control of their interactions with information and knowledge. For instance, Marc Prensky (2008, n.p.) argues for a 'new pedagogy of kids teaching themselves with the teacher's guidance'. This sense of providing young people with opportunities to influence the direction of institutional change is reflected in Donald Tapscott's (1999, p.11) advice to 'give students the tools, and they will be the single most important source of guidance on how to make their schools relevant and effective places to learn'. While none of these commentators are suggesting the complete abolishment of the school *per se*, they all point towards a substantial alteration and refocusing of what schools are and what they do. More important still, such ideas and proposals are gaining increasing credence and influence among mainstream education and policy communities.

Recognising the ideological nature of these suggestions for reconstruction

While increasingly influential, these are ongoing debates that have not reached any satisfactory conclusions – not least because of their highly ideologically-driven nature. The forms of digitally-driven change being proposed from within the educational technology community are not merely neutral, technical readjustments to schooling. Whether intentional or not, these proposals are all highly political in nature. Indeed, as Henri Lefebvre observes, such forms of techno-utopianism tend to constitute a profoundly political project:

> these ideologies do not think that they are interpreting the techniques, but that they are estimating them objectively. They refuse to concede that they are pre-senting, or representing, a tendentious political project. To them, the project seems to follow logically from the technology. Is not technologising the social and political, as opposed to socialising and politising technology, a choice and a decision? A political standpoint that presents itself as objective meaning? (Lefebvre 1981, p.149).

Of course, any suggestion for change or innovation will be informed by underlying values, principles, beliefs and intentions. Yet, the proposals for the reconstruction of the school outlined above can be said to promote a particularly divisive techno-cen-tric ideology that goes against many of the critical principles that have underpinned this book. As such, the proposals outlined above for abandoning the industrial-era school in the digital age merit questioning and challenging in the strongest terms possible.

Above all, questions need to be asked with regards to the distinct mistrust of the school and formal education that pervades these proposals for change. This is per-haps most evident in the unsubstantiated over-valorising of informal learning that runs throughout these accounts. In particular, the devaluing of current forms of school-based education feeds into a wider anti-school discourse that has long found a receptive audience within discussions of education and technology. From one per-spective, this anti-schooling agenda is based upon a set of ostensibly compelling anti-establishment ideals that many readers of this book may well have some sympathy with (see Robertson 2003). Indeed, the anti-school intentions of most technologists are often justified as being rooted in benign counter-cultural sensibilities – drawing on the spirit of 1960s' Californian 'hippy' philosophy that informed the beginnings of the home-brew computer movement, early programmer communities and, more recently, the notions of open-source software and social software. As Danah Boyd (2007, p.17) points out, for many technologists these forms of digital technology are not seen merely as neutral artefacts but also as a rallying call for a new age of activities which are made 'by the people, for the people' rather than centred around official, institutional interests.

In this sense it is evident how many of the current proposals outlined above for the discontinuation of schooling in favour of technological means advocate a form of deschooling of society along digital lines, thus (un)consciously updating the arguments of Ivan Illich (1971) for the early twenty-first century. At first glance, Illich's thesis fits well with many of the issues raised throughout this book – most notably his condemnation of institutionalised learning as inhibiting individual growth due to its function as product of capitalist society and emphasis on 'progress' through mass production and consumption. This reading of school and schooling therefore fits well with contemporary rhetorics of digital technologies and education. As Charles Leadbeater (2008a, p.44) reasoned recently, 'in 1971 [deschooling] must have sounded mad. In the era of eBay and MySpace it sounds like self-evident wisdom'. Indeed, the tendency of academic commentators and technologists to celebrate individuals' self-determination of their learning via digital technologies feeds into a wider enthusiasm shared among many in education for the inherent benefits of episodes of informal learning that take place outside the control of formal education organisations and settings (see Sefton-Green 2004). This in turn can be seen as part of a wider societal idealisation of the informal (Misztal 2000), and the networked individualism of everyday life (see Beck and Beck-Gernsheim 2002).

While the intentions of many commentators may well be rooted in such counter-cultural sensibilities, the spirit of these arguments is now being used to support a number of less obvious ideological standpoints – most notably the removal of the state from the provision of public education by a range of more neo-conservative and neo-liberal interests (see Apple 2004; Kovacs 2007). The prospect of the digital replacement of the school has also been enrolled into recent neo-liberal articulations of the 'end of school' and realising the 'dream of education without the state' (Tooley 2006). Here digital technology is valorised in decidedly different terms than outlined above – i.e. as an ideal vehicle for the establishment of 'a genuine market in education, where there was no state intervention of any kind, in funding, provision or regulation' (Tooley 2006, p.26). For example, Tooley (2006, p.22) talks of 'the technological capability to allow inspiring teachers to reach millions of young people [rather than] forc[ing] all teachers into an egalitarian straight-jacket'. In this sense, many of the arguments for the increased 'technologification' of schools could be said to feed into the wider libertarian discourses that have long pervaded societal and political discussion of digital technology – a trend identified by writers such as Langdon Winner (1997) as 'cyber-libertarianism'. Here the power of technology and the power of the individual – what Kelemen and Smith (2001, p.371) term 'two ideas which lie at the heart of modern civilisation' – converge into an argument for the creation of new forms of action and organisation that do not require the appropriation of traditional spaces or structures. In this sense digital technology is positioned as nothing less than 'a moral enterprise set to rescue the world' (Kelemen and Smith 2001, p.370), underpinned by an ideological faith in the power of radical individualism, market forces and the pursuit of rational self-interest.

Although these agendas may appear unlikely bedfellows, such neo-liberal sentiments have proved to meld surprisingly well with the counter-cultural heritage of the fields of computer programming, IT development and the so-called 'hacker ethic'. Both these world-views can be said to espouse a shared respect for individualism – in particular the celebration of individual choice over state intervention. As Charlie Gere (2008, p.144–145) argues:

> It might seem at first that, both in theory and in practice, neo-liberalism would be at odds with counter-cultural thinking. But in fact . . . there is a remarkable degree of consensus. Both neo-liberalism and the counter-culture elevated the individual over the collective. Both also proclaimed the necessity of freeing the individual's capacity to act from the tyranny of organisations and bureaucracies [. . .] Like Adam Smith's market system, neo-liberal economics instantiate a kind of cybernetic fantasy of self-regulation [. . .] Accompanying these naturalisations of capitalism and technology is an active denial of the role of government.

Thus while the general premise of the individualised, non-institutionalised visions of digitally-based learning may be seductive, it should be remembered that such arguments support a number of political ends that run counter to the critical principles of equality, social justice and democratic empowerment outlined from the beginning of this book onwards – not least laissez-faire arguments for the dismantling of the state and public sector. It may well be that the convenience of digital technology allows the 'privilege and convenience' of education to be provided 'without the unsightly mess' of state provision (Dean 2002, p.3). Yet, if these terms are accepted as the basis upon which education in the digital age is to follow, then a number of important principles of mass schooling in society such as collective responsibility and empowerment are weakened, if not rejected altogether. As Raymond Williams (1981) asserts, a neo-liberal perspective requires that it is the successful individual that is constantly making an individual effort and crucially an individual success of themselves. The overriding question that faces this book as it draws to a conclusion is what alternatives can be proposed to these prevailing visions of individualised and atomised learning?

Towards a fairer future schooling in the digital age

The political nature and the political importance of schools and digital technology should, by now, be clear. Debates about schools in the digital age are not about matters of bandwidth or the technical efficiencies of tablet computers or micro-blogging. Instead, the main debates surrounding schooling in the digital age are about questions of benefit and power, equality and empowerment, structure and agency and social justice. As Michael Apple (2002, p.442) reasons:

> the debate about the role of the new technology in society and in schools is not and must not be just about the technical correctness of what computers can and cannot do. These may be the least important kinds of questions, in fact. Instead, at the very core of the debate are the ideological and ethical issues concerning what schools should be about and whose interests they should serve.

In these terms there is clearly much to oppose in the emerging received wisdom in current educational technology discussions and debates concerning the digital re-schooling or even de-schooling of compulsory education in the twenty-first century. Such arguments present an overly deterministic stance on technology and place far too much emphasis on the disembodied individual learner. In particular, these arguments rely upon an overly simplistic view of groups of like-minded individuals somehow transcending the wider social, economic, political and cultural contexts of education. As such, there are as many critical silences within these current agendas for change as there are unfeasible solutions. Where, for example, does corporate capitalism feature in these individualised visions of virtual learning? What concern is there for inequalities of access, skills, resourcing or know-how?

Current thinking about the future of schools in the digital age is perhaps most misguided in its persistence in seeing digital technology as capable of enacting new arrangements and forms of education. If anything is to be learnt from the last seven chapters of this book, it should be that digital technologies are associated with few, if any, disjunctures and novelties. To reiterate a point made throughout latter chapters of this book, schooling in the digital age marks a set of continuities rather than discontinuities with schooling in the pre-digital age. In this sense, many of the current proposals for reconfiguring schools in the digital age replicate the long-standing celebration of 'the new' that is characteristic of techno-utopian thinking. As Lefebvre (1981, pp.142–143) again reasons:

> with each new means of communication and information . . . people anticipate miracles: the transfiguration of daily life. As if it could come from a means or medium. These means or media can only transmit what existed prior to the mediating operation, or what occurs outside it. Today, communication *reflects* – nothing more, nothing less.

So how can current critics of schools and schooling in the digital age do any better? The remainder of this book pursues a different set of arguments to those presented in this chapter – i.e. that a more successful approach to reimagining schools in the digital age could involve two principles often absent from discussions of educational technology – (i) working with the 'messy realities' of schools as they currently stand; (ii) seeking to alter the politics of schools technology rather than the technical aspects of schools in the digital age.

The first aspect of this approach recognises that while it may be tempting to denounce the many technological frustrations of the 'industrial-era' school, such thinking sets a dangerous precedent where the interests of technology outweigh all other social, cultural and political concerns. Aside from the presumed requirements of digital technology and the knowledge economy, it could be argued that there are actually few compelling reasons to assume that formal schooling is set to lose significance and status in contemporary society. In fact, the continued persistence of a top-down, hierarchal configuration of formal schooling could be seen as testament to what Steven Kerr identified as the 'historical flexibility of schools as organisations, and of the strong social pressures that militate for preservation of the existing institutional structure' (Kerr 1996, p.7). Thus, whether they like it or not, there is little historical reason for educational technologists to anticipate the imminent institutional decline of the industrial-era school.

Making this point is not intended to convey or endorse a conservative mis-remembering of a 'golden age' of traditional schooling and high standards. On the contrary, retaining the notion of the school as it currently stands can be justified on simple grounds of quality, fairness and democracy. From a social justice perspective alone, the argument could be advanced that educational technologists (however well-intentioned) have no *right* to legitimise calls for the cessation of the publically provided industrial-era school. For all its intuitive appeal, the widespread valorisation of informal learning and the growing 'curricularisation' of children's digitally-based leisure activities (Buckingham 2000) dangerously depoliticises the act of learning – overemphasising the technology-empowered individual learner and distracting attention away from matters of structural inequality and oppression (see Gorman 2007). Conversely, it could be argued that, for all its faults, current forms of mass schooling play a significant role in the improvement of life chances for all young people. Amidst their enthusiasm for new digital technologies, educational technologists should therefore remain mindful that while functioning as instruments of cultural transmission and state power, systems of compulsory formal schooling also fulfil a societal purpose as a valuable source of 'powerful knowledge' and social mobility for all, not just the technologically-privileged few (Young and Muller 2009).

This notion of 'powerful knowledge' is an important one – referring to specialist knowledge that can lead to powerful outcomes, such as new ways of thinking about the world, new abilities to act in the world and so on. On one level this can be seen as the 'high-status learning' that most school-based learning entails, i.e. learning that is directly related to formalised and assessed curricular forms of knowledge. Yet powerful knowledge can also take the form of other knowledge that can be said to lead to meaningful, useful and empowering outcomes for students; i.e. forms of knowledge that 'lead to forms of understandings – power and knowledge of a specifically political kind – that can act as the basis for agency in the real world' (Hassan 2008, p.31). This, as Michael Young (2007) claims, is context independent or 'theoretical knowledge' developed to provide generalisations and makes claims to universality – providing a basis for making judgments and usually, but not solely, associated with the sciences. Young (2007) goes on to make the point that schools should be seen as fulfilling an important democratic role in the transmission of these kinds of knowledge – not 'transmissive' in the sense of one-way, mechanical passive model of rote-learning which is associated with a conservative view of education but acting to enable students to acquire the powerful knowledge that for most of them cannot be acquired at home or in the community. Crucially, this is often knowledge that is not accessible through informal learning elsewhere and can only be transmitted through the school. In the case of such powerful knowledge, it is therefore argued that the school plays a crucial enabling and supporting role – not least if 'learners cannot actually 'construct' their own learning (because, in Foucault's pithy phrase, they cannot know what they do not know) the role of teachers cannot be reduced to that of guide and facilitator rather than as a source of strategies and expertise' (Young and Muller 2009, p.7). If this is the case then it surely would be foolhardy to give up on the notion of the school retaining some form of pedagogic authority and responsibility.

The second focus of this argument refers to the pressing need to concentrate on the politics of schools and digital technologies – i.e. the social, economic, cultural and political arrangements and relationships that surround technology use, rather than the technologies themselves. Indeed, moving the focus of the educational technology debate *away* from digital technology is a crucial first step in this process. Most of the 'problems' of schools in the digital age highlighted in this book are profoundly social in nature – thereby requiring social rather than technical solutions. As Lewis Mumford argued nearly eighty years before, 'the belief that the social dilemmas created by the machine can be solved merely by inventing more machines is today a sign of half-baked thinking which verges close to quackery' (Mumford 1934, p.367). Instead, educational technologists must set about thinking of ways of engineering a new politics of schools technology. The use of digital technology has been shown throughout this book to be linked to a very specific professional-managerial division of labour within schools associated with prevailing concerns of efficiency, employability, audit culture and credentialism. As Anthony Wilhelm reflects, 'social justice and fairness have been lost in the bustle to increase efficiency, often at the expense of equity' (Wilhelm 2004, p.xiii). From this perspective it would seem that there is an urgent need to alter the nature and direction of the educational technology discourse along more democratic and equitable lines – away from the current configuration of neoliberal, libertarian and individualistic forces that currently shape prevailing understandings of what schools technology is, and what it could be.

Conclusions

As Chapter 9 will go on to discuss, it could well be that these changes are best pursued through exploring relatively modest possibilities for subtler 'readjustments' to schools' technological practices that do not disrupt existing institutional structures and boundaries. Instead of giving up on the entire notion of the industrial-era school as it currently exists, it may be more productive and certainly more practical to set about addressing the 'problem' of schools and technology in subtler and less disruptive ways that work *with* rather than *against* the politics of schools and schooling. It could well be more sensible for educational technologists to seek, as Wilhelm (2004, p.xii) puts it, to 'meet people where they are, not where [they] would like them to be'. This present chapter, therefore, concludes on the point that it makes little sense – and is of little practical help – to argue that the only way that digital technologies can be properly used in education is by radically altering the school. As Julian Sefton-Green (2004, p.32) reasons, 'nothing is going to replace the importance of schools in educating the young in our society, nor is any other system likely to be able to play a role in overcoming social inequalities'.

These sentiments are all well and good, but they leave the final chapter of this book facing as many questions as the first eight chapters have so far offered answers. So what does it mean to try to work with (rather than against) the notion of the school as it currently exists? How can academics, educational technologists and other concerned parties pursue a renewal and reshaping of existing education technologies and educational arrangements, rather than attempting to force the rupturing of established ways-of-doing and forcing the development of new tools and new schools? The present chapter has made some progress in identifying some ways forward – not least in arguing that change can be possible if it is accepted that digital technologies 'emerge as the expressions of social forces, personal needs, technical limits, markets and political considerations' (Nye 2007, p.49) and are therefore flexible both in their meanings and design. If digital technologies are approached as social constructions, then opportunities surely exist for educational interests to have a shaping influence on digital technologies. Deciding on what forms these opportunities can take provides the focus for the final chapter of the book.

9 Readjusting schools and schooling in the digital age

Introduction

It should now be clear that schooling in the digital age is a complex, compromised and often contradictory affair. Although schools and schooling may not have been transformed completely, digital technologies certainly lie – for better and for worse – at the heart of the processes and structures of contemporary schooling. It therefore follows that although digital technology is unlikely – at least in the short to medium term – to be the stimulus for any far-reaching revolution in the nature of schools and schooling, this is not to say that technology cannot act as a focus for improvement in the immediate future. This final chapter therefore takes care to avoid either a false optimism or a fatal cynicism – recognising instead 'what might be done, even while remaining fully aware of inauspicious forces of circumstance' (Ball 2007b, p.154). Over the last eight chapters of this book, a strong case has been made for understanding the politics of schools technology. Previous chapters have shown, for example, how the logic of digital technology use in schools currently often follows – in Torin Monahan's words – a set of 'neo-liberal orders' with technology use replicating and sometimes reconfiguring the long-standing articulation between education and wider structures of society, economy, politics and culture. Moreover, it has been argued that schools technology is often best understood in terms of power, inequality, democracy, structure and agency. These are all highly 'inauspicious' and powerful forces of circumstance to work within and against.

Much of the discussion over the past eight chapters has reflected the ways in which digital technology is enrolled into the wider politics of schooling, which in turn is enrolled into the wider politics of society. In this sense, as Levinson and Sadovnik (2002, p.2) observe, 'schools are a Pandora's box for visualising a number of conundrums currently facing liberal democratic societies'. Viewing schools technology through a broad socio-political lens has often steered this book towards focusing on the areas of tension, conflict and problem that envelop technology use in schools. As was reasoned in the book's opening chapters, this has been a necessary step to move beyond the often anodyne and relentlessly optimistic analyses of schools and digital technology that dominate the academic literature on educational technology. Yet it is now worth returning to the warning offered by Jim Wresch at the end of Chapter 3 against over-compensating for the techno-utopian tone of much current thinking about technology and education and entering instead into a 'counter-orthodoxy of pessimism'. As has been asserted throughout, this book has not been written from a wilfully pessimistic perspective. In this sense there is a strong need to now retain a balanced perspective on the future of digital technology, schools and schooling – especially in terms of considering what realistic opportunities for change are on offer.

It should not be concluded from the tone of the preceding chapters that schools are locked forever more in an oppressive, permanent digital hegemony. As is now often acknowledged by sociologists of education, it is unwise to overstate the correspondence between schools and society. Instead, it should be recognised that what takes place inside a school is not determined wholly by economic or social pressures. Not only is 'the message that nothing changes within the deep structure of schooling' a highly conservative one (Brehony 2002, p.187), but it also avoids the crucial questions of who creates the apparently dominant structures and grammars of schooling and most importantly how this situation can be altered or adjusted in any way. There is perhaps value, then, in re-examining the politics of digital technology and schools, and attempting to set about addressing the obvious tensions that exist between the rhetoric and reality of technology use in schools. It therefore makes sense to approach the immediate future of schools and schooling in the digital age with at least a modicum of optimism, and not lose sight of the potentially beneficial aspects and advantages of digital technology use in schools.

As Stephen Ball (2008) has argued, there is some merit in continuing to approach the digital as a 'frontier' in education – i.e. as a space between what is known and what is not yet known. Like all frontiers, then, schooling in the digital age should be seen as a space of opportunities and risks, expectations and unknowns, benefits and threats, winners and losers, new imaginaries and freedoms. As this book has sought to convey, schooling in the digital age is certainly a frontier that is being fought over, and remains a frontier that is worth fighting over. Indeed, a recurring theme throughout this book is how digital technology use in schools is a site of intense ongoing struggle. As Ivor Goodson has observed, 'educational innovation comes to represent a new arena for the contestation of educational goals and purposes, in which stakeholders attempt to redraw the borders of institutional control' (Goodson *et al.* 2002, p.6). In this sense there is certainly value in the increased engagement of critically-minded commentators with the struggle that characterises the social shaping of schools technology. The remainder of this chapter therefore concludes the book's analysis by considering the prospects for future change – in Henri Lefebvre's (1981) words, looking for opportunities to force difference where there is homogeneity, to force unity where there is fragmentation and division, and to encourage equality where there is hierarchy.

This book is not the first to address the daunting question of how best to set about re-engineering the social relations implicit in the organisation of schooling in contemporary capitalist society. As such, inspiration can be drawn from previous critical studies of schools and schooling that have concluded that such macro-level intentions are often best addressed through micro-level means. To take the approach of the activist-educator Michael Apple, for example, it can be argued that there is room to 'deal absolutely seriously with class and the materialities of capitalist relations' while also engaging seriously with the material and ideological realities of schools' day-to-day struggles (Apple 2006, p.680). It is therefore worthwhile considering the opportunities that may exist for altering the politics of schools and digital technology in ways that are perhaps more equitable, effective and centred on the needs of the individuals who operate within the school setting. As Torin Monahan contends:

> actors in school systems do possess agency to negotiate the dominant trajectories being established, and information technologies can be used to catalyse student learning and collective empowerment. Intelligent tactical resistance on the local level is required to conjure these alternate realities into existence and to leverage them against the silencing forces of neoliberal orders (Monahan 2005, p.19).

These sentiments are all laudable and well-intentioned, but what exactly does this 'intelligent tactical resistance' constitute? What options exist for (re)shaping schools in the digital age along more democratic and just lines? How, then, can some of the less dominant and powerful actors in the 'game' of educational technology be empowered to exercise agency in relation to how they encounter digital technology? How can those actors in and around the school setting be supported in the social shaping of schools technology, even though they may never be able to 'exercise complete control over technology any more than we can other parts of culture' (Boody 2001, p.20)? In other words, where are the spaces for the devolution of power in the school – spaces for the democratic use of digital technology use to flourish? What are the opportunities to engender a more critically informed and critically aware debate to take place about education and technology? How may educational interests, priorities and agendas be better represented in the design and development of technological artefacts and practices?

These are, of course, simple questions for which there are no ready simple answers. The remainder of this chapter will therefore consider five areas for the potential readjustment of the politics of school technology use at the macro, meso and micro levels of analysis. Some readers may well consider certain suggestions to be more plausible and workable than other suggestions. Other readers may well consider all the suggestions to be unwieldy and unworkable. Yet what is most important is that serious consideration and debate begins to take place about how the *next* thirty years of digital technology use in schools can more successful than the last thirty years in terms of making a difference to the lives of those who operate within the school setting. It is in this spirit that the following areas of potential change are discussed.

Encouraging an 'open source' approach to schools' procurement of digital technology

The first area for possible change is how school-level actors may be involved more fully in the shaping of the digital technologies that enter, and are then used in, the school setting. These suggestions therefore build upon one of the recurrent themes throughout this book's analysis of the ways in which dominant social interests are reflected and reproduced through technology design – what Andrew Feenberg (2008) refers to as technological hegemony. While the propriety interests of commercial developers and producers of digital technologies may appear all-defining it could be that opportunities exist to disrupt existing arrangements and thereby increase opportunities for school staff and students to intervene and participate in shaping the terms on which technology is used in educational contexts (Hamilton and Feenberg 2005). Such activities would therefore seek to disrupt the 'correspondence' between schools technology and the wider concerns of commercial profit, global economy and political mandate – realising the notion that 'the contents of schooling are not something imposed by society but as arising from within the school' (Brehony 2002, p.181).

One of the most obvious opportunities along these lines is the adoption of open source approaches to technology use within individual school communities. The notion of 'open source' is gaining in popularity across many sectors of society – from its origins in software development to the production of carbonated soft-drinks (Open Cola) and even vehicle production (the OScar). The premise underlying all these examples is that communities of user/developers can take collective responsibility for the ongoing scrutiny and refinement of existing technological artefacts as well as the bespoke development of new technologies. In the terms of interest of this book, therefore, the open source ethos offers a possibility of moving beyond the limited and linear ways in which digital technologies are being currently articulated within schools and, instead, setting about reshaping digital technology around the needs and demands of teachers and students. Thus, instead of altering their practice to fit around the constrained forms of computing offered by off-the-shelf Office software packages, laptop computers and the like, it could be argued that teachers and students are more than capable of assuming control of the means of technological production and developing forms of digital technology for themselves. As Hamilton and Feenberg (2005, p.117) contend, 'there is now wide latitude for faculty intervention and participation in shaping the terms on which [digital technologies] will impact the academic labour process, the division of academic labour, and ownership of intellectual resources'.

The idea of teachers and students eschewing the purchase of commercial IT products altogether and turning instead to the use of open-source software and hardware is gaining momentum among some technologists and more radically minded educators. This support for the open source movement in education stems largely from the increased flexibility and control it is seen to offer to teachers and students, as well as the potential for collaborative creation in the direct shaping of the software being used for learning (Raymond 1998). Thus, as Van De Bunt-Kokhuis (2004, p.269) enthuses, 'open source software like Linux, might serve to democratise [education] and allow greater grassroots input'. Alongside 'legitimate' open-software platforms like the Linux operating system, students and teaching staff have been urged by more radical commentators to also find ways and means of breaking open the 'black box' of proprietary software code and modify commercial software according to their own need and demands, much as 'games modders' do with video games (Kirkpatrick 2004). In this sense, any piece of educational software is a negotiable and malleable text rather than a predefined artefact. These open source and critical procurement arguments therefore seek to engineer a reversal of the currently limited forms of 'built pedagogy' which see non-educationally focused values, ideologies and power relations 'hardwired' into education technologies. By encouraging educators to identify and encourage alternate uses of digital technology that challenge the existing technological hegemony, these calls for open source development and the modification of digital technology pursue a deeper political agenda than just the personalisation of technology-based education.

Such open source, recoding and modification arguments mark an interesting return to the grass-roots 'home-brew' origins of 1970s computing and programming – seeking to disrupt the proprietary power of the corporatised IT industry which is seen by some technologists to have compromised the ideals and purity of the early educational technology movement. Indeed, educational enthusiasm for open source solutions has been growing in prominence of late, fuelled by a desire by some within the educational technology community for a return to the 'hobbyist' era when self-programming of computer code and even self-assembly of computer hardware was the norm. The persuasiveness of this argument also draws provenance from forty years of computer 'counterculture' as typified in the activities of games enthusiasts, amateur software modifiers and the early computer hobbyists, and a prevailing mood among many technologists to reject the increasing commercialisation and homogenisation of digital technology and rediscover the value of developing a deep understanding of how computers and computing can be controlled and creatively shaped (see Aarseth 2005). Thus it is understandable that the open source approach has been heralded as an antidote 'to the currently prevailing dependency on large commercial organisations and proprietary products in the field of education . . . offer[ing] an opportunity for educators, network administrators and software developers to participate in the development of resources appropriate to local needs while developing their own skills' (Carmichael and Honour 2002, p.47).

The appeal of these suggestions should be obvious in light of this book's preceding discussion of schools and technology. Indeed, despite their regulated nature schools are seen by some commentators to be especially appropriate and conducive settings within which the open source ethos can thrive 'around the edges' of the use of proprietary digital resources – not only for reasons of cost reduction. Given the long-established legacy of shared responsibility and 'distributed development' of teaching practice, as well as the culture of peer review, evaluation and regular revision in the light of experience, open source could be argued to fit well with certain established academic cultures within schools. The prospect of reskilling and re-empowering otherwise deskilled teachers or engaging otherwise disengaged learners is also attractive. It is perhaps understandable that many critically-minded commentators are seizing on the use of open source as a panacea to educational technology's woes. Such suggestions fit well an activist ethos, constituting a mild form of insurgency and organised tactical resistance within schools, mobilising teachers and students against structural inertia through a deliberate 'pollution' of commercially constructed digital technology. Open source practices also tap into the socialist ideal of collaboration leading to 'better' outcomes. Richard Sennett (2007), among others, has passionately argued for the benefits of the 'craft approach' that underpins the production of open source software. This celebrates the 'slowing down' of the collaborative production process where technological artefacts are carefully and imaginatively crafted. All of these sentiments have obvious appeal to those seeking to change schools and schools technology along more equitable lines.

Encouraging a 'loosening-up' of schools' uses of digital technology

There are clear rationales for radical educators to promote and valorise such 'open' approaches to controlling the means of technology production in the school setting – based as these ideas are on radically-minded notions of 'indy media', 'hacktivism' and disruptive forms of creation and distribution (Atton 2004). Yet to project unproblematically these uses and ideals into the more regulated and restricted confines of the school (without also tackling the nature of the school itself) is perhaps as unrealistic and utopian a shift as the suggestions for the total technological reconstruction of schools outlined in Chapter 8. It could be argued that it is more realistic to seek out opportunities for change that engage directly with the micro-politics of the school – not least the social, political and cultural practices and sensibilities that surround technology use in schools. In contrast to the arguments outlined in the previous chapter, this focus on engaging with the micro-politics of digital technology use in schools seeks to be more sympathetic to the existing nature, priorities and grammar of the industrial-era school. The emphasis here is certainly not on the redefinition of pedagogy, the reconstitution of the curriculum, or the reformation of assessment procedures to accommodate digital practice. Instead, it could be that less disruptive and more realistic opportunities for change are available. As Tyack and Tobin (1995, p.455) reason, the most fruitful changes to contemporary forms of schooling could well be those that focus on altering and adjusting spaces, places, locations and practices that are not integral to the grammar of schooling – changes that in other words take place 'on the periphery of the system'.

So what form may these 'subtler', 'less disruptive' approaches to the 'peripheries' of digital technology use within schools take? One option worthy of consideration is to view the processes and practices surrounding digital technology use in schools in terms of a 'formality-informality span' – i.e. the varying 'extent and strictness of the social rituals which bind the behaviour of people' in their dealings with technology and each other (Misztal 2000, p.8). As this book's discussion has so far suggested, much digital technology use within the school context could be characterised as being highly formalised – i.e. planned, goal-directed, determinate, procedural and risk-adverse. Conversely, much digital technology use outside of the school setting could be characterised as rather more informalised – i.e. spontaneous, indeterminate, fragmented and risky. As Chapters 6 and 7 discussed in particular, it is not surprising that informal domestic modes of technology use do not transfer easily into highly ritualised and regulated school settings.

It would seem appropriate, therefore, for anyone seeking to improve schools as sites of digital technology use to seek to develop appropriate and undisruptive ways of lessening the gaps between these differing formalities of engagement – in other words to seek to increase, where possible, the sense of informality surrounding technology processes and practices in school. As Barbara Misztal (2000, p.229) describes:

Although the process of formalisation is the dominant trend in modern social life, informality is the essential element in constructing trust relationships and, thus, in any cooperative arrangement aimed at improving the quality of life . . . only a society that achieves an optimal balance between the informality and formality of interactional practices is in a position to create the conditions for cooperation and innovation.

As Misztal infers, rebalancing school technology practices along more informalised lines would be a cooperative process, with members of a school community contributing to conditions within school settings that may relax and de-restrict the expectations, guidelines, rules and regulations that surround technology use. This is not to argue for the de-regulation of school technology use into some form of digital 'free-for-all'. Instead it may be that changes can be made 'around the edges' of the industrial-era school that may permit, or even encourage, a wider range of digital practices than is currently possible, while posing minimal threat to the overall social order and wider vested interests of the school as organisation. As such, serious thought needs to be given to how in-school technology use can be refined in ways that complement rather than challenge all of the dominant institutional priorities of curriculum, assessment, performativity and so on that have been highlighted in earlier chapters.

An initial stage in supporting a meaningful but sympathetic informalisation of in-school digital practice would be to encourage a negotiated governance of technology use among all members of a school community that is predicated around conditions of trust, democracy and co-operation. Within most school settings, these conditions are likely to arise from the encouragement of sustained dialogue between all adults and young people about digital technologies. Indeed, as the ultimate 'end users' of technology in schools it would seem self-evident that more attention is paid to the views, opinions, ideas and expertise of students as well as staff.

Encouraging inter-generational conversations about digital technology within schools could take a number of formal and informal lines. There has been much interest of late in many countries in the notion of facilitating 'learner voice' within schools, i.e. allowing students to enter into dialogue and bring about change with regards to the schools and learning (see Flutter and Ruddock 2004; Rudd *et al.* 2006). The ways and means in which such dialogue can take place are now well-established in many schools, from whole 'school councils' of elected pupil representatives to daily classroom negotiations between individual teachers and their students (see Kirby *et al.* 2003). While current enthusiasm for learner voice relates to many aspects of school life (from encouraging dialogue on the school meals and toilet facilities, to the nature of policies on uniforms and bullying), the topic of digital technology use is not usually seen to be a suitable area for democratic negotiation. This oversight is curious, as in-school technology use could be considered to be a highly appropriate topic for dialogue and debate between schools and students, not least given children and young people's presumed expertise and interest in the area.

Of course, establishing digital technology use as a site for meaningful negotiation and collaboration between all members of the school community cannot be considered to be a straightforward task. In the first instance, the relations surrounding school technology need to be moved on from the 'climates of unease' that presently surround students' and teachers' engagement with technology in many schools, to a set of more cooperative, consensual and civilised relations of trust. While school authorities may see increasing trust in students as a potentially risky step to take, there is little evidence to suggest that students cannot be trusted when it comes to reaching sensible, practical and realistic suggestions for technological change. Indeed, empirical studies suggest that most students have an acute awareness of the educational structures and requirements within which in-school technology use is located, with many children and young people mindful of the risks involved in fully 'opening-up' classroom settings, often sharing institutional concerns over the 'usefulness' and 'safety' of unfettered technology use (Selwyn 2006; Selwyn *et al.* 2010). In this sense there are few reasons to suggest that allowing students to play an increased part in the governance of school technology would result in a slew of unreasonable or unrealistic demands. While the democratisation of other areas of school life may well be more problematic and disruptive, digital technology could well be an area where increased trust in the opinions and actions of students is merited. Indeed, given the affinity and expertise that children and young people are presumed to have with digital technology, in-school technology use is surely a conducive site for the development of 'warmer, more interactive relationships between teachers and students' (Deuchar 2009, p.30).

Assuming that cultures of trust and mutual respect can be developed successfully between schools and students, then what form might negotiations over the informalities of technology use take? Here, it would seem appropriate to focus attention on a subtle 'loosening' of school technology use rather than seeking to force radical or disruptive change. In this sense, inspiration can be drawn from recent debates among academic geographers, planners and architects on the nature of 'loose space' (see Franck and Stevens 2007). As discussed in Chapters 6 and 7, in-school technology use can be conceived as an activity that is situated within a number of spatial, temporal and behavioural boundaries that are the product of continual negotiation and contestation between students, teachers and school authorities. The need remains, therefore, to ask what negotiable boundaries exist within the school setting where 'looser', less formal engagements with digital technologies may take place – in particular where the 'lived space' of the school may be reconfigurable and open to change. As Gulson and Symes (2007) observe, school space consists both of architectural plans and floor layouts, but also results from the practices that take place therein. In this manner, school spaces are constantly subject to redesign and reformation: 'educational spaces [are] fluid and ephemeral, being ever re-written and re-inscribed, formed and deformed as each pedagogic moment is transformed into another and as they are acted out in time' (Gulson and Symes 2007, p.105).

Serious thought therefore needs to be given to identifying the spaces within the school setting that may easily be loosened and reformed through the informal uses of digital technologies. When considering such issues in relation to the general built environment, geographers and planners often turn for inspiration to the loose qualities of (quasi) public spaces such as parks, plazas and public squares, as well as more liminal and derelict spaces such as underpasses and side-alleys that are overlooked or disregarded in formal planning processes. Such spaces can be described as allowing people to pursue a variety of spontaneous or serendipitous activities often not originally intended for these locations (Franck and Stevens 2007). Of course, the organisational environment of the school is a relatively 'tight' space in contrast to these (quasi) public spaces, but they illustrate the general point that looseness can, and will, arise in even the tightest and most formalised of spaces – not least through the activities and actions of individuals that take place without official permission and sanction. Indeed, many of the digital practices and actions most likely to generate looseness may not appear to be especially productive or reproductive, as is the case with the archetypal 'loose' acts of playing or simply 'hanging out'. Yet even the loosest of activities should play a vital role in providing a necessary counterbalance to tighter and more formal arrangements elsewhere. In this sense, permitting a 'loose use' of digital technology in some areas of the school setting should be seen as a necessary element of the successful formal use of technology in other areas. Thus, sustained and ongoing negotiations between students, teachers and administrators over what is (and what is not) permissible within the school space should be seen as a vital element of the ongoing development of technology use within the school.

Many of these changes in behaviour would be associated with a readjustment of the places, spaces and times where digital technologies may be engaged with within the school structure – in particular subtle adjustments 'around the edges' of the current organisation of time and space within schools. In seeking to (re)use the environments that already exist in schools rather than build new environments that are somehow more technology-friendly, it would seem appropriate to concentrate on the times and spaces that are connected less directly to the formal bureaucratic concerns of the school. In this spirit, school communities could explore where informal digital technology practices may be encouraged in already 'slack times' of the school day such as lunchtimes, free times before and after school, and in-between lessons. Similar explorations could consider the 'loose spaces' within the physical environment of schools that have no prescribed formal pedagogic function, such as playgrounds, dining halls, atria and corridors. It may also be that technology use could be encouraged in less obvious 'found spaces' within the school – i.e. spill over, liminal or 'niche' spaces such as stairwells, bicycle sheds and other hidden spaces of the school (Rivlin 2007). In short, negotiations could be held over the propagation of various 'technological public commons' within the wider bounded nature of the school, 'where definitions and expectations are less exclusive and more fluid, where there is greater accessibility and freedom of choice for people to purpose a variety of activities' (Franck and Stevens 2007, p. 3).

The development of such 'breathing spaces' for informalised modes of digital technology use could be negotiated without excessive disruption to the wider organisational structures and relationships that constitute the 'school' and 'schooling'. For instance, negotiations could be encouraged between students and schools regarding the formalised rules, regulations, structures and sanctions that currently shape most forms of technology engagement within schools – ranging from when and where specific technologies can be used, to the form of online content that can be accessed. The rules, regulations and other structures of control that surround these aspects of technology use would seem to be especially appropriate areas for negotiation between all members of the school community, exploring the leeway that exists for rules to be relaxed or even subverted at certain times with impunity. The overall aim here would be – where possible – to make technology use in schools more of a self-governing process that is acceptable both to students and teachers.

In a similar vein, attention could also be given to the negotiated loosening of the nature and scope of technology-based behaviours that are tolerated within schools. From this perspective there may well be opportunities to expand the tacit permission for digital activities and practices not necessarily associated with the formal 'business' of schooling, but nevertheless may provide a balance to more formalised pedagogic and administrative uses of technology. These 'other' activities could include technology-based play and entertainment, informal communication and interaction with others, expressive activities and even the practices of simply 'hanging out' and 'messing around' with digital technologies. While not immediately productive, such activities nevertheless constitute an integral element of participating with digital technology. Thus increased emphasis could be placed on school communities reconsidering their stance towards students' seemingly inconsequential, risky or transgressive technology-based activities highlighted towards the end of Chapter 7 that at present many schools attempt to suppress.

There are obvious parallels in these arguments with wider calls from educational commentators regarding the possibilities for the development of democratic schools and schooling, and the general 'need for a more participative approach to school organisation' (Deuchar 2009, p.23). Philip Woods (2005) writes, for example, of the benefits of developing 'free spaces' and 'independent zones' within the school where students and staff can suspend their usual hierarchical relationships – if only for a brief period – and be allowed to be free, creative agents. Similarly, Michael Fielding (2009) talks of the benefits of engineering spaces for 'restless encounters' within the school day, where students and staff can come to re-assess their relationships with each other. It could well be that similar opportunities exist for a reshaping of digital technology use along more inclusive and more expansive lines of 'democratic experimentalism', where major, long-term change can be achieved within schools through cumulative, piecemeal reforms (see Fielding and Moss 2010).

Of course, adjusting school settings in any of these ways would be dependent on significant shifts in the organisational cultures of schools. It is therefore important to expect any refinements and changes to school technology use to be incremental and gradual (Sørensen *et al.* 2007). As has already been acknowledged, while no public space could be considered to be absolutely free, the school should be seen as a particularly tight institutional setting, 'where rules, meanings and physical structure are explicit and relatively fixed' (Franck and Stevens 2007, p. 26). Thus all of the instances of possible 'looseness' described above should be seen in a dialectic rather than an absolute sense, where loosenings and tightenings of digital technology use within a school setting will develop continually in relation to the other. While it would be naïve to assume that realising these increased flexibilities would be easy, achieving some shifts in understandings of what is considered acceptable, appropriate and permissible with technology should be possible in even the most tightly regulated and bounded of school settings.

Toward the promotion of a critical digital literacy in schools

Advancing these suggestions for the negotiated adjustment of school technology use is certainly not intended to propose a complete relaxation of the formal aspects of school organisation and provision. Indeed, it should be remembered that the formal provision of schooling could be seen to provide a relative certainty, homogeneity and order to technology use, often providing students with opportunities to use digital technologies in ways that they may otherwise not have. Thus while calling for increased freedoms from rule-bound conduct, it is important to acknowledge that schools can play a valuable authoritative role in educating, informing and directing the activities of children and young people – in particular providing an environment where the social contexts surrounding digital technology use allow students to be more informed about their choices than they may otherwise be. From this perspective further thought could also be given to how schools go about helping students and teachers learn *about* (as opposed to learn *with*) digital technologies. As discussions throughout this book have indicated, the actual implementation of digital technologies in schools more often than not involves either the learning of curriculum content through the use of computers and the internet, or else the training of students to develop the technical skills required to use these technologies – what can be seen as 'functional' media literacy. At very few points are students given the prolonged opportunity to think about and reflect upon the role of digital technology itself in their learning, or indeed their everyday lives. Thus there is a growing contention among some commentators that schools could better support students to develop forms of 'critical' digital literacy – i.e. 'cultivat[ing] the habit of uncovering and critiquing both [students'] own constructed and contingent experiences and resulting worldviews, particularly those that influence society's relation with technology' (Duffelmeyer 2001, p.243).

In this sense, growing numbers of media educators are beginning to argue that digital technologies need to be introduced to students within their schools in a questioning and challenging rather than passively accepting manner – therefore introducing 'a reflective and critical discourse to an increasingly normalised and controlled environment' (Muffoletto 2001, p.4). While the notion of instilling critical thinking about computers in students has almost as long a heritage as educational computing itself, in practice the development of students' critical digital literacy in schools has remained a peripheral educational concern, overshadowed by the imperative to develop 'hands-on' skills and aptitudes. Of course, technology is not the only societal issue that has been felt to merit critical reflection and scrutiny within schools. The 1970s and 1980s saw sustained calls for schools to foster a 'public understanding of science' among students through the integration of a 'science-technology-society' approach into science education (e.g. Royal Society 1985; Power 1987). Similarly, the needs for schools to encourage critical understanding of economics and personal finance have also been called for as financial fortunes fluctuate around the world. Although differing in substantive focus, the tenor of all these debates follows a similar form. In the case of science education, for example, proponents of the public understanding of science have long argued for education that 'helps citizens make informed decisions [about science and technology], particularly those which involve social responsibility' (Power 1987, p.5) and therefore informs everyday thinking about scientific issues (Ratcliffe and Grace 2003).

Rather than declining in relevance, it could be argued that there is a heightened imperative for the provision of a critical digital literacy in twenty-first century school curricula. For example, Jane Kenway and Elizabeth Bullen (2005) reason that there is now a pressing need for spaces to be provided within school curricula for students to develop a sense of critical agency that goes beyond that made available by consumer–media culture as experienced outside of the classroom (see also Steinberg and Kincheloe 1997). These authors talk of giving students the time to 'look between the scenes' of the technological cultures they live within, and consider the many social, ethical and political issues which surround technology consumption and use. The school can therefore be re-appropriated as a space to help young people reach a better understanding of the processes and power relations involved in 'why they want what they want' (Walkerdine 1991, p.89) and even, it could be argued, 'why they get what they get'. As Bromley and Shutkin (1998, p.1) contend:

> we think it crucial that our students develop the habit of examining what conventionally goes unexamined and unchallenged, so as to foreground and problematise the taken-for-granted workings of power; we wish them to ask what interests shape technology and its use, what meanings are attached to it, who benefits from it, in what ways, and who does not.

These arguments have featured prominently in the work of the UK media educator David Buckingham, who has long called for schools to help children and young people learn about media in more critical and empowered ways. In his recent writing, Buckingham (2007) proposes a revitalisation of media education within the contemporary school curriculum, reasoning that there needs to be a reworking of curricular definitions of literacy beyond the medium of print to also include questions such as who controls the content of digital media and how these new media represent the world. Thus schools are urged to 'place a central emphasis on developing children's critical and creative abilities with regards to new media', and promote 'a form of 'digital media literacy' as a basic educational entitlement' (Buckingham 2007, p.144). In light of young people's current media practices Buckingham suggests that schools could help students, for instance, to develop a critical internet literacy or a critical computer games literacy which could be supported by the 'informed intervention' and 'collaboration' of teachers and peers. As with Kenway and Bullen's thesis, at the heart of these proposals is the re-imagining of the school along modernist lines as 'a key public sphere' (Buckingham 2007, p.182), providing a managed 'forum for open public communication and critical debate' and occupying a neutral and benign nexus 'between the citizen and the operations of the market and the state'.

Such arguments are not only concerned with supporting students to become more effective and 'savvy' consumers of technology, but are also intended to establish the school as a supporting and guiding presence that can help young people develop into effective digital age citizens. In this way, the notion of a school-based critical digital literacy feeds into wider contemporary concerns over the need for all technology users to be able to understand the coded mechanics of how digital tools and applications actually work rather than merely understanding what they are programmed to do. For writers such as Kirkpatrick (2004), for example, a 'deep understanding' of digital technology is seen to be a crucial element of an individual's empowerment, agency and equal citizenship in the digital age. Conversely, exclusion from such understanding is seen as leading to an almost inevitable marginalisation if not disenfranchisement. Thus it can be argued strongly that developing and encouraging a critically reflexive engagement with digital technology within the relative neutrality of the school environment makes good sense for students as well as their teachers. As Duffelmeyer (2001, p.242) contends:

> Educators absolutely must begin to demand more intellectualism and ruthless questioning from teachers and students alike. A productive and responsible marriage of digital technology and education is possible, if educators can develop this necessary agency in themselves and their students.

A number of areas can be suggested where there are clear and practical opportunities for schools to support young technology users in this way. Within the context of in-class technology use, for example, teachers could play important roles in managing students' experiences of using digital technologies and supporting their attempts to apprehend the structures and meanings of digitally-based information (Ljoså 1998). Teachers could assume joint responsibility with their students for the goals and methods of interactions with digital technology – supporting self-directed activities and providing the initial impetus for collaborative activities that underpin digital scholarship (Rosenblum 2008). Both these suggestions highlight the valuable authoritative role that teachers can play in educating, informing, managing and directing the technological activities of students. Kennedy *et al.* (2008, p.490) suggest, for example, that teachers and school authorities should seek to provide 'appropriate fora in which students can engage meaningfully with challenges and issues associated with using emerging technologies in [educational] contexts' – not least issues such as authenticity, academic integrity, shifting academic authority and the changing nature of public and private (see Chang *et al.* 2008; Sefton-Green *et al.* 2009). There may also be scope to encourage increased awareness, discussion and challenging of the more overtly political and disciplinary uses of technologies within schools. As Andrew Hope (2009, p.15) reasons, 'the ethics underlying such practices need to be more explicitly understood, lest individuals remain unaware while values embedded in the educational system start to change, possibly for the worse.'

Towards a critical public awareness of schools and digital technology

Having made the case for the promotion and promulgation of a 'critical digital literacy' among students and teachers this logic could – and should – be extended to the other end-users, stakeholders and interested parties identified in Chapters 4 and 5. In other words, critical understanding and awareness could also be fostered among the general publics of schools technology. As has been highlighted throughout the last eight chapters of this book, popular and professional views of schools and digital technology range from the wildly enthusiastic to the defiantly disinterested. More often than not, however, active discussion of educational technology has tended to be captured by what Charlie Gere terms the 'soothsayers of the digital age' – i.e. 'futurologists, futurists and techno-utopians whose message of combined technological and social progress charms us into complacency' (Gere 2008, p.20). Very rarely is schools technology the focus for intense public scrutiny, debate or controversy – despite the high levels of public funding directed towards it. More often than not, the use of digital technology in schools is accepted by parents, employers and the wider population as an inherently 'good thing' that merits little, if any, sustained thought or attention.

Of course, the trivialisation of technological implementation is not limited to education (see Ellul 1984), yet schools technology seems especially prone to be thought about in neutral terms of 'a de-politicised conformity, effectively limiting our goals and actions only to those realisable within the framework of capitalism' (Paterson 2006, p.27). While schools technology may be a relatively trivial matter for public debate and discussion in comparison to issues such as nuclear disarmament, climate change or bio-technology, contemporary society would surely benefit from an improved, expanded public understanding of education and technology. In particular there is a clear need to re-politicise the debate over technology and education – refocusing discussion away from the presumed transformation of social relations and towards more realistic readings of the technological that 'recover a language of and for education articulated in terms of ethics, moral obligations and values' (Ball 2007a, p.191). In short, concerted efforts are required to make schools technology use what Fine and Weis (2003) term 'a scene of extraordinary conversation' rather than a 'scene of silencing'.

Following this line of reasoning, efforts could be made to 'capture' the common-sense understandings that surround schools and technology. As Antonio Gramsci observed, those responsible for the entrenchment of hegemony are well versed at attaching their positions to other people's good sense. Crucially, then, the struggle for common-sense should be seen as being absolutely essential if public understandings of schools and schooling in the digital age are to take on more critical and socially-focused tones. In these terms, adding a critical perspective to prevailing common-sense public understandings of schools and technology would appear a vital initial step in engineering counter-hegemonic practice. As Jodi Dean reasons:

> publicity is the solution to the problem of instrumental reason: the system shouldn't run things, people should, and the way they should do this is by communicating and discussing in a free and open manner. People have to take things into their own hands, politicise the processes of decision-making and stop allowing scientific and technocratic imperatives to organise all of social life (Dean 2002, p.108).

In this sense there is a clear need to identify spaces where it is possible to engage in practices that challenge and even disrupt current orthodoxies and common-sense understandings of technology and schools. This may well involve a consensual rather than conflicting approach to engaging with all sectors of the educational technology community – from parents and employers to IT firms, neo-conservative groups, and technology advocates. This need for an inclusive ongoing debate stems from the general lack of *any* debate over education and technology at present. It can be argued that educational technology is too important a topic to be left to elected members of legislatures or specialist interest groups. Neither can markets alone be left to deal with the deeply political questions surrounding schools' use of digital technology. Instead, 'before citizens can think well about such matters they need information . . . open debate and the exchange of ideas' (Nye 2007, p.148), all leading to the emergence of a 'new performative counter-politics' (Amin and Thrift 2005, p.235).

What form and focus, then, could a 'performative counter-politics' of schools technology take? As has been highlighted throughout this book, there is a range of issues that need to be considered and discussed. Above all, any discussion of schools and schooling in the digital age should include consideration of issues such as disconnection, disempowerment, inequality, commercialisation, bureaucracy, power, control and regulation. Central to these conversations are questions of what human subjects, knowledges and societies are schools are intended to produce. For instance, if schools exist to produce empowered, questioning, lively citizens then surely empowered, questioning, lively forms of digital technology use are required in schools? A sustained debate also needs to take place over the meaning of public service values in relation to schools in the digital age, not least the articulation between schools technology and wider economic and wider societal requirements. As discussed in Chapter 4, many people's understandings of schools technology are so far embedded in the discourse of the knowledge economy that alternatives are often overlooked or even discounted as irrational or illogical. Although the notion of the knowledge economy has become so influential that it has become accepted as the status of a hegemonic truth, it nevertheless denies the possibilities of alternative forms of economy that exist and could just as easily be aligned with the use of digital technology in school – not least the gift economy, the libidinal economy or the survival economy (see Kenway *et al.* 2006). These economic models present alternative forms of educational technology that could be implemented in schools – raising questions, for example, of whether digital technology has such benefits that should necessitate giving it away (rather than selling it for commercial gain), or whether technologies should be used to privilege and maintain knowledges that are otherwise marginalised under the knowledge economy – e.g. arts instead of commerce, indigenous rather than global knowledges. In all these instances, it is clear how alternate constructions of what schools technology is and what roles is may play are possible given the favourable conditions for such discussions to take place.

These are all extreme examples of the issues that could be discussed as part of a wider (and undoubtedly often more mundane) 'consciousness-raising' regarding schools and schooling in the digital age. Before such discussions can take place there needs to be considerable expansion of public interest in schools technology. As Chapter 8's analogy of educational technology as a 'game' implied, at the moment it appears that few people are overly concerned with the plight of schools technology beyond a general feeling that digital tools and applications are a desirable feature of contemporary society. Despite the increased tendency of parents to exert their 'consumer rights' in other areas of education, there is often a distinct agnosticism and apathy among the general public when it comes to the precise nature of the digital technology use that takes place in schools. Thus perhaps the most important change that could be sought is the (re)formation of new coalitions of interested and engaged stakeholders from beyond the dominant producer interests of the current educational technology complex as outlined in Chapters 4 and 5.

The first stage in enabling an enhanced critical public awareness would be encouraging as many people as possible to get involved in the shaping of schools technology through the development and the stimulation of a democratised discourse about the capabilities and purpose of digital technology in schools. As William Davies (2005, p.2) has argued, 'we have to keep alive a belief that politics can determine what sort of digitally-enabled society we live in, and the extent to which we pursue change at all'. This would involve recapturing the schools technology agenda from the relatively closed educational technology complex highlighted in Chapters 4 and 5 and creating and supporting informed public discourse on such matters as internet safety, the quality of internet based learning and so-forth. Just as there are growing calls for the development of public understanding of science and public understanding of the past given the increasing importance of science and history in people's lives, so too should there be increased public engagement with issues surrounding schools and technology.

Towards a rigorous scholarship of schools and digital technology

The obvious interest group that has remained as yet absent from these suggestions for improving societal understanding of schools technology is the academic educational technology community – i.e. those responsible for the plethora of academic writing, research and commentary that is produced annually on schools, schooling and digital technology. As has been argued from the outset of this book, the study of schools and technology is a rather underpowered, and some would argued impoverished, area of academic educational scholarship (which itself could be said to be a rather impoverished area of social science research). The critical studies of schools and digital technologies drawn upon in the latter chapters of this book to illustrate the complexities of schooling in the digital age are few and far between. For every rich ethnographic study of classroom struggles over technology, there are literally thousands of anodyne, a-critical and occasionally substandard pieces of 'research' pertaining to 'prove' some 'impact' or other that can be associated with digital technology. As was implied in Chapter 3, educational technology scholarship is in need of a more critical, realistic and reasoned intellectual base from which to operate. In this sense, there is clear scope to improve and expand the academic questions that are asked of schools and digital technology – as well as improving and expanding the people who ask these questions and the ways that these questions are asked.

In terms of the first of these issues, there is clearly a need for further academic writing and research that focuses on the present realities rather than future possibilities of technology-based education. As discussed in Chapter 3, the topic of technology use in schools understandably invites a forward-looking 'state-of-the-art' perspective. As latter chapters of this book have shown, the social importance of a forward-looking perspective on technology and schools is, at best, limited. As David Nye acknowledges, 'all technological predictions and forecasts are in essence little narratives about the future. They are not full-scale narratives of utopia, but they are usually presented as stories about a better world to come' (Nye 2007, p.35). In the face of the continuing excitement within the academic literature over the perennially new dynamics of digital education there is clearly a need to inject educational technology scholarship with an enhanced 'commitment to the here and now, the empirical and the demonstratable' (Cavanagh 2007, p.7). This reiterates Beer and Burrow's (2007, 1.1) plea for academic accounts of the digital that concentrate on developing 'thick' descriptive accounts of the present uses of technologies in situ:

> At a time of rapid socio-cultural change a renewed emphasis on good – critical, distinctive and thick – sociological descriptions of emergent digital phenomena, ahead of any headlong rush into analytics, seems to us to be a sensible idea. We need to understand some of the basic parameters of our new digital objects of sociological study before we can satisfactorily locate them within any broader frames of theoretical reference.

One aspect of these 'thick' accounts is a rigorous analysis of how particular inequalities are reproduced or perhaps challenged in schools through technology – an issue that has only been touched upon in this book. As was suggested in Chapter 7, the use of digital technology in schools is often implicated with the sorting and stratification of social groups and individuals in terms of gender, race, social class and so on. Yet more research is certainly required that addresses the changing dynamics of digital technology use in schools along these lines. As Kahn and Kellner (2007) observe, more questions need to be asked of who is being excluded and why, as well as to what extent schools technology is simply serving to reproduce existing inequalities, or to what extent new forms of stratification are apparent.

Aside from a focus on the inequalities of the 'here and now', there is undoubtedly room for further academic critiques of school technology that offer culturally plausible suggestions as to how current inequalities and hegemonies may be countered, and how digital technology use in schools may be reshaped along fairer and more equitable lines. This suggests a sociology of schools technology that builds upon Ann Oakley's (2000) notion of social science research that is democratic, interventionist and emancipatory. In particular there is a need to first detail and then test the opportunities available to teachers, learners and other interested parties to take advantage of the inherently political processes of technology production and use in schools. Academic researchers and writers can identify spaces where opportunities exist to resist, disrupt and alter the technology-based reproduction of the 'power differential that runs through capitalist society' (Kirkpatrick 2004, p.10). In this sense there is an ongoing need for academic analyses that test and extend the ideas and issues raised in this book – not least highlighting the tensions and liminal spaces where digital technologies can be challenged and reconfigured in school settings.

In terms of how research questions are asked and analyses constructed of schools and technology, developing this clarity of questioning would necessitate a variety of appropriate yet imaginative methodological approaches. Researchers working in the area of education and technology could reconsider not only the ways in which they formulate research questions, but also the methods they choose to collect and analyse data to address these questions. In particular, there is a need to take a broad approach to the methodology of technology research. While many research approaches are available, the field of educational technology has tended towards a methodological conservativism based around observational case studies, action research and limited forms of interviewing (see McDougall *et al.* 2009). Unlike other areas of social science research, educational technology is subject to far fewer studies that utilise properly ethnographic and visually-informed methods, or large-scale cross sectional survey research and randomised-controlled-trials. There is also an obvious need for macro-studies and meta-analyses of schools and technology – thereby moving the field away from the preference for studies that are 'determinedly local, small-scale and particular' (Webster 2005, p.453). Yet schools technology is not exclusively a matter for micro-investigation or macro-investigation – rather a combination of both. There is clear scope for education researchers to adopt a more expansive and imaginative approach to investigating schools and digital technology, utilising the methods of data collection and analysis that best fit their research questions rather than personal convenience or habit.

This increased clarity of questioning and methodology would contribute greatly to the establishment of a body of educational technology scholarship which could be considered 'fit for purpose'. Yet in seeking to increase the quality of debate and inquiry in the field it is perhaps necessary for researchers and writers to also reflect upon what the purposes of their endeavours actually are – i.e. why questions are being asked of schools and digital technology. In particular, there is a need to challenge the underlying personal and political intentions of those writers and researchers who have long been working in the field and have come to assume leading roles within the academic educational technology 'community'. In raising these issues it is important to recognise, of course, that all social researchers will assume that they are 'doing good works or creating useful knowledge' (Scheurich 1997, p.1). Yet few educational technologists could deny that their identification of research topics, formulation of questions and choice of methods of study were not shaped by personal interests and agendas.

In this sense it could be argued that the current concerns and grades of educational technology scholarship have been restricted by a particular set of intellectual and professional agendas which have left much research and writing imbued with a distinct techno-centric bias. An implicit agenda of many researchers has been to demonstrate the 'effectiveness' of education technologies and to prove that technology 'works' – engendering a corresponding reluctance to address some of the more problematic and 'untidy' issues highlighted throughout this book. For some researchers this belief in the power of technology stems from professional experience, personal interest or even passion for their own new media use or pedagogical preferences. Yet however motivated, it should be argued that it is not the role of education researchers to 'sell' the latest technologies to the wider education community. There is therefore a need to move research agendas away from overtly pro-technology or anti-school stances, and towards producing more disinterested analyses that seek to reconcile schooling and technology. Instead of advocating de-schooling perspectives on technology, the role of education research should be to reconcile the currently de-contextualised debate over new digital education with the messy realities of the use of these technologies in practice.

Conclusions

While the arguments developed throughout the nine chapters of this book have striven to be comprehensive and all-encompassing, it is important to remain mindful of the gaps, silences and deficiencies of the picture that has been painted. The book has developed what will undoubtedly be seen by some readers as an 'excessive' argument – a phrase that should be seen in Henri Lefebvre's (1981, p.26) words as denoting an argument that is 'hypercritical, but not meaningless'. Yet it could be argued that any excess in this book's analysis stems from the necessity to counter the excessive mainstream eulogising of digital technology in education. Perhaps a more valid criticism that can be levelled at the book is that its take on schooling in the digital age has been an especially privileged Western-centric one – focusing largely on the school systems of the (over)developed world and therefore addressing issues that are of marginal interest to the majority of the world's population who experience entrenched political repression and poverty. It should be recognised that much of this book remains irrelevant to the 1.3 billion people in the world who exist on less than a dollar a day, and for whom any kind of schooling is a privilege rather than a problem.

These limitations notwithstanding, this book has attempted to advance a modest case for exploring ways of 'loosening up' the structures and social relations that surround schools technology. In particular, the case has been made throughout this concluding chapter for changing the nature and the content of the educational conversations that surround digital technology use, and giving serious and sustained consideration to the socio-political nature of schools and schooling in the digital age. As such the book has perhaps finished with more questions than it has provided answers – not least the underlying question of how feasible any of the changes outlined in this last chapter with be to achieve in practice. Indeed, having read this book, one could be forgiven for concluding resignedly that the ways in which digital technologies are used in schools are, in the final analysis, simply endemic to the neo-liberal logic of capitalist society. Schools technology could well be dismissed simply as just another example of the constrained and 'cynical' application of technology in contemporary society. If this is so, then nothing less than a wholesale re-engineering of the dominant capitalist economic system and its incentives would achieve any meaningful and lasting change. While this is an argument that many readers of this book may well have some sympathy for, it is an unhelpful basis for those seeking to re-engineer educational technology along more equitable and benevolent lines. It is perhaps more helpful to at least attempt to seek ways of working with – rather than railing against – the prevailing political, economic, social, cultural and historical conditions that schools technology is located within. As Ash Amin and Nigel Thrift conclude, it is no longer acceptable to simply decry the neo-liberal mis-shaping of technology and society without also reaching suggestions for working with this situation:

> capitalism is no longer an unambiguously easy target to attack. Capitalism comes in many varieties, some of which are undoubtedly cruel and exploitative, while others in the Left have managed to secure compromises that have improved the lives of many (Amin and Thrift 2007, p.113).

With these thoughts in mind, this book has itself concluded with at least a degree of optimism for the future of schools and schooling as the twenty-first century advances. It may well be that increased questioning and challenging of the politics of schools technology offers the best basis from which to enable a more equitable reconstruction of digital technology use in school settings. Leveraging such changes will, of course, be a monumental task. It is likely that any specific improvements to schools technology will be incremental and often imperceptible in and of themselves. Yet the sooner that the non-technological issues surrounding schools technology are engaged with in a sustained and serious manner then the sooner that the undoubted potential of digital technologies for schools and schooling can be realised.

References

Aarseth, E. (2005) 'Game studies: what is it good for?' *The International Digital Media and Arts Association Journal* 2, 1, pp.3–7.

Abbott, C. and Alder, W. (2009) 'Social networking and schools: early responses and implications for practice' in Hatzipanagos, S. and Warburton, S. (eds.) *Handbook of Research on Social Software and Developing Community Ontologies,* Hershey PA, IGI Global.

Amin, A. and Thrift, N. (2005) 'What's Left? Just the future', *Antipode*, 37, pp.220-238.

—— (2007) 'On being political', *Transactions of the Institute of British Geographers*, 32, pp.112–115.

Angrist, J. and Lavy, V. (2002) 'New evidence on classroom computers and pupil learning', *The Economic Journal*, 112, pp.735–765.

Angus, L. (1993) 'The sociology of school effectiveness', *British Journal of Sociology of Education*, 14, 3, pp. 333–345.

Apple, M. (1979) *Ideology and Curriculum*, London: Routledge & Kegan Paul.

—— (1986) 'National reports and the construction of inequality', *British Journal of Sociology of Education*, 7, 2, pp.171–190.

—— (1992) 'Educational reform and educational crisis', *Journal of Research in Science Teaching* 29, 8, pp.779–789.

—— (1994) 'Computers and the deskilling of teaching', *CPSR Newsletter*, 12, 2, pp.3–5.

—— (2002) 'Is the new technology part of the problem or part of the solution in education?' in Darder, A., Baltodano, M. and Torres, R. (eds.) *The Critical Pedagogy Reader*, London: Routledge.

—— (2004) 'Are we wasting money on computers in schools?' *Educational Policy*, 18, 3, pp.513–522.

—— (2006) *Educating the 'Right' Way: Markets, Standards, God, and Inequality*, London: Routledge.

Apple, M. and Jungck, S. (1990) 'You don't have to be a teacher to teach this unit: teaching, technology, and gender in the classroom', *American Educational Research Journal*, 27, 2, pp.227–251.

Arum, R. and Beattie, I. (2000) 'Introduction: the structure of schooling' in Arum, R. and Beattie, I. (eds.) *The Structure of Schooling: Readings in the Sociology of Education*, New York: McGraw Hill.

Atton, C. (2004) *An Alternative Internet*, Edinburgh: Edinburgh University Press.

Austin, R. and Anderson, J. (2008) *E-schooling: Global Messages from a Small Island*, London: Routledge.

Ball, S. (1987) *The Micro-Politics of the School: Towards a Theory of School Organisation*, London: Routledge.

—— (1993) 'What is policy? Texts, trajectories and toolboxes', *Discourse: Studies in the Cultural Politics of Education*, 13, 2, pp.10–17.

—— (1998) 'Big policies/small world: an introduction to international perspectives in education policy', *Comparative Education* 34, 2, pp.119–130.

—— (2003) 'The teacher's soul and the terrors of performativity', *Journal of Education Policy*, 18, 2, pp.215–228.

—— (2007a) *Education Plc: Understanding Private Sector Participation in Public Sector Education*, London: Routledge.

—— (2007b) 'Reading Michael Apple: the sociological imagination at work', *Theory and Research in Education*, 5, 2, pp.153–159.

—— (2008) 'The use of technologies in education and the promotion of social inclusion: discussant comments' presentation to '*Education, Equality and Social Justice in Brazil, India, South Africa and UK*' symposium, Campo Grande, Brazil, 24 April.

Ball, S. and Lacey, C. (1984) 'Subject disciplines as the opportunity for group action: a measured critique of subject subcultures' in Hargreaves, A. and Woods, P. (eds.) *Classrooms and Staffrooms: The Sociology of Teachers and Teaching*, Milton Keynes: Open University Press.

Barker, R. and Gardiner, J. (2007) *Focus on the Digital Age: E-learning and E-skills*, London: National Statistics.

Barrera-Osorio, F. and Linden, L. (2009) *The Use and Misuse of Computers in Education: Evidence from a Randomised Experiment in Colombia*. World Bank Policy Research Working Paper, Washington DC: World Bank.

Barton, L. and Walker, S. (1985) *Education and Social Change*, London: Routledge.

Bassett, C. (2006) 'Cultural studies and new media' in Hall, G. and Birchall, C. (eds.) *New Cultural Studies: Adventures in Theory*, Edinburgh: Edinburgh University Press.

Bauman, Z. (2005) *Liquid Life,* Cambridge: Polity.

BBC News (2008) 'Dell joins cut-down laptop market', *BBC News Online*, 29 May.

—— (2009) 'Slump in school computer lessons' *BBC News Online*, 3 March.

Beck, U. and Beck-Gernsheim, E. (2002) *Individualisation*, London: Sage.

Becker, H. (2000) 'Findings from the teaching, learning and computing survey' in *Proceedings of the 2000 State Educational Technology Conference*, Washington DC, Council of Chief State School Officers.

Beer, D. and Burrows, R. (2007) 'Sociology of and in web 2.0: some initial considerations' *Sociological Research Online*, 12, 5, [www.socresonline.org.uk/12/5/17.html]

Behr, R. (2009) 'The good and the bad of digital dependency', *The Observer*, 22 February, Review supplement, p.22.

Bennet, A. and Bennet, D. (2008) 'E-learning as energetic learning', *VINE: The Journal of Information and Knowledge Management Systems* 38, 2, pp.206–220.

Bennett, R. (1995) 'School-business links: clarifying objectives and processes', *Policy Studies*, 16, 1, pp.23–48

Bennett, S., Maton, K. and Kervin, L. (2008) 'The 'digital natives' debate', *British Journal of Educational Technology*, 39, 5, pp.775–786.

Bentley, T. (2000) 'Learning beyond the classroom', *Educational Management, Administration and Leadership*, 28, pp.353–364.

Berker, T., Hartmann, M., Punie, Y. and Ward, K. (2006) *Domestication of Media and Technology*, Buckingham: Open University Press.

BESA (2009) *Information and Communication Technology in UK State Schools*, London: British Educational Suppliers Association.

Beynon, J. and Mackay, H. (1992) *Technological Literacy and the Curriculum*, London: Routledge.

Bigum, C. and Kenway, J. (1998) 'New information technologies and the ambiguous future of schooling: some possible scenarios' in Hargreaves, A., Lieberman, A. and Fullan, M. (eds.) *International Handbook of Educational Change*, Berlin: Springer.

Bigum, C. and Rowan, L. (2008) 'Landscaping on shifting ground: teacher education in a digitally transforming world', *Asia-Pacific Journal of Teacher Education*, 36, 3, pp.245–255.

Bijker, W. (1995) *Of Bicycles, Bakelites and Bulbs*, Cambridge MA: MIT Press.

Bijker, W., Hughes, T. and Pinch, T. [eds.] (1987) *The Social Construction of Technological Systems: New Directions in the Sociology and History of Technology*, Cambridge MA: MIT Press.

Bijker, W. and Law, J. (1992) *Shaping Technology/Building Society: Studies in Sociotechnical Change*, Cambridge MA: MIT Press.

Blair, T. and Schroeder, G. (1999) *The Third Way/Die Neue Mitte*, London: Labour Party.

Blau, P. (1974) *On the Nature of Organisations*, New York: John Wiley.

Bloomfield, B. and Coombs, R. (1992) 'Information technology, control and power: the centralisation and decentralisation debate revisited', *Journal of Management Studies* 29, 4, pp.459–484.

Blythman, J. (2004) *Shopped: The Shocking Power of British Supermarkets*, London: Fourth Estate.

Bogin, R. (2009) 'Once the dust has settled', *Willmott Magazine*, issue 41, May/June, pp.50–51.

Bolter, J. and Grusin, R. (1999) *Remediation: Understanding New Media*, Cambridge MA: MIT Press.

Boody, R. (2001) 'On the relationships of education and technology' in Muffoletto, R. (ed.) *Education and Technology: Critical and Reflective Practices*, Cresskill NJ: Hampton Press.

Boud, D. (1995) 'Assessment and learning: contradictory or complementary?' in Knight, P. (ed.) *Assessment for Learning in Higher Education*, London: Kogan Page.

Bowers, C. (1988) *The Cultural Dimensions of Educational Computing: Understanding the Non-neutrality of Technology*, New York: Teachers College Press.

Boyd, D. (2007) 'Why youth social network sites: the role of networked publics in teenage social life' in Buckingham, D. (ed.) *MacArthur Foundation Series on Digital Learning – Youth, Identity, and Digital Media,* Cambridge MA: MIT Press.

Boyd-Barrett, O. (1990) 'Schools' computing policy as state-directed innovation', *Educational Studies*, 16, 2, pp.169–185.

Brabazon, T. (2007) *The University of Google*, Aldershot: Ashgate.

Bragg, S. (2003) 'Review: Consuming children', *British Journal of Sociology of Education*, 24, 4, pp.522–526.

Brehony, K. (2002) 'Researching the 'grammar of schooling': an historical view' *European Educational Research Journal*, 1, 1, pp.178–189.

Brint, S. (1998) *Schools and Societies*, Thousand Oaks CA: Pine Forge Press.

Brockes, E. (2007) 'A punk and a preacher: interview with Vivienne Westwood', *The Guardian*, 12 May, Weekend supplement, p.18.

Bromley, H. (2001) 'The influence of context: gender, power and the use of computers in schools' in Muffoletto, R. (ed.) *Education and Technology: Critical and Reflective Practices*, Cresskill NJ: Hampton Press.

Bromley, H. and Shutkin, D. (1998) 'Social power and practices of science and technology within education', *Educational Policy* 12, 5, pp.467–483.

Brown, M. and Murray, F. (2005) 'A culture of technology critique' in Cooper, M. (ed.) *Proceedings of the 33rd Annual Australian Teacher Education Association Conference*, Griffith University, Centre for Professional Development.

Brown, M. and Stratford, R. (2007) 'Problematising the ICT movement: learning for which future?' paper presented to *ITTE 2007 Conference*, Leicester, July.

Brown, P. (2003) 'The opportunity trap: education and employment in a global economy', *European Educational Research Journal*, 2, 1, pp.141–179.

Brush, T. (1999) 'Technology planning and implementation in public schools', *Computers in the Schools*, 15, 2, pp.11–23.

Buckingham, D. (2000) *After the Death of Childhood*, Cambridge: Polity Press.

—— (2007) *Beyond Technology*, Cambridge: Polity Press.

Bugeja, M. (2006) 'Facing the Facebook', *The Chronicle of Higher Education*, 52, 21, 27 January, p.C1.

Buschman, J. (2009) 'Information literacy, 'new' literacies and literacy', *The Library Quarterly*, 79, 1, pp.95–118.

California Office of the Governor (2009) *Leading the Nation into a Digital Textbook Future,* State of California: Office of the Governor [http://gov.ca.gov/index.php?/fact-sheet/12455/]

Carmichael, P. and Honour, L. (2002) 'Open source as appropriate technology for global education', *International Journal of Educational Development* 22, 1, pp.47–53.

Carolan, B., Natriello, G. and Rennick, M. (2003) '*Rethinking the Organisation and Effects of Schooling*', EdLab research paper, Teachers College, Columbia University, New York.

Caron, A. and Caronia, L. (2001) 'Active users and active objects: the mutual construction of families and communication technologies', *Convergence*, 7, 3, pp.38–61.

Cascio, J. (2009) 'Get smarter', *The Atlantic*, July/August [www.theatlantic.com/doc/200907/intelligence]

Castells, M. (1996) *The Rise of the Network Society*, Oxford: Blackwell.

—— (2000) 'Materials for an exploratory theory of the network society', *British Journal of Sociology*, 51, 1, pp.5–24.

—— (2008) *Internet Beyond Myths: The Record of Scholarly Research* presentation to London School of Economics, 24 October.

Cavanagh, A. (2007) *Sociology in the Age of the Internet*, Buckingham: Open University Press.

Chandler, D. (1995) *Technological (or Media) Determinism* [www.aber.ac.uk/media/Documents/tecdet/tecdet.html]

Chang, R., Kennedy, G. and Petrovic, T. (2008) 'Web 2.0 and user-created content: students negotiating shifts in academic authority' in Atkinson, R. and McBeath, C. (eds.) *Hello! Where Are You in the Landscape of Educational Technology? Proceedings Ascilite Melbourne 2008* [www.ascilite.org.au/conferences/melbourne08/procs/index.htm]

Chomsky, N. (1968) *Language and Mind*, San Diego: Harcourt Brace Jovanovich.

Clark, B. (1998) *Creating Entrepreneurial Universities*, New York: Elsevier.

Clegg, S., Hudson, A. and Steel, J. (2003) 'The emperor's new clothes', *British Journal of Sociology of Education*, 24, 1, pp.39–53.

Code, J. and Zaparyniuk, N. (2009) 'The emergence of agency in online social networks' in Hatzipanagos, S. and Warburton, S. (eds.) *Handbook of Research on Social Software and Developing Community Ontologies*, Hershey PA, IGI Global.

Cole, M. (2008) *Marxism and Educational Theory*, London: Routledge.

Coleman, J., Campbell, E., Hobson, C., McPartland, J., Mood, A., Weinfeld, F. and York, R. (1966) *Equality of Educational Opportunity*, Washington DC: Government Printing Office.

Collins, A. and Halverson, R. (2009) *Rethinking Education in the Age of Technology*, New York: Teachers College Press.

Collins, R. (1975) *Conflict Sociology*, London: Academic Press.

Comino S. and Manenti, F. (2005) 'Government policies supporting open source software for the mass market', *Review of Industrial Organisation* 26, 2, pp.217–240.

Condie, R. and Munro, R. (2007) *The Impact of ICT in Schools: A Landscape Review*, Coventry: Becta.

Connell, J. (2007) 'We are on the verge of profound change', *The Guardian*, 7 January, Education Supplement (part three), p.7.

Considine, M. (2005) *Making Public Policy*, Cambridge: Polity.

Convery, A. (2009) 'The pedagogy of the impressed: how teachers become victims of technological vision', *Teachers and Teaching*, 15, 1, pp.25–41.

Cooley, M. (1999) 'Human-centred design' in Jacobson, R. (ed.) *Information Design*, Cambridge MA: MIT Press.

Corbett, H., Firestone, W. and Rossman, G. (1987) 'Resistance to planned change and the sacred in school cultures', *Educational Administration Quarterly*, 23, 4, pp.36–59.

Cowan, R. (1987) 'The consumption junction' in Bijker, W., Hughes, T. and Pinch, T. (eds.) *The Social Construction of Technological Systems: New Directions in the Sociology and History of Technology*, Cambridge MA: MIT Press.

Cox, A. (2008) 'Flickr: a case study of web 2.0', *Aslib Proceedings*, 60, 5, pp. 493–516.

Crook, C. (2002) 'The social character of knowing and learning: implications of cultural psychology for educational technology', *Journal of Information Technology in Teacher Education*, 10, pp.19–36.

—— (2008) 'Theories of formal and informal learning in the world of web 2.0' in Livingstone, S. (ed.) *Theorising the Benefits of New Technology for Youth*, University of Oxford/ London School of Economics.

Crook, C. and Harrison, C. (2008) *Web 2.0 Use for Learning at Key Stage Three and Four: Final Report*, Coventry: Becta.

Cuban, L. (1986) *Teachers and Machines: The Classroom Use of Technology Since 1920*, New York: Teachers College Press.

—— (2001) *Oversold and Underused: Computers in the Classroom*, Cambridge MA: Harvard University Press.

Cuban, L., Kirkpatrick, H. and Peck, C. (2001) 'High access and low use of technologies in high school', *American Educational Research Journal*, 38, 4, pp.813–834.

Curtis, P. (2009) 'McDonald's to sponsor Australian maths lessons', *The Guardian*, 20 March, p.23.

Dale, R. (2009) 'Renewing or rupturing the sociology of education?' *British Journal of Sociology of Education*, 30, 3, pp.379–387.

Dale R., Robertson S. and Shortis T. (2004) 'You can't not go with the technological flow, can you?' *Journal of Computer Assisted Learning* 20, pp.456–470.

D'Andrea, A. (2006) 'Neo-nomadism: a theory of post-identitarian mobility in the global age', *Mobilities*, 1, 1 pp. 95–119.

Daniel, J. (2010) *Mega-schools, Teachers and Technology: Achieving Education for All*, London: Routledge.

Davidson, J. (2003) 'A new role in facilitating school reform: the case of the educational technologist', *Teachers College Record*, 105, 5, pp.729–752.

Davies, B. (1976) *Social Control and Education*, London: Methuen.

Davies, W. (2005) *Modernising With Purpose: A Manifesto for a Digital Britain*, London: Institute for Public Policy Research.

Day, C. and Gu, Q. (2010) *The New Lives of Teachers*, London: Routledge.

Dean, J. (2002) *Publicity's Secret: How Technoculture Capitalised on Democracy*, Ithaca NY: Cornell University Press.

de Certeau, M. (1984) *The Practice of Everyday Life*, Berkeley: University of California Press.

Deem, R. (2004) 'New managerialism, academic capitalism and entrepreneurialism' in Tight, M. (ed.) *Higher Education Reader*, London: Routledge.

Department for Education and Employment [DfEE] (1998) *Connecting the Learning Society*, London: Department for Education and Employment.

Department for Education and Skills [DfES] (2005) *E-learning Strategy: The Key to Personalised Learning*, London: Stationery Office.

Deuchar, R. (2009) 'Seen and heard, and then not heard: Scottish pupils' experience of democratic educational practice during the transition from primary to secondary school', *Oxford Review of Education* 35, 1, pp.23–40.

Dittoe, W. (2006) 'Seriously cool places: the future of learning-centered built environments' in Oblinger, D. (ed.) *Learning Spaces*, Washington DC: Educause.

Downey, J. (1999) 'XS 4 all? Information society policy and practice in the European Union' in Downey, J. and McGuigan, J. (eds.) *Technocities*, London: Sage.

Duffelmeyer, B. (2001) 'Using digital technology to augment a critical literacy approach to first-year composition' in Muffoletto, R. (ed.) *Education and Technology: Critical and Reflective Practices*, Cresskill NJ: Hampton Press.

Dutton, B. (2008) 'Discussant comments on 'Developing the technological imagination'' in Livingstone, S. (ed.) *Theorising the Benefits of New Technology for Youth: Controversies of Learning and Development*, University of Oxford/ London School of Economics [www.education.ox.ac.uk/esrcseries/uploaded/08_0314%20ESRC%20report_web.pdf]

Dynarski, M., Agodini, R., Heaviside, S., Novak, T., Carey, N., Campuzano, L., Means, B., Murphy, R., Penuel, W., Javitz, H., Emery, D. and Sussex, W. (2007) *Effectiveness of Reading and Mathematics Software Products: Findings from the First Student Cohort*, Washington DC, National Centre for Educational Evaluation, US Department of Education [http://ies.ed.gov/ncee/pdf/20074005.pdf]

Edson, J. (2007) 'Curriculum 2.0: user-driven education', *The Huffington Post*, 25 June [www.huffingtonpost.com/jonathan-edson/curriculum-20userdri_b_53690.html]

EdTechActionNetwork (2009) *Ed Tech Action and You* [www.edtechactionnetwork.org]

Edwards, P. (1996) *The Closed World: Computers and the Politics of Discourse in Cold War America*, Cambridge MA: MIT Press.

Ellul, J. (1984) 'The latest developments in technology and the philosophy of the absurd', *Research in Philosophy and Technology*, 7, pp.77–97.

Eraut, M. (1991) *The Information Society: A Challenge for Education Policies?* London: Cassell.

Facer, K. and Green, H. (2007) 'Curriculum 2.0 educating the digital generation', *Demos Collection*, no. 24, pp.47–58.

Fairclough, N., Jessop, R., and Sayer, A. (2002) 'Critical realism and semiosis', *Journal of Critical Realism*, 5, 1, pp.2–10.

Feenberg, A. (2008) 'From critical theory of technology to the rational critique of rationality?' *presentation to London Knowledge Lab*, 27 May 2008.

Fielding, M. (2009) 'Education, identity and the possibility of democratic public space in schools' presentation to 'Digital Identities' ESRC seminar, 2 March, London School of Economics.

Fielding, M. and Moss, P. (2010) *Radical Education and the Common School*, London: Routledge.

Fine, M. and Weis, L. (2003) *Silenced Voices and Extraordinary Conversations: Re-imagining Schools*, New York: Teachers College Press.

Fisher, M. and Baird, D. (2009) 'Pedagogical mashup: Gen Y, social media, and digital learning styles' in Hin, L. and Subramaniam, R. (eds.) *Handbook of Research on New Media Literacy at The K-12 Level*, Hershey PA, IGI Global.

Flutter, J. and Ruddock, J. (2004) *Consulting Pupils: What's in it for Schools?* London: Routledge.

Foucault, M. (1979) *Discipline and Punish*, Harmondsworth: Penguin.

Franck, K. and Stevens, Q. (2007) 'Tying down loose space' in Franck, K. and Stevens, Q. (eds.) *Loose Space: Possibility and Diversity in Urban Life*, London: Routledge.

Friedkin, N. (1985) 'The sociology of school organisation – book review' *Contemporary Sociology*, 14, 2, p.207–208.

Friedman, T. (2007) '*The World is Flat*' [Release 3.0] New York, Farrar, Straus and Giroux.

Fuchs, T. and Woessmann, L. (2004) 'What accounts for international differences in student performance?' *Econometric Society 2004 Australasian Meetings* 274.

Fuller, M. (2003) *Behind the Blip*, Brooklyn NY: Autonomedia.

Gall, M. and Breeze, N. (2007) 'The sub-culture of music and ICT in the classroom', *Technology, Pedagogy and Education*, 16, 1, pp.41–56.

Gane, N. (2005) 'An information age without technology', *Information, Communication and Society*, 8, 4, pp.471–476.

Garnham, N. (2000) 'Information society as theory or ideology?' *Information, Communication and Society*, 3, 2, pp.139–152.

Garrison, M. and Bromley, H. (2004) 'Social contexts, defensive pedagogies, and the (mis)uses of educational technology', *Educational Policy*, 18, pp.589–613.

Gee, J. (2006) *Don't Bother me Mom – I'm Learning!* London: Paragon House.

—— (2008) *What Video Games Have to Teach Us About Learning and Literacy* [second edition], London: Palgrave Macmillan.

Gere, C. (2008) *Digital Culture* [second edition], London: Reaktion.

Gibson, J. (1979) *The Ecological Approach to Visual Perception,* Boston MA: Houghton Mifflin.

Gitlin, A. and Margonis, F. (1995) 'The political aspect of reform: teacher resistance as good sense', *American Journal of Education,* 103, 4, pp.377–405.

Goffman, E. (1959/1990) *The Presentation of Self in Everyday Life*, Harmondsworth: Penguin.

Goodson, I., Knobel, M., Lankshear, C. and Mangan, J. (2002) *Cyberspaces/Social Spaces,* London: Palgrave Macmillan.

Goodson, I. and Mangan, J. (1996) 'Computer literacy as ideology', *British Journal of Sociology of Education*, 17, 1, pp.65–80.

Gorard, S. (2001) 'International comparisons of school effectiveness: the second component of the 'crisis account' in England?' *Comparative Education* 37, 3, pp.279–296.

Gorman, R. (2007) 'The Feminist standpoint and the trouble with 'informal learning': a way forward for Marxist-Feminist educational research' in Green, A., Rikowski, G. and Raduntz, H. (eds.) *Renewing Dialogues in Marxism and Education*, London: Palgrave Macmillan.

Grant, L. (2009) *Children's Role in Home–school Relationships and the Role of Digital Technologies*, Bristol: Futurelab.

Green, H., Facer, K., Rudd, T., Dillon P. and Humphreys, P. (2006) *Personalisation and Digital Technologies*, Bristol: Futurelab.

Green, H. and Hannon, C. (2007) *Their Space: Education for a Digital Generation*, London: Demos.

Green, W. and Bigum, C. (1993) 'Aliens in the classroom', *Australian Journal of Education*, 37 2, pp.119–41.

Greener, I. and Perriton, L. (2005) 'The political economy of networked learning communities in higher education', *Studies in Higher Education*, 30, 1, pp.67–79.

Greenfield, S. cited in Lords Hansard (2009) 'Children: social networking sites: debate', *Lords Hansard*, vol. 707, no. 33 (February 12th) columns 1290–1293 [www.publications.parliament.uk/pa/ld200809/ldhansrd/index/090212.html]

Griffith A. and Andre-Bechely, L (2008) 'Institutional technologies: coordinating families and schools, bodies and texts' in DeVault, M. (ed.) *People at Work: Life, Power, and Social Inclusion in the New Economy*, New York: New York University Press.

Grint, K. and Woolgar, S. (1992) 'Computers, guns, and roses: what's social about being shot?' *Science Technology and Human Values,* 17, pp.366–380.

—— (1997) *The Machine at Work*, Cambridge: Polity.

Guernsey, L. (2001) 'Learning, one bullet point at a time', *New York Times* (Technology Section) 31 May, p.1.

Gulson, K. and Symes, C. (2007) 'Knowing one's place: space, theory, education', *Critical Studies in Education*, 48, 1, pp.97–110.

Gunter, H. (2009) 'The 'C' word in educational research', *Critical Studies in Education*, 50, 1, pp.93–102.

Haigh, G. (2007) *Inspirational, and Cautionary Tales for Would-be School Leaders*, London: Routledge.

Hall, S. (2003) 'New Labour's double-shuffle' *Soundings*, 24, pp.10–24.

Hamilton, E. and Feenberg, A. (2005) 'The technical codes of online education', *e-Learning*, 2, 2, pp.104–121.

Hansard (2002a) *Culture, Media and Sport: Minutes of Evidence Select Committee Report,* 22 January.

—— (2002b) *Science and Technology: Sixth Special Report House of Commons Commission report* 16 October.

—— (2003) *Hansard Written Answers for 4 Feb 2003 (pt 22)*, 4 February.

Hargadon, S. (2008) *Web 2.0 is the Future of Learning,* 4 March [www.stevehargadon.com/2008/03/web-20-is-future-of-education.html]

Hargreaves, D. (1967) *Social Relations in a Secondary School*, London: Routledge.

Harris, S. (1994) 'Entitled to what? control and autonomy in school', *International Studies in Sociology of Education*, 4, 1, pp.57–76.

Hassan, R. (2008) *The Information Society*, Cambridge: Polity.

Hattam, R., Prosser, B. and Brady, K. (2009) 'Revolution or backlash? The mediatisation of education policy in Australia', *Critical Studies in Education*, 50, 2, pp.1–10.

Haydn, T. (2002) 'Subject discipline dimensions of ICT and learning: history, a case study', *International Journal of Historical Learning, Teaching and Research*, 2, 1, pp.17–36.

Haythornthwaite, C. (2005) 'Social networks and internet connectivity effects', *Information, Communication and Society*, 8, 2, pp.125–147.

Held, D. and McGrew, A. (2002) *Governing Globalisation: Power, Authority and Global Governance*, Cambridge: Polity.

Heppell, S., Chapman, C., Millwood, R., Constable, M. and Furness, J. (2004) *Building Learning Futures*, CABE / RIBA 'Building Futures' programme.

Hess, F. and Leal, D. (2001) 'A shrinking digital divide? The provision of classroom computers across urban school systems', *Social Science Quarterly*, 82, 4, pp.765–778.

Hinchey, P. (2008) 'Educational technology' in Hill, D. (ed.) *Knowledge and Power in the Global Economy*, New York: Lawrence Erlbaum.

Hodas, S. (1996) 'Technology refusal and the organisational culture of schools' in Kling, R. (ed.) *Computerisation and Controversy: Value Conflicts and Social Choices*, San Diego: Academic Press.

Holloway, S. and Valentine, G. (2003) *Cyberkids: Children in the Information Age,* London: Routledge.

Hope, A. (2005) 'Panopticism, play and the resistance of surveillance: case studies of the observation of student internet use in UK schools', *British Journal of Sociology of Education*, 26, 3, pp.359–373.

—— (2006) 'School internet use, youth and risk: a social-cultural study of the relation between staff views of on-line dangers and students' ages in UK schools', *British Educational Research Journal*, 32, 2, pp.307–329.

—— (2007) 'Risk taking, boundary performance and intentional school internet 'misuse'', *Discourse: Studies in the Cultural Politics of Education*, 28, 1, pp.87–99.

—— (2008) 'Internet pollution discourses, exclusionary practices and the 'culture of over-blocking' within UK schools', *Technology, Pedagogy and Education*, 17, 2, pp.103–113.

—— (2009) 'CCTV, school surveillance and social control', *British Educational Research Journal*, 35, 6, pp.891–907.

Hutchby, I. (2001) 'Technologies, texts, and affordances', *Sociology* 35, 2, pp.441–456.

—— (2003) 'Affordances and the analysis of technologically mediated interaction: a response to Brian Rappert', *Sociology*, 37, 8, pp.581–589.

Illich, I. (1971) *Deschooling Society*, Harmondsworth: Penguin Books.

Information Infrastructure Task Force (1993) *The National Information Infrastructure: Agenda for Action*, Washington DC: Information Infrastructure Task Force.

Ito, M., Horst, H., Bittanti, M., Boy, D., Herr-Stephenson, R., Lange, P., Pascoe, C. and Robinson, L. (2008) *Living and Learning with New Media: Summary of Findings from the Digital Youth Project*, Chicago: MacArthur Foundation.

Jencks, C., Smith, M., Acland, H., Bane, M., Cohen, D., Gintis, H., Heyns, B., and Michelson, S. (1972) *Inequality: A Reassessment of the Effect of Family and Schooling in America*, New York: Basic Books.

Jenkins, H. (1998) 'Childhood innocence and other modern myths' in Jenkins, H. (ed.) *The Children's Culture Reader*, New York: New York University Press.

—— (2004) 'Why Heather can write', *Technology Review* [BizTech], 6 February [www.technologyreview.com]

Jensen, C. and Lauritsen, P. (2005) 'Reading Digital Denmark: IT reports as material-semiotic actors', *Science, Technology and Human Values*, 30, 3, pp.352–373.

John, P. and La Velle, L. (2004) 'Devices and desires: subject subcultures, pedagogical identity and the challenge of information and communications technology', *Technology, Pedagogy and Education*, 13, 3, pp.307–326.

Johnson, N. (2009) 'Teenage technological experts' views of schooling', *Australian Educational Researcher*, 36,1, pp.59–72.

Johnston, C. (2001) 'Mounting opposition to the Beeb's big idea', *Times Educational Supplement*, Online supplement, 7 September, p.7.

Kahn, R. and Kellner, D. (2007) 'Paulo Freire and Ivan Illich: technology, politics and the reconstruction of education', *Policy Futures in Education*, 5, 4, pp.431–448.

Keen, A. (2007) *The Cult of the Amateur*, London: Nicholas Brealey.

Kelemen, M. and Smith, W. (2001) 'Community and its 'virtual' promises: a critique of cyber-libertarian rhetoric', *Information, Communication & Society*, 4, 3, pp.370–387.

Kellner, D. (2004) 'Technological transformation, multiple literacies and the re-visioning of education', *e-Learning*, 1, 1 [www.wwwords.co.uk]

Kelly, F., McCain, T. and Jukes, I. (2008) *Teaching the Digital Generation: No More Cookie-cutter High Schools*, Thousand Oaks CA: Corwin Press.

Kennedy, G., Dalgarno, B., Bennett, S., Judd, T., Gray, K. and Chang, R. (2008) 'Immigrants and natives: investigating differences between staff and students' use of technology' in Atkinson, R. and McBeath, C. (eds.) *Hello! Where Are You in the Landscape of Educational Technology? Proceedings Ascilite Melbourne 2008* [www.ascilite.org.au/conferences/melbourne08/procs/index.htm] pp.484–492.

Kenway, J., Bigum, C., Fitzclarence, L., Collier, J. and Tregenza, K. (1994) 'New education in new times', *Journal of Education Policy*, 9, 4, pp.317–333.

Kenway, J. and Bullen, E. (2005) 'Globalising the young in the age of desire: some educational policy issues' in Apple, M., Kenway, J. and Singh, M. (eds.) *Globalising Public Education: Policies, Pedagogies and Politics*, New York: Peter Lang.

—— (2007) 'The global cultural economy and the young cyberflaneur: a pedagogy for global citizenship' in Dolby N. and Rizvi, F. (eds.) *Youth Moves, Identities and Education in Global Perspective*, London: Routledge.

Kenway, J., Bullen, E., Fahey, J. with Robb, S. (2006) *Haunting the Knowledge Economy*, London: Routledge.

Kerr, S. (1996) 'Toward a sociology of educational technology' in Jonassen, D. (ed.) *Handbook of Research on Educational Communications and Technology*, New York: Macmillan.

King, R. (1983) *The Sociology of School Organisation*, London: Methuen.

Kirby, P., Lanyon, C., Cronin, K. and Sinclair, R. (2003) *Building a Culture of Participation: Involving Children and Young People in Policy, Service Planning, Development and Evaluation*, London: Department for Education and Skills.

Kirkpatrick, G. (2004) *Critical Technology: A Social Theory of Personal Computing*, Aldershot: Ashgate.

Kling, R. (1992) 'When gunfire shatters bone: reducing sociotechnical systems to social relationships', *Science Technology and Human Values*, 17, 3, pp.381–385.

Knight, P (1995) 'Introduction' in Knight, P. (ed.) *Assessment for Learning in Higher Education*, London: Kogan Page.

Kovacs, P. (2007) 'The anti-school movement' in Gabbard, D. (ed.) *Knowledge and Power in the Global Economy: The Effects of School Reform in a Neoliberal/Neoconservative Age*, London: Routledge.

Kruk, M. (1999) 'The internet and the revival of the myth of the universal library', *The Australian Library Journal*, 48, 2, pp.137–147.

Kupchik, A. and Monahan, T. (2006) 'The New American School: preparation for post-industrial discipline', *British Journal of Sociology of Education*, 27, 5, pp.617–631.

Ladwig, J. (1994) 'For whom this reform: outlining educational policy as a social field', *British Journal of Sociology of Education*, 15, 3, pp.341–363.

Lally, E. (2002) *At Home with Computers*, Oxford: Berg.

Lameras, P., Paraskakis, I. and Levy, P. (2009) 'Using social software for teaching and learning in higher education' in Hatzipanagos, S. and Warburton, S. (eds.) *Handbook of Research on Social Software and Developing Community Ontologies*, Hershey PA: IGI Publishing.

Lankshear, C. and Bigum, C. (1999) 'Literacies and new technologies in school settings', *Pedagogy, Culture and Society*, 7, 3, pp.445–465.

Latour, B. (1987) *Science in Action: How to Follow Scientists and Engineers Through Society*, Milton Keynes: Open University Press.

—— (2005) *Reassembling the Social: An Introduction to Actor-Network-Theory*, Oxford: Oxford University Press.

Laurillard, D. (2008) *Digital Technologies and Their Role in Achieving Our Ambitions for Education*, London: Institute of Education.

Lauven, E., Lindahl, M., Oosterbeek, H. and Webbink, D. (2003) *The Effect of Extra Funding for Disadvantaged Students on Achievement*, Department of Economics, University of Amsterdam.

Law, J. (1987) 'Technology and heterogeneous engineering: the case of Portuguese expansion' in Bijker, W., Hughes, T. and Pinch, T. (eds.) *The Social Construction of Technological Systems: New Directions in the Sociology and History of Technology*, Cambridge MA: MIT Press.

Lave, J. and Wenger, E. (1991) *Situated Learning: Legitimate Peripheral Participation*, Cambridge: Cambridge University Press.

Law, N., Pelgrum, P. and Plomp, T. (2008) *Pedagogy and ICT use in Schools Around the World: Findings from the IEA SITES 2006 Study*, Berlin: Springer.

Lawn, M. and Grosvenor, I. (2005) *Materialities of Schooling: Design, Technology, Objects, Routines*, Oxford: Symposium.

Leadbeater, C. (2008a) *We-think*, London: Profile.

—— (2008b) 'People power transforms the web in next online revolution', *The Observer*, 9 March, p.26.

Leathwood, C. and O'Connell, P. (2003) 'It's a struggle: the construction of the "new student" in higher education', *Journal of Education Policy*, 18, 6, pp.597–615.

Lee, J. and Caldwell, B. (2010) *Changing Schools in an Era of Globalisation*, London: Routledge.

Lefebvre, H. (1975/ 2009) 'The state in the modern world' in Brenner, N. and Elden, S. (eds.) *State, Space World: Selected Essays*, Minneapolis MN: University of Minnesota Press.

—— (1981/2007) *Critique of Everyday Life: Volume Three – From Modernity to Modernism* [trans. Elliott, G.] London: Verso.

Levin, D. and Arafeh, S. (2002) *The Digital Disconnect*, Washington DC: Pew Internet and American Life Project.

Levinson, D. and Sadovnik, A. (2002) 'Education and society: an introduction' in Levinson, D., Cookson, P. and Sadovnik, A. (eds.) *Education and Sociology*, London: Routledge.

Lim, S. (2006) 'From cultural to information revolution: ICT domestication by middle-class Chinese families' culture' in Berker, T., Hartmann, M., Punie, Y. and Ward, K. (eds.) *Domestication of Media and Technology*, Buckingham: Open University Press.

Lindblom, C. (1977) *Politics and Markets: The World's Political-Economic Systems*, New York: Basic Books.

Lingard, B., Rawolle, S. and Taylor, S. (2005) 'Globalising policy sociology in education: working with Bourdieu', *Journal of Education Policy*, 20, 6, pp.759–777.

Livingstone, S. (2009) *Children and the Internet*, Cambridge: Polity.

Ljoså, E. (1998) 'The role of university teachers in a digital era' paper presented to the *EDEN Conference*, Bologna, June.

Lohnes, S., and Kinzer, C. (2007) 'Questioning assumptions about students' expectations for technology in college classrooms', *Innovate*, 3, 5, [http://innovateonline.info]

Long, S. (2005) 'Digital natives: if you aren't one, get to know one', *New Library World* 106, 3–4, pp.187–189.

Lortie, D. (1975) *Schoolteacher: A Sociological Study*, Chicago: University of Chicago Press.

—— (2002) 'Preface to the 2002 edition' in *Schoolteacaher: A Sociological Study*, Chicago: University of Chicago Press.

Louis, K. and Firestone, W. (1997) 'Schools as cultures' in Murphy, J. and Louis, K. (eds.) *Handbook of Research on Educational Administration*, San Francisco CA: Jossey Bass.

Lovink, G. (2004) *Uncanny Networks*, Cambridge MA: MIT Press.

Luckin, R. (2010) *Learning, Context and the Role of Technology*, London: Routledge.

Luckin, R., Clark, W., Graber, R., Logan, K., Mee, A. and Oliver, M. (2009a) 'Beyond web 2.0: mapping the technology landscapes of young learners', *Journal of Computer Assisted Learning* 25, pp.56–69.

Luckin, R., Clark, W., Logan, K., Graber, R., Oliver, M. and Mee, A. (2009b) 'Do web 2.0 tools really open the door to learning: practices, perceptions and profiles of 11-16 year olds learners', *Learning, Media and Technology* 34, 2, pp.87–104.

Luhmann, N. (2000) *The Reality of the Mass Media*, Stanford CA: Stanford University Press.

Luke, C. (2003) 'Pedagogy, connectivity, multimodality, and interdisciplinarity', *Reading Research Quarterly*, 38, 3, pp.397–413.

Lyon, D. (2006) *Theorising Surveillance: The Panopticon and Beyond*, Uffculme: Willam.

MacKenzie, D. and Wajcman, J. (1985) *The Social Shaping of Technology: How the Refrigerator Got its Hum*, Milton Keynes: Open University Press.

Madden, A., Ford, N., Miller, D. and Levy, P. (2005) 'Using the internet in teaching', *British Journal of Educational Technology*, 36, 2, pp.255–280.

Mäkitalo-Siegal, K., Kaplan, F., Zottmann, J. and Fischer, F. (2009) *Classroom of the Future: Orchestrating Collaborative Spaces*, Rotterdam: Sense.

Mann, S. (2001) 'Alternative perspectives on the student experience', *Studies in Higher Education* 26, 1, pp.7–19.

Markoff, J. (2006) 'For $150, third-world laptop stirs big debate', *New York Times*, 30 November [www.nytimes.com/2006/11/30/technology/30laptop.html]

Marshall, G. (2005) 'Mind the gap! Policy issues for e-learning proponents', *Educational Media International*, 42, 2, pp.153–159.

Martin, B. (1996) 'Technological determinism revisited', *Metascience*, 9, pp.158–160.

Mason, R. and Rennie, F. (2007) 'Using web 2.0 for learning in the community', *Internet and Higher Education*, 10, pp.196–203.

McCahill, M. and Finn, R. (2010) 'The social impact of surveillance in three UK schools: angels, devils and teen mums' paper presented to ESRC Seminar on Surveillance *'Exclusion and Inclusion'* University of Sheffield, 24 February.

McDougall, A., Murnane, J., Jones, A. and Reynolds, N. (2009) *Researching IT in Education*, London: Routledge.

McLoughlin, C. and Lee, M. (2008) 'Mapping the digital terrain: new media and social software as catalysts for pedagogical change' in 'Hello! Where are you in the landscape of educational technology?' *Proceedings ascilite Melbourne 2008* [www.ascilite.org.au/conferences/melbourne08/procs/mcloughlin.html]

McNeil, L. (1986) *Contradictions of Control: School Structure and School Knowledge*, London: Routledge.

McNeil, M. (1991) 'The old and new worlds of information technology in Britain' in Corner, J. and Harvey, S. (eds.) *Enterprise and Heritage: Cross Currents of National Culture*, London: Routledge.

Mee, A. (2007a) 'E-learning funding for schools: a policy paradox?' *British Journal of Educational Technology*, 38, 1, pp.63–71.

Mee, A. (2007b) 'E-learning policy and the 'transformation' of schooling: a UK case study', *European Journal of Open, Distance and E-Learning* 2007/II, [www.eurodl.org]

Meier, K., Polinard, J., and Wrinkle, R. (2000) 'Bureaucracy and organisational performance: causality arguments about public schools', *American Journal of Political Science*, 44, 3, pp.590–602.

Menchik, D. (2004) 'Placing cybereducation in the UK classroom', *British Journal of Sociology of Education*, 25, 2, pp.193–213.

Meyer, H. and Rowan, B. (2006) *The New Institutionalism in Education*, Albany NY: State University of New York Press.

Miller, R. (2006) 'Equity in a twenty-first century learning intensive society: is schooling part of the solution?' *Foresight* 8, 4, pp.13–22.

Mingers, J. (2004) 'Realising information systems: critical realism as an underpinning philosophy for information systems', *Information and Organisation*, 14, 2, pp.87–103.

Misztal, B. (2000) *Informality: Social Theory and Contemporary Practice*, London: Routledge.

Mitchell, W. (1995) *City of Bits: Space, Place, and the Infobahn*, Cambridge MA: MIT Press.

Molnar, A. (2005) *School Commercialism: From Democratic Ideal to Market Commodity*, London: Routledge.

Molnar, A., Miron, G. and Urschel, J. (2008) *Profiles of For-Profit Educational Management Organisations: Tenth Annual Report*, Boulder CO, Education and the Public Interest Center, University of Colorado.

Monahan, T. (2004) 'Technology policy as a stealth agent of global change', *Globalisation, Societies and Education* 2, 3, pp.355–376.

—— (2005) *Globalisation, Technological Change, and Public Education*, London: Routledge.

Monahan, T. and Torres, R. (2010) *Schools Under Surveillance: Cultures of Control in Public Education*, Piscataway NJ: Rutgers University Press.

Monchinski, T. (2007) *The Politics of Education*, Rotterdam: Sense.

Monke, L. (2008) 'Better informed – but poorly educated?' *The Guardian* 23 September, 'Time to learn' supplement, p.4.

Morgan, G. (1997) *Images of Organisation*, London: Sage.

Morgan, M., Ludlow, L., Kitching, K., O'Leary, M. and Clarke, A. (2010) 'What makes teachers tick? Sustaining events in new teachers' lives', *British Educational Research Journal*, 36, 2, pp.191–208..

Mörtberg, C., Stuedahl, D. and Alander, S. (2010) 'Why do the orders go wrong all the time? Exploring sustainability in an e-commerce application in Swedish public school kitchens', *Information, Communication & Society*, 13, 1, pp.68–87.

Muffoletto, R. (2001) *Education and Technology: Critical and Reflective Practices*, Cresskill NJ: Hampton Press.

Mulderrig, J. (2007) 'Textual strategies of representation and legitimation in New Labour policy discourse' in Green, A., Rikowski, G. and Raduntz, H. (eds.) *Renewing Dialogues in Marxism and Education*, London: Palgrave Macmillan.

Mulgan, G. (1998) *Connexity: How to Live in a Connected World*, Cambridge MA: Harvard Business School Press.

Mumford, L. (1934/1963) *Technics and Civilisation*, London: Harvest.

Murdock, G. (2004) 'Past the posts: rethinking change, retrieving critique', *European Journal of Communication*, 19, 1, pp.19–38.

Negroponte, N. (1995) *Being Digital* London, Coronet.

Nespor, J. (1997) *Tangled up in School: Politics, Space, Bodies and Signs in the Educational Process*, London: Routledge.

Newton, L. (2005) 'Data, information and questions of pupil progress' in Tatnall, A., Osorio, J. and Visscher, A. (eds.) *Information Technology and Educational Management in the Knowledge Society*, Berlin: Springer.

New Zealand Government (2008) *The Draft Digital Strategy 2.0: Achieving our Digital Potential*, Wellington: Ministry of Economic Development.

Ng, R. (1997) 'A woman out of control' in Bryson, M. and de Castell, S. (eds.) *Radical In(ter)ventions*, New York: SUNY Press.

Nicholas, D., Rowlands, I. and Huntington, P. (2008) *Information Behaviour of the Researcher of the Future – Executive Summary* [www.jisc.ac.uk/media/documents/programmes/reppres/gg_final_keynote_11012008.pdf]

Nivala, M. (2009) 'Information society strategies: simple answers for complex problems: education and ICT in Finnish', *Media Culture and Society*, 31, pp. 433–448.

Noble, D. (1997) 'A bill of goods: the early marketing of computer-based education and its implications for the present moment' in Biddle, B.J. (ed.) *International Handbook of Teachers and Teaching*, Netherlands: Kluwer.

—— (2002) *Digital Diploma Mills*, New York: New York University Press.

Norman, D. (1999) 'Affordances, conventions and design', *Interactions* 6, 3, pp. 38–43.

Norton L., Tilley A., Newstead S. and Franklyn-Stokes A. (2001) 'The pressure of assessment in undergraduate courses and their effect on student behaviours', *Assessment and Evaluation in Higher Education* 26, pp.269–284.

Nunes, M. (2006) *Cyberspaces of Everyday Life*, Minneapolis: University of Minneapolis Press.

Nye, D. (2007) *Technology Matters: Questions to Live With*, Cambridge MA: MIT Press.

Oakley, A. (2000) *Experiments in Knowing: Gender and Method in the Social Sciences*, Cambridge: Polity.

OfCOM (2009) *Communications Market Report 2009*, London: Office of Communications.

OLPC [One Laptop Per Child] (2008) *One Laptop per Child – Mission Statement* [www.laptop.org/vision]

Orton-Johnson, K. (2007) 'The online student: lurking, chatting, flaming and joking', *Sociological Research Online*, 12, 6, [www.socresonline.org.uk/12/6/3.html]

Oudshoorn, N and Pinch, T. (2003) *How Users Matter*, Cambridge MA: MIT Press.

Oudshoorn, N., Rommes, E. and Stienstra, M (2004) 'Configuring the User as Everybody: Gender and Design Cultures in Information and Communication Technologies', *Science, Technology, & Human Values*, 29, 1, pp.30–63.

Paechter, C. (1995) 'Subcultural retreat: negotiating the design and technology curriculum', *British Educational Research Journal*, 21, 1, pp.75–87.

Paige, R. (2005) *Remarks for U.S. Secretary Of Education Rod Paige at the National Education Technology Plan Release 'Technology & No Child Left Behind: Transforming Education'*, Washington, DC, January 7, 2005.

Papert, S. (1984) 'Trying to predict the future', *Popular Computing*, 3, 13, pp.30–44.

—— (1998) 'Does easy do it? Children, games, and learning', *Game Developer* June/September, pp.88–92 [www.papert.org/articles/Doeseasydoit.html]

Paterson, M. (2006) *Consumption and Everyday Life*, London: Routledge.

Paton, G. (2007) 'Google aims to net teenagers for life', *The Telegraph*, 13 June, p.11.

Pearlman, R. (2009) 'Making twenty-first century schools: creating learner-centred school-places/ workplaces for a new culture of students at work', *Educational Technology*, 49, 5, pp.14–19.

Perelman, L. (1992) *School's Out: Hyperlearning, the New Technology and the End of Education*, New York: Avon.

Peters, M. and McDonough, T. (2008) 'Editorial', *Critical Studies in Education*, 49, 1, pp.127–142.

Pettigrew, A. (1973) *The Politics of Organisational Decision-making*, London: Tavistock.

Pfaffenberger, B. (1992) 'Technological dramas', *Science, Technology and Human Values*, 17, 3, pp.282–312.

Pinch, T. and Bijker, W. (1984) 'The social construction of facts and artefacts: or how the sociology of science and the sociology of technology might benefit each other', *Social Studies of Science* 14, pp.399–441.

Plowman, L., Stephen, C. and McPake, J. (2010) *Growing up with Technology: Young Children Learning in a Digital World*, London: Routledge.

Poster, M. (1995) *The Second Media Age*, Cambridge: Polity.

—— (2005) 'History in the digital domain' in Land, R. and Bayne, S. (eds.) *Education in Cyber-space*, London: Routledge.

Potter, J. (2005) 'Book review: telling tales on technology', *Technology, Pedagogy and Education*, 14, 1, pp.141–143.

Power, C. (1987) 'Science and technology towards informed citizenship', *Castme Journal* 7, 3, pp.5–18.

Prenksy, M. (2001) 'Digital natives, digital immigrants', *On the Horizon*, 9, 5, pp.1–6.

Prensky, M. (2008) 'The role of technology in teaching and the classroom', *Educational Technology*, 48, 6, November/December.

Preston, P. (2009) 'The media of our discontent', *The Observer*, 22 February, Business and Media supplement, p.10.

Progress and Freedom Foundation (2010) *Mission statement* [www.pff.org/about]

Qvortrup, L. (2006) 'Understanding new digital media: medium theory or complexity theory?', *European Journal of Communication*, 21, 3, pp.345–356.

Rappert, B. (2003) 'Technologies, texts and possibilities: a reply to Hutchby', *Sociology*, 37, 8, pp.565–580.

Rassool, N. (1993) 'Post-Fordism? Technology and new forms of control', *British Journal of Sociology of Education* 14, 3, pp.227–244.

Ratcliffe, M. and Grace, M. (2003) *Science Education for Citizenship: Teaching Socio–scientific Issues*, Buckingham: Open University Press.

Raymond, R. (1998) 'The cathedral and the bazaar', *First Monday*, 3, 3 [www.firstmonday.org/issues/issue3_3/]

Readings, W. (1996) *The University in Ruins*, Cambridge: Harvard University Press.

Reedy, G. (2008) 'PowerPoint, interactive whiteboards, and the visual culture of technology in schools', *Technology, Pedagogy and Education*, 17, 2, pp.143–162.

Reid, C. (2009) 'Technology-loving Luddites? Declining participation in high school computing studies in Australia', *British Journal of Sociology of Education*, 30, 3, pp.289–302.

Reynolds, D., Treharne, D. and Tripp, H. (2003) 'ICT – the hopes and the reality', *British Journal of Educational Technology* 34, 2, pp.151–167.

Rheingold, H. (1994) *The Virtual Community*, London: Secker and Warburg.

Rivlin, L. (2007) 'Found spaces: freedom of choice in public life' in Franck, K. and Stevens, Q. (eds.) *Loose Space: Possibility and Diversity in Urban Life*, London: Routledge.

Robertson, J. (2003) 'Stepping out of the box: rethinking the failure of ICT to transform schools', *Journal of Educational Change* 4, 4, pp.323–344.

Robins, K. and Webster, F. (1989) *The Technical Fix: Education, Computers and Industry*, London: Macmillan.

—— (2002) 'Prospects of a virtual culture', *Science as Culture*, 11, 2, pp.235–256.

Robinson, B. (1993) 'The cultural dimension of information technology' in King, A. and Reiss, M. (eds.) *The Multicultural Dimension of the National Curriculum*, London: Routledge.

Rosenblum, B. (2008) 'Developing new skills and expertise to support digital scholarship and scholarly communication' paper presented to *World Library and Information Congress: 74th IFLA General Conference and Council*, Quebec, August.

Roszak, T. (1994) *The Cult of Information: A Neo-luddite Treatise on High-tech, Artificial Intelligence, and the True Art of Thinking*, Berkeley CA, University of California Press.

Royal Society (1985) *The Public Understanding of Science*, London: The Royal Society.

Rudd, T., Colligan, F. and Naik, R. (2006) *Learner Voice*, Bristol: Futurelab.

Rutkowski, D. (2007) 'Converging us softly: how intergovernmental organisations promote neoliberal educational policy', *Critical Studies in Education*, 48, 2, pp.229–247.

Rutter, M., Maughan, B., Mortimore, P. and Ouston, J. (1979) *Fifteen Thousand Hours*, London: Paul Chapman.

Sackmann, S. (1992) 'Culture and subcultures: an analysis of organisational knowledge', *Administrative Science Quarterly*, 37, 1, pp.140–161.

Saltman, K. and Gabbard, D. (2010) *Education as Enforcement*, London: Routledge.

Sarason, S. (1990) *The Predictable Failure of Educational Reform*. San Francisco: Jossey Bass.

Saunders, L. (1992) 'Education, work and the curriculum', *Policy Studies*, 12, 2, pp.13–26.

Scheurich, J. (1997) *Research Method in the Postmodern*. London: Routledge.

Schiller, H. (1995) *Information Inequality: The Deepening Social Crisis in America*, New York: Routledge.

Schofield, J. (1995) *Computers and Classroom Culture*, Cambridge: Cambridge University Press.

Schwarzenegger, A. (2009) *Leading the Nation into a Digital Textbook Future*, State of California, Office of the Govenor [http://gov.ca.gov/index.php?/fact-sheet/12455/]

Sefton-Green, J. (2004) *Literature Review in Informal Learning with Technology Outside School*, Bristol: Futurelab.

Sefton-Green, J., Nixon, H. and Erstad, O. (2009) 'Reviewing approaches and perspectives on digital literacy', *Pedagogies: an International Journal*, 4, 2, pp.107–125.

Selwood, I. (2005) 'Primary school teachers' use of ICT for administration and management' in

Tatnall, A., Osorio, J. and Visscher, A. (eds.) *Information Technology and Educational Management in the Knowledge Society*, Berlin: Springer.

Selwyn, N. (2001) 'Turned on/switched off: exploring children's engagement with computers in primary school', *Journal of Educational Computing Research*, 25, 3, pp.245–266.

Selwyn, N. (2006) 'Exploring the 'digital disconnect' between net-savvy students and their schools', *Learning, Media and Technology*, 31, 1, pp.5–17.

Selwyn, N., Potter, J. and Cranmer, S. (2010) *Primary Schools and ICT: Learning from Pupil Perspectives*, London: Continuum.

Sennett, R. (2003) *Respect: The Formation of Character in a World of Inequality*, London: Allen Layne.

—— (2007) *The Craftsman*, London: Allen Layne.

Shaffer, D. (2008) 'Education in the digital age', *The Nordic Journal of Digital Literacy*, 4, 1, p.39–51.

Shepherd, J. (2009) 'Someone to watch over you', *The Guardian* 4 August, Education supplement, p.1–2.

Shirky, C. (2008) *Here Comes Everybody: The Power of Organising without Organisations*, London: Allen Lane.

Shoup, B. (1984) 'Television: friend, not foe of the teacher', *Journal of Reading*, 27, 7, pp.629–31.

Shuttleworth, D. (2003) *School Management in Transition: Schooling on the Edge*, London: Routledge.

Siemens, G. (2004) *Connectivism: A Learning Theory for the Digital Age* [www.elearnspace.org/Articles/connectivism.htm]

Sigman, A. (2009) 'Well connected', *The Biologist*, 56, 1, pp.14–20.

Silverstone, R. (1993) 'Time, information and communication technologies and the household', *Time and Society*, 2, 3, pp.283–311.

—— (2006) 'Domesticating domestication: reflections on the life of a concept' in Berker, T., Hartmann, M., Punie, Y. and Ward, K. (eds.) *Domestication of Media and Technology*, Buckingham: Open University Press.

Silverstone, R. and Hirsch, E. (1992) *Consuming Technologies: Media and Information in Domestic Spaces*, London: Routledge.

Silverstone, R., Hirsch, E. and Morley, D. (1992) 'Information and communication technologies and the moral economy of the household' in Silverstone, R. and Hirsch, E. (eds.) *Consuming Technologies: Media and Information in Domestic Spaces*, London: Routledge.

Singh, P. (1993) 'Institutional discourse and practice: a case study of the social construction of technological competence in the primary classroom', *British Journal of Sociology of Education*, 14, 1, pp.39–58.

Siskin, L. (1991) 'Departments as different worlds: subject subcultures in secondary schools', *Educational Administration Quarterly*, 27, 2, pp.134–160.

Slaughter, S. and Leslie, L. (1997) *Academic Capitalism: Politics, Policies, and the Entrepreneurial University*, Baltimore: Johns Hopkins University Press.

Small, G. and Vorgon, G. (2008) *iBRAIN: Surviving the Technological Alteration of the Modern Mind*, London: Collins.

Smith, M. (1994) 'Recourse of empire' in Smith, M. and Marx, L. (eds.) *Does Technology Drive History? The Dilemma of Technological Determinism*, Cambridge MA: MIT Press.

Solomon, G. and Schrum, L. (2007) *Web 2.0: New Tools, New Schools*, Washington DC: International Society for Technology in Education.

Somekh, B. (2007) *Pedagogy and Learning with ICT: Researching the Art of Innovation*, London: Routledge.

Sørensen, B., Danielsen, O. and Nielsen, J. (2007) 'Children's informal learning in the context of schools of the knowledge society', *Education and Information Technologies*, 12, 1, pp.17–27.

Sproull, L. and Kiesler, S. (1991) *Connections: New Ways of Working in the Networked Organisation*, Cambridge MA: MIT Press.

Sreenivasulu, V. (2000) 'The role of a digital librarian in the management of digital information systems', *The Electronic Library* 18, 1, pp.12–20.

Steinberg, S. and Kincheloe, J. (1997) *Kinderculture: The Corporate Construction of Childhood*, Boulder CO: Westview Press.

Stodolsky, S. (1993) 'A framework for subject matter comparisons in high schools', *Teaching & Teacher Education*, 9, pp.333–346.

Street, B. (1987) 'Models of computer literacy' in Finnegan, R., Salaman, G. and Thompson, K. (eds.) *Information Technology: Social Issues*, Milton Keynes: Open University Press.

Suoranta, J. and Vadén, T. (2010) *Wikiworld*, London: Pluto Press.

Suppes, P. (1965) *Computer-assisted Instruction in the Schools: Potentialities, Problems, Prospects*, Stanford University: Institute for Mathematical Studies in the Social Sciences, Technical Report Number 81 [http://suppes-corpus.stanford.edu/techreports/IMSSS_81.pdf]

Sussman, G. (1997) *Communication, Technology and Politics in the Information Age*, Thousand Oaks CA: Sage.

Sutherland, R., Robertson, S. and John, P. (2008) *Improving Classroom Learning with ICT*, London: Routledge.

Swain, H. (2009) 'Dawn of the cyberstudent', *The Guardian*, 20 January, 'University challenge' supplement, p.1.

Tapscott, D. (1999) 'Educating the net generation', *Educational Leadership*, 56, 5, pp.6–11.

Tapscott, D. and Williams, A. (2008) *Wikinomics: How Mass Collaboration Changes Everything*, London: Atlantic.

Tasker, M. and Packham, D. (1993) 'Industry and higher education: a question of values', *Studies in Higher Education*, 18, 2, pp.127–136.

Taylor, A. (1998) 'Employability skills: from corporate 'wish list' to government policy', *Journal of Curriculum Studies* 30, 2, pp.143–164.

Taylor, E. (2010) 'If I wanted to be on Big Brother, I would have auditioned for it: the rise of the surveillance school in the UK' paper presented to ESRC Seminar on Surveillance '*Exclusion and Inclusion*' University of Sheffield, 24 February.

Thompson, J. (1995) *The Media and Modernity*, Palo Alto CA: Stanford University Press.

Thompson, R. (2007) 'University degree not the only route to an IT job', *Computer Weekly*, 24 August [www.computerweekly.com]

Toffler, A. (1970) *Future Shock*, London: Bodley Head.

Tooley, J. (2006) 'Education reclaimed' in Booth, P. (ed.) *Towards a Liberal Utopia?* London: Continuum.

Trucano, M. (2005) *Knowledge Maps: ICTs in Education*, Washington DC: World Bank.

Tufte, E. (2003) 'PowerPoint is evil', *Wired*, September [www.wired.com/wired/archive/11.09/ppt2.html]

Tyack, D. and Tobin, W. (1995) 'The 'grammar' of schooling: why has it been so hard to change?', *American Educational Research Journal*, 31, 3, pp.453–479.

Urry, J. (2007) *Mobilities*, London: Sage.

Van de Bunt-Kokhuis, S. (2004) 'Globalisation and the freedom of knowledge', *Higher Education in Europe* 29, 2, pp.269–284.

Van Zoonen, L. (2002) 'Gendering the internet: claims, controversies and cultures', *European Journal of Communication* 17, 1, pp.5–23.

Vyas, D., Chisalita, C. and van der Veer, G. (2006) 'Affordance in interaction' in *Proceedings of*

ECCE – Thirteenth European Conference on Cognitive Ergonomics, Zürich: European Association of Cognitive Ergonomics.

Wajcman, J. (2004) *Technofeminism,* Cambridge: Polity.

—— (2008) 'Life in the fast lane? Towards a sociology of technology and time', *The British Journal of Sociology* 59, 1, pp.59–77.

—— (2010) 'Feminist theories of technology', *Cambridge Journal of Economics* 34, 1, pp.143–152.

Walkerdine, V. (1991) *Schoolgirl Fictions,* London: Verso.

Wang, S. and Chern, J. (2008) 'The new era of 'school 2.0' – teaching with pleasure, not pressure' in *Proceedings of World Conference on Educational Multimedia, Hypermedia and Telecommunications 2008,* Chesapeake VA: Association for the Advancement of Computing in Education.

Warschauer, M., Knobel, M. and Stone, L. (2004) 'Technology and equity in schooling: deconstructing the digital divide', *Educational Policy* 18, 4, pp.562–588.

Warner, D. (2006) *Schooling in the Knowledge Era,* Victoria, Australian Council for Education Research.

Webb, J., Schirato, A. and Daniher, G. (2002) *Understanding Bourdieu,* Sydney: Allen and Unwin.

Webb, P. (2008) 'Re-mapping power in educational micropolitics', *Critical Studies in Education,* 49, 2, pp.127–142.

Webster, F. (2005) 'Making sense of the information age', *Information, Communication & Society,* 8, 4, pp.439–458.

Weizenbaum, J. (1976) *Computer Power and Human Reason: From Judgment to Calculation,* San Francisco: W. H. Freeman.

Wellman, B., Haase, A., Witte, J. and Hampton, K. (2001) 'Does the internet increase, decrease, or supplement social capital?', *American Behavioral Scientist* 45, 3, pp.436–455.

Whitney, P., Grimes, J. and Kumar, V. (2007) *Schools in the Digital Age,* Chicago: MacArthur Foundation.

Wilhelm, A. (2004) *Digital Nation: Toward an Inclusive Information Society* Cambridge MA, MIT Press

Williams, P. (2008) 'Leading schooling in the digital age: a clash of cultures', *School Leadership and Management,* 28, 3, pp.213–228.

Williams, Raymond (1974) *Television: Technology and Cultural Form,* London: Fontana.

—— (1981) *Keywords: A Vocabulary of Culture and Society,* London: Fontana.

Williams, Robin and Edge, D. (1996) 'What is the social shaping of technology?' *Research Policy* 25, pp.856–899.

Williams, Robin and Sørensen, K. (2002) *Shaping Technology, Guiding Policy: Concepts Spaces and Tools,* Cheltenham: Elgar.

Williams, Rosalind (1994) 'The political and feminist dimensions of technological determinism' in Smith, M. and Marx, L. (eds.) *Does Technology Drive History? The Dilemma of Technological Determinism,* Cambridge MA: MIT Press.

Willis, P. (1977) *Learning to Labour,* Farnborough: Saxon House.

Windschitl, M. and Sahl, K. (2002) 'Tracing teachers' use of technology in a laptop computer school: the interplay of teacher beliefs, social dynamics, and institutional culture', *American Educational Research Journal,* 39, pp.165–205.

Winner, L. (1993) 'Upon opening the black box and finding it empty: social constructivism and the philosophy of technology', *Science Technology and Human Values,* 18, 3, pp.362–378.

—— (1997) 'Cyberlibertarian myths and the prospects for community', *Computers and Society,* 27, 3, pp.14–19.

Withers, K. with Sheldon, R. (2008) *Behind the Screen: The Hidden Life of Youth Online,* London: Institute for Public Policy Research.

Woods, P. (2005) *Democratic Leadership in Education*, London: Paul Chapman.

Woolgar, S. (1997) 'Science and technology studies and the renewal of social theory' in Turner, S. (ed.) *Social Theory and Sociology: The Classics and Beyond*, Cambridge: Blackwell.

—— (2002) *Virtual Society? Technology, Cyberbole, Reality*, Oxford: Oxford University Press.

Woolgar, S. and Cooper, G. (1999) 'Do artefacts have ambivalence? Moses' bridges, Winner's bridges and other urban legends in S&TS', *Social Studies of Science*, 29, 3, pp.433–449.

Wresch, W. (2004) 'Review article: the information age', *The Information Society*, 20, pp.71–72.

Wright, W., Knight, P. and Pomerleau, N. (1999) 'Portfolio people: teaching and learning dossiers and the future of higher education', *Innovative Higher Education*, 24, 2, pp.89–102.

Xuereb, K. (2006) 'A comparative study of information and communications technology policy in primary education in two small islands', *Technology, Pedagogy and Education* 15, 1, pp.31–45.

Yinger, J. (1960) 'Contraculture and subculture', *American Sociological Review* 25, 5, pp.625–635.

Youdell, D. (2010) *School Trouble: Identity, Power and Politics in Education*, London: Routledge.

Young, M. (1971) *Knowledge and Control*, London: Collier Macmillan.

—— (2007) *Bringing Knowledge Back in: From Social Constructivism to Social Realism in the Sociology of Education*, London: Routledge.

Young, M. and Muller, J. (2009) *Three Scenarios for the Future: Lessons from the Sociology of Knowledge*, paper for Department for Children, Schools and Families 'Beyond Current Horizons' programme.

Younie, S. (2006) 'Implementing government policy on ICT in education: lessons learnt', *Education and Information Technologies*, 11, pp.385–400.

Zhao, Y., Lei, J. and Conway, P. (2005) 'A global perspective on political definitions of e-learning' in Weiss, J., Nolan, J. and Hunsinger, J. (eds.) *International Handbook of Virtual Learning Environments*, Netherlands: Kluwer.

Index

access: to technology 4, 23, 26, 35, 98, 111
actor network theory 48
affordances 7, 30, 34, 47
agency 43–44, 62, 100–101, 103, 115, 131, 133, 136–139, 147
alienation 31, 107–108, 111–112
anti-determinism 43–49
anti-essentialism 43–45, 52, 56
Apple, Michael ix, 27, 73–74, 107–108, 119, 131, 137–138
assessment 17–18, 25, 27, 93, 97, 103, 106–110, 128, 141
authority *see* power

Ball, Stephen 9, 19, 56–57, 66–67, 71, 77, 137
BBC 84–85
boosterism 13
Buckingham, David 71, 80, 147
buildings: school architecture 3–4, 27, 30, 35, 128
bureaucracy 17, 29, 79–81, 89–90, 92, 97, 131, 144, 150

California: state purchasing of flex-books 93–94
Castells, Manuel 29, 48, 61
CCTV (close circuit television) 108–110
Chomsky, Noam 88
classroom 3–4, 11, 13, 15, 18, 23, 28–35, 55, 87–88, 91, 95–96, 98–99, 102–116, 143–151
commercial 11, 42, 68–86, 119, 122, 138–140, 150
connectivism 14
conservatism iix, 27–29, 32, 84–85, 90, 104, 133, 137
control *see* power
counterculture: in computing 129–131

critical digital literacy 146–148
critical sociology 5, 9–10, 49–52, 137–138, 140, 150, 155
Crook, Charles 14, 50
Cuban, Larry ix, 11, 26, 34, 74, 124
culture of schooling 29–30, 34, 67, 90–96, 106, 140–145
curriculum 34, 59, 82, 95–97, 112–113, 127–128, 141–146

De Certeau, Michel 112–113
defensive: defensive teaching / defensive learning 106–107, 114–116
democracy: within school 18, 133, 141–146
deprofessionalisation 107–108
deschooling 130
deskilling 107–108, 140
digital: definition of 'the digital' 6–8
digital age 5–8
digital immigrants 31
digital natives 30–31
disciplinary structures of schools 88, 90, 96–99, 104–107, 113–114, 148
disconnection: student experience of 29–31, 110
discourse 13, 27, 36, 39, 42, 46, 50–51, 57–59, 62–67, 82, 93, 98–99, 104, 129–130, 134, 146, 150–151
domestication of technology 46, 115

economy: economic linkages 57, 67, 83–84, 93–94, 119–122, 150
educational technology community viii, 80, 120, 124–126
edutainment 70–72, 83
efficiency 20, 60, 62, 68, 76, 83, 102, 104, 134
emotion 12, 32, 82, 108, 112
equity 9, 134

Estonian 'Learning Tiger Programme' 23
ethnographic studies 9, 105–107, 111–112, 114, 151
examinations *see* assessment

feminist perspectives of technology 47–48
for-profit 69–70. 74, 94
foucault 96–98

games 11, 41, 126, 139–140, 147
gender 47–48, 111–112
globalisation 49, 60–61, 67, 122
Goodson, Ivor 92, 96, 102, 121
grammar of schooling 88–89, 99, 102–104, 137, 141

hidden curriculum 113
hierarchical organisation of schools 7–8, 18, 28–29, 87–89, 100, 103, 127–128, 132
Hodas, Steven ix, 90–92, 99, 106
home schooling 70–72, 85
home use of technology 10, 30, 46, 50, 70, 72, 83, 126

ideologies of educational technology 47, 57–59, 61–67, 120–125, 129–131
individualised learning 7, 16–17, 20, 28, 90–91, 120, 130–134
industrial-era schools 28–29, 35, 100, 125–129, 132–134
informal learning 7, 15–16, 83, 130–133
informalisation 130–144
interactive whiteboard: smartboard 3–4, 18, 25, 69–71, 77–78, 89, 91, 105
international development 58, 81
internet 5–7, 13–19, 23–30, 35, 40–42, 55, 58–59, 61, 65–66, 69–70, 81–82, 98, 104, 109, 146–147, 151
IT industry 4, 11, 70–86, 102, 120, 123–125, 150
Ito, Mimi 16, 30

knowledge 7–8, 14, 24, 28–29, 33, 59, 61, 66, 88, 90, 92, 97–100, 103, 112, 122
knowledge economy 49, 60, 62, 132, 150

laptop computer 3, 68, 71–75
learning 13–17
Lefebvre, Henri 11, 20, 36, 51, 78, 115, 121, 129, 137, 154
libertarianism 125, 130, 134
lobby groups 78, 80, 82, 84–85

macro level analysis 7, 51–60, 87, 122–124, 137–138
materiality 4, 43–45, 47
McDonalds 85
mega-schools 15
meso level analysis 51, 56
micro level analysis 7, 50–51, 102–109, 110, 137–138
micro-economy of the classroom 109–110
micropolitics 92, 101, 120, 141
mobile phones 5–7, 13, 30, 42, 82
Monahan, Torin 76, 98, 107–108, 136–138
Mumford, Lewis 136
MySpace 75

national policy agendas 23–24, 55–67, 33–34
neo-Corporativism 78
neo-liberalism 9, 61, 73, 102, 125, 130–131, 136, 154
networking logic 7, 14, 28–29, 35, 49
new managerialism 93

One Laptop per Child 73
open source 138–140

Papert, Seymour 34, 80, 125
parents 4, 11, 19, 70, 79, 82–84
pedagogy 27–28, 50, 91, 95, 127–128, 141
performativity 62–64, 93, 105–106, 142
personalisation 11, 14, 16, 20, 25
philanthropy 72–75
policy as discourse 55–67
policy as text 55–67
political economy of technology 46
power 5–9, 11, 15–26, 46–49, 55, 67–68, 85–86, 87–110, 112–115, 130–136, 146–148
PowerPoint 25, 76, 91, 95
Prensky, Marc 15, 30–31
privatisations 68–86
public/private partnership 73, 77–78, 86
public debate and awareness of schools technology 139–140

regulation 8–9, 28–31, 97–98, 106, 120, 130–131, 142–144
remediation 7
reschooling 137–139
research 151–154
research evidence 24–26, 106, 111, 123, 143
resistance 20, 90, 99, 105–108, 112–114, 120–123, 138–140

risk 29, 33, 39, 65, 83–84, 98, 143
rules *see* regulation

school funding 4, 19, 23–24, 27, 35, 56–58, 64–65, 93, 149
school management 18–19, 25, 69–72, 87, 93–98
school organisation 8, 19, 33, 59, 90–100, 146
science and technology studies 43
skills 13, 24–27, 59–62, 83, 109–112, 127–128, 146
social class 82–83, 111, 137, 152
social construction of technology 46, 68, 112, 120, 135
social justice 5, 10, 50, 131–134
social media [web 2.0] ix, 6, 12, 15, 16, 76, 82, 126–138
social shaping of technology 38, 45–55, 92, 137
socio-cultural theories of learning 14, 20, 121
sociology of schools 9, 152
sousveillance 113
space: as part of schooling 8, 19, 88, 96–98, 100, 113, 116, 128, 141–146
state: state involvement in school technology 23–24, 55–67
stratification 9, 66, 109, 111, 152

structuration 100, 123
students 29–31, 102–103, 108–116
subject disciplines 95–96
surveillance 25, 28, 70, 96–99, 103, 113
symbolism of educational technology 22, 26, 64, 75, 83

teachers 31–32, 102–108, 114–116
technical fix 10, 12, 62, 100
technological determinism 40–47, 62
technology as text 43–47
Tesco: computers for schools 72
testing *see* assessment
time: as part of schooling 28, 87–91, 96–98, 100–110, 143–145
Toffler, Alvin 28
trust 98, 142–145

universities 62, 80, 112

values: values associated with technology use 17, 49, 51, 55, 57–61, 63, 66, 69, 78, 90, 96, 99, 115, 129, 139, 148
virtual learning environment 25, 72, 91, 107–108

Williams, Raymond 41, 44, 131

Young, Michael 133